All Abroad

All Abroad

A Memoir of
Travel and Obsession

Geoffrey Weill

THE UNIVERSITY OF WISCONSIN PRESS

The University of Wisconsin Press
728 State Street, Suite 443
Madison, Wisconsin 53706
uwpress.wisc.edu

Gray's Inn House, 127 Clerkenwell Road
London ECR 5DB, United Kingdom
eurospanbookstore.com

Printed in the United States of America
This book may be available in a digital edition.

Library of Congress Cataloging-in-Publication Data
Names: Weill, Geoffrey, 1949- author.
Title: All abroad : a memoir of travel and obsession / Geoffrey Weill.
Description: Madison, Wisconsin : The University of Wisconsin Press, [2021]
Identifiers: LCCN 2020017002 | ISBN 9780299330804 (cloth)
Subjects: LCSH: Weill, Geoffrey, 1949- | Travel agents—Biography.
Classification: LCC G154.5.W45 A3 2021 | DDC 338.4/791092 [B]—dc23
LC record available at https://lccn.loc.gov/2020017002

To my cousin TERRY,
without whom this book would never
have been started.

To my tolerant and devoted wife, NOA,
without whom this book would never
have been finished.

To my children—BENJAMIN, ZOË, and LIAM—
who hate my being on the road so often but who enjoyed and
enjoy traveling as much as I.

For my part, I travel not to go anywhere, but to go.
I travel for travel's sake. The great affair is to move.

ROBERT LOUIS STEVENSON,
Travels with a Donkey in the Cévennes, 1878

Contents

Preface

This is not a travel book per se; it is a memoir of how an obsession was fashioned. Memoirs are often about celebrities or politicians or generals or royalty or about those who have a claim to some measure of fame. Other memoirs are of interesting nobodies who, at times, because of the charm or uniqueness of the story or the writing, become notable. This is a story of an English boy then man in desperate need of escape from a childhood and adolescence that were outwardly charmed, all calm and happiness, yet inwardly all of these were laced with claustrophobic insecurity, regimentation, blame, and torment. Others might have turned to crime, to booze, to drugs. But because my need to escape started early—long before any of those avenues would have been remotely achievable—I sought solace elsewhere, ultimately in travel.

My fancies were not about touring the Taj Mahal or climbing the Matterhorn or admiring Iguazú Falls. My fascination, like Robert Louis Stevenson's, was about the actual journeys. Briefly, I also flirted with theater, ballet, Zionism—each a kind of escape—but those all paled in the wake of traveling. It wasn't about the sights. Mine was and is an obsession with the conveyances, the planes, the airports, the ships, the trains . . . and the hotels that await journey's end.

Moreover, there was no dream of actually being a pilot or being a train driver or being a Basil Fawlty commanding a quaint hotel on the English shore. No, it was all about being a passenger. About being a guest. There were no diagrams of engine rooms or locomotives: it was a torrent of timetables, schedules, hotel guides, and glossy brochures. There was not the slightest interest in the sort of travel that required hiking boots, backpacks, and tents. It was the getting there, the staying there, the feeling at home on six continents. Ultimately, I was able to turn my curiously eclectic obsession into a career.

It is a memoir that is thematic rather than chronological. Yet to assist the reader in keeping pace with what and how and where, each chapter is titled not numerically or with a name but by the year to which much of it refers. It is perhaps a somewhat curious tale, made even more curious by the torrent of eccentric characters with which it is inundated. It is an account full of events, distresses, injustices, joys, friendships, relationships, discoveries, sexual awakenings, illnesses, deaths, histories, and happenings— of which many are tangentially, directly, or literally associated with travel. It is a twentieth-century story, but one that has lashings of the Victoriana and Edwardiana that had expired long before my birth. And it is a story whose crucial escape is, at the age of twenty-three, my move to the United States. Which is where and how and when, in 1973, this actual story takes flight.

Several but by no means all names in this memoir have been changed so as not to embarrass the victims of my recollections.

I am immensely grateful to Joel Gonchar, Raphael Kadushin, Dennis Lloyd, Janet K. Rodgers, and Asher Weill, without whose support this book could never have seen the light of day.

All Abroad

Check-In

THE PHOTOGRAPH IS BLACK AND WHITE. I am smiling sheepishly and I am kneeling in my pajamas and my woolly robe behind a card table erected in my bedroom in our flat in London. The table is covered with a variety of objects arranged as if in a store window display. There is a dark-green leather writing case from my cousins in Paris. There is a tan leather box emblazoned with my initials, containing two hairbrushes. There is a Waterman fountain pen from Colin—a disappointment to my mother, who caustically commented he should have given me a watch. There are two pairs of gold cuff links. There are at least ten books, a brass letter opener, and matching bookmark. And a stud box. There is a portable typewriter from my parents and a German-made Kodak camera from my brother. There is a navy-blue leather writing case for traveling. With a squeeze of its golden hinges, it snaps open to reveal a temporary writing desk, complete with cream-colored blotter and pouches bulging with matching cream stationery. There is a large pigskin folder lined with moiré silk. It looks like an attaché case, but actually it's for pajamas. There's a leather map holder complete with Perspex window for outlining a route with a grease pencil. There is a prayer book bound in brass.

It is January 1963 and it is the morning after my Bar Mitzvah. I am posing with my gifts—or some of my gifts. For it would have been unthinkable to have photographed the checks, including the breathtakingly exotic check for fifty dollars from my aunt, uncle, and cousin in America, or the check for ten pounds from Shirley and Lionel, or the check for ten shillings and sixpence—half a guinea—from cousin Harry Isaacs, a sum that even in 1963 was absurd. In retrospect, I see clearly how many of the gifts were,

Me with my Bar Mitzvah gifts, 1963. (Author collection)

even then, purposefully connected to traveling, albeit travel with a sense
of the chronically dated: the stationery folder ideal for letters penned in
my polished mahogany compartment on the Berlin to Baghdad railway.
The pajama case perfect for the cabin steward to unpack in my stateroom
aboard the *Mauretania*. The map planner suitable for an outing in my 1928
Hillman roadster. The case snugly holding my hairbrushes after a two-
handed Jeeves-and-Wooster brilliantining. The camera. Even the portable
typewriter. But my favorite of all the gifts is not in the picture. It was a gift
from my father: a one-year subscription to the *ABC World Airways Guide*,
a pair of tomes to be delivered monthly, each telephone-directory thick,
revealing in six- and eight-point type the routings, timings, and fares of the
world's airways.

At thirteen, I was obsessed. And, evidently, my obsession was publicly
acknowledged and generously indulged.

Boarding

IT IS THE FIRST DAY OF NOVEMBER 1997 and I'm sitting in the courtyard of Au Bar, a small restaurant behind the Metropole Hotel in Hanoi.
The air is fresh, like May in New York, quite unlike the steam and sweat
and slime I've encountered almost everywhere before in Southeast Asia. I
sit facing the wrought iron gates that front the avenue and gaze at the
Metropole across the street. It soars seven stories high. Its porte cochère
thrusts out from the building with an iron-and-glass art nouveau flourish. Beneath it, teenaged porters in red tunics and red pillbox hats port;
doormen greet; and westerners sweep in and out, clutching their bargains,
rushing to appointments, busy with all the busyness that has made them
prosperous enough to be here.

I have been in the capital of Vietnam precisely forty-eight hours, and I
have yet to descend from the high of falling in love. A friend had told me
that "Hanoi is a dream," and from the moment my plane from Bangkok
descended over rice paddies glistening in the late-afternoon sun, the hazy
points of mountains forming so flawless a backdrop that it almost seemed
clichéd, I realized Hanoi was finally the Asia I had been hoping to find
since my first visit twenty-seven years earlier.

En route from the airport, I had passed those glistening rice paddies
as well as dozens of grazing, pointy-shouldered cows tended by teams of
conical-hatted farmers. In Hanoi, peeling ocher and vanilla buildings lined
dozens of avenues. Old trees provided tunnels and arches of shade. The
buildings were crammed together higgledy-piggledy, each quite different
yet somehow projecting a curious uniformity. The city's residents sat by
the dozen on the sidewalks, buying, selling, drinking, eating, daydreaming,

hawking, spitting. There were few cars, even fewer buses. But there were hundreds and thousands of bicycles. They were simple, no-gear contraptions. They gusted in waves east and west, north and south, like vast, monochrome schools of fish, veering, careening, whooshing, but miraculously never touching. Some bicycles had a passenger straddling the rear wheel, arms around the driver. There was no obvious bicycle sexism, for women were riding bikes with or without crossbars, as were the men. But then I noticed a far more ancient form of sexism: for the bikes the women were riding all appeared to have capacious, often brimming baskets attached to the front, while the men's bikes were invariably sleekly unencumbered, as if ready for the Tour d'Indochine.

The bicycles stream past the courtyard. As do the "cyclos," Hanoi's bicycle-powered rickshaws. Some cyclos are ratty and rusting, others have stylish mudguards, curvy chrome armrests, and fan-shaped sunshades, their drivers riding high at the rear, sporting military-green pith helmets. Every now and then, small boys come inside, point at my footwear, and inquire, "Shoe-shy?" Around me sit other westerners. On my left sits a shatteringly handsome young Englishman with his even more shatteringly handsome Eurasian wife. He is wearing a kind of hedgehog crew cut and gold circular wire glasses. She wears a blue sweater and size 2 pants, an Hermès scarf tied with studied nonchalance into a perfect small knot. She chats with her mother-in-law, clearly fresh off the plane from London, and also with her picture-perfect four- or five-year-old son, dangling from Daddy's knee. To my right, another tall Eurasian sips a cappuccino. He too is breathtakingly handsome. To his left, a young Frenchman—imagine the magical product of placing Alain Delon and Brad Pitt in a blender—chatters fluently in Vietnamese to an exquisite, heart-stoppingly nubile young woman, whose impossibly large, oyster-shaped eyes, hooded by ski-jump eyelashes, survey the scene with blasé indifference. And it suddenly flashes through my mind that the kind of Paris or London or Frankfurt or New York yuppies dispatched for a year or two to such foreign parts by the world's megacorporations are indeed a kind of superstar.

I munch my croque monsieur and pommes frites, sip my draft Tiger beer, and consider that this six-dollar snack is going to cost more than any cyclo rider outside the gates will earn today, and possibly tomorrow too. And it occurs to me that nothing has changed in sixty years, except the numbers. For the Vietnamese are still schlepping westerners for less than a dollar an hour to their hundreds-of-dollars-a-day hotels, and the westerners are still sitting on the terrace downing Sancerre, debating whether or not to buy that handbag in the Metropole's ludicrously cavernous Louis Vuitton boutique. Except that now, I reason, it's the Vietnamese who are holding the cards, who are doing all this scurrying as an investment. Because they know that ten or twenty years from now—when Hanoi, like Bangkok and Shanghai, is all fumes and skyscrapers and only children will be riding bicycles—Vietnam, already eighty million strong, will undoubtedly be a major world player.

My fleeting sense of guilt expunged, I down my beer and return to the Metropole. I slow my pace for the umpteenth time to admire its mahogany corridors, its teak-floored terrace overlooking the pool, where oversized rattan armchairs are lazily cooled by swirling ceiling fans. I unlock the door of my third-floor aerie. It is a newly built bedroom, I'm told, but a perfect re-creation of a cabin on the long-lost SS *Normandie*, where I start to pack, trying artfully to stuff into my luggage the mounds of booty purchased in my countless forays into the markets. I speak with my wife and eleven-year-old son in New York, impatient with my call at the zenith of a children's Halloween party. They are both slightly irritated, I fancy, that after a numbing twenty-four-hour journey to the other side of the globe and four fourteen-hour days of tedium-laced meetings, I haven't immediately inserted myself back into an aluminum tube for the twenty-two-hour flight home but have elected instead to delay the torture by spending the weekend in Hanoi.

I feel a pang of guilt, indeed several pangs—but they're pangs derived less, I know, from having missed the orange and black design accents, the tricks, the treats, the goblins and monsters, but from my once again experiencing the sickly kind of remorse associated with undeserved and illicit pleasure. It is a sensation to which—for more than half a century—I've been accustomed. A sensation that demands, quite boldly, "How dare you enjoy this so much?" It is as if I'm continually questioning my right to experience such a sense of euphoria from a mere takeoff or landing, or an ocean voyage, or a train ride, or an airport Jetway, or a hotel room—particularly a hotel room such as this, so flawlessly nostalgic with its moderne desk, its art deco lamp, its tub-shaped fauteuil upholstered in lemon brocade with scarlet welting, its matching bedspread, its crisply starched pillows, its gold-cornered navy leather stationery folder filled with orderly lines of crisp paper and card that somehow recalls the folder in my Bar Mitzvah display, and its salver of custard apples and persimmons nestled next to a plate, knife, fork, and stiffly starched napkin.

I am in travel heaven. And even though I recognize that in the general scheme of things it's an obsession that is relatively harmless, an obsession it is nonetheless.

All Abroad

1973

FOR MANY YEARS, THE MAIN FLOOR OF 587 Fifth Avenue was one of those numerous Midtown Manhattan stores where hapless tourists are intimidated into buying overpriced cameras, luggage, cell phones, and hideous sculptures in a fluorescent atmosphere of impatience and thinly veiled contempt. More recently, it has become a discount clothing store.

But in 1973, the year I arrived in New York from England, 587 Fifth Avenue remained very grand. It was the North American headquarters of Thomas Cook, the world's oldest travel agency. And I had been dispatched here from the London head office both to learn and to teach.

Cook's occupied the entire ten-story building. At street level, Manhattan's premier retail travel agency sold tickets and tours to the populace of metropolitan New York. A side door led to two antiquated, attended elevators that rose to the management and accounting floors. Bronze arrows above the elevators' bronze doors juddered around dials that indicated each car's current location. Waiting to be conveyed upstairs, staring up at those arrows swooshing cartoonlike around those dials, one was hard-pressed not to assume Tom would momentarily screech around the corner as he chased Jerry down the surrounding staircase.

Architecturally, the main floor was imposing. It exuded an air of trust and formality. There was a distinct sense that this was the place to come to make travel arrangements that were reliable, even sporadically patrician. Two stories in height, it stretched far back to a wall painted marine blue and emblazoned with letters of brushed chrome spelling "Cook's." At its base, gentlemen in cages sold travelers' checks, and bookkeepers hunched over adding machines. In the front of the store, some fifteen travel "consultants" stood at counters or sat at desks, their names engraved into a gray Formica sign: just Mr., Miss, or Mrs. and surname—as if it were a congressional hearing. We were never to refer to those who came to us as clients, nor as customers. They were to be ennobled with the title of "passengers."

I was a consultant-in-training. I had been apprenticed to the debonair James, a handsome man in his mid to late forties with swept-back silver hair, twinkling eyes, and a waxed moustache with Hercule Poirot points. James had a way with the ladies. As they sat at his desk, he would lean forward earnestly and seductively, conveying his knowledge and suggestions with a courtliness spiced with more than just a soupçon of flirtatiousness. Several of his female clients would return more often than necessary for further advice and guidance and, on occasion, an invitation to an after-work whiskey sour at the Top of Sixes.

Harry, a nattily dressed gentleman in his sixties, was based at the reception counter, handing out brochures and directing clients back toward the rest of us in the rear. Edward, the head salesman, stood at the front of the counter, nearest to Fifth Avenue. Surrounded by untidy piles of passenger files and the paraphernalia of travel teasing, he worked his magic on his clients, unfurling vast maps and deck plans to obscure the mess. Myron, the most knowledgeable of us all, was oversensitive, irritable, and sporadically witty. Chivalrous and amiable Raymond, tall and dashing with lush waves of silver hair and a goatee, had a dual client base. While graciously tending to the requirements of the grandes dames who wafted into the store, he was also fashioning trips for small and intimate groups of leather-harnessed friends to the bars and backrooms of Amsterdam and Hamburg. Raymond was the first gentleman I was ever to encounter with an unused pierced ear: he kept it discreetly unbejeweled during working hours.

Further back were Louise and Laura. Louise, at twenty-five, was a product of her time, her class, her birthright. Born of an aristocratic WASP family, she had married into an even better one. Her Carol Burnett smile lit up the room; her demeanor was one of calm and grace, of New Canaan, Connecticut, integrity. And it was evident that at the moment she were to become pregnant, her career would draw to an instant close. Laura was younger, of similar breeding with a slightly naughtier edge. There was the tranquilly erotic Helena with the come-to-bed eyes; the delicately long-haired Melanie from Little Italy; and Aggie, who wore shapeless shifts and the air of a hippie. There was the young Eduardo with the outrageously handsome face despite its pockmarks, who had escaped Cuba by swimming to Key West and who exuded smiles and raging sexuality. There was the elderly Cedric, whose role was not to sell but to act as a Cook's greeter and escort at the West Side docks and at Newark and Kennedy Airports. And then there was Millie, in her sixties, with thinning orange hair and an unfocused demeanor, whose exact role, apart from gossiping with Cedric and sourly trashing us all, I was never able to divine.

In 1973 the travel business was on the cusp of dramatic change, indeed of complete revolution. There was not a computer or a microchip in the building, nor even the expectation that there might soon be. (Yet by the end of the decade, each of those desks would have a clunky monitor and keyboard.) Reservations for virtually everything—from a bus tour to an airline ticket to a hotel room—were made by telephone. Each call required requesting an outside line from Blanche, the cheery telephone operator, our very own Ermengarde, perched on a mezzanine balcony crammed with consoles, Bakelite headsets, and jungles of fabric-coated wires.

Communication overseas was accomplished via a telex machine the size of a gas range. It sat up in a second mezzanine, where out-of-work actors boldly flirted and typed our Dictaphone-recorded letters into IBM Selectrics and onto carbon sets. Each transmission of a telex caused a giant clatter as yards of ticker tape were fed through its intestines, tape that miraculously emerged at the other end as a graciously intelligible request for a double room with private bath at the Negresco, with a view of the Mediterranean if you please.

Yet as archaic as it all somehow sounds, the future was not merely dawning, it had arrived. The Boeing 747 had been flying for three years, the DC-10 for two. The Concorde was on the horizon. Conversely, a little booklet published monthly by Cook's affirmed that elegant ocean liners were still regularly plying the Atlantic: the *Queen Elizabeth 2*, the *France*, the *Rafaello*, the *Nieuw Amsterdam*, even Poland's less stylish *Stefan Batory*. Each would steam periodically up the Hudson, parking itself at the crumbly docks on Twelfth Avenue and inspiring novelist Dan Greenburg (*How to Be a Jewish Mother*) to describe a Park Avenue socialite with the withering "the only time she went to the West Side was on her way to Europe."

It was the era before security concerns were to forever mangle the grandeur and romance of the travel experience. Every cruise and ocean voyage was preceded by a shipboard party. Passengers' friends and families would board the ship for an envy-laced tour and to cram into their friends' state-room to munch canapés and toast the travelers with champagne. The loud-speakers' increasingly panicked calls of "all ashore who's going ashore" would bring a close to the revelry. After farewell hugs and sloppy kisses, friends and family would tipsily descend the gangplank and—to the strains of a brass band—turn to wave and catch streamers as the liners' giant pro-pellers began to growl, their whistles whistled, and tugs towed the giant ships gently out into the Hudson.

Yet it was the swan song of the transatlantic passenger ship. In 1968 the SS *United States*, the pride of the United States Line, had been withdrawn from service, taking with it to its dry dock in Newport News the secrets of its strength and speed, secrets considered so militarily sensitive that to this day they remain classified. In the summer of 1974, the French unions engi-neered a strike while the *France* was docked in New York and the pride of France's merchant marine lumbered passenger-less back to Le Havre, only to return several years later as the *Norway*, her elegance and chic diminished by the emancipated constitution of cruising. Shortly, the Ital-ian and Polish liners stopped coming too—leaving the Atlantic the sole property of the *Queen Elizabeth 2* and, thirty thousand feet above it, ever-burgeoning fleets of 747s.

Mankind's yearning for speed had ended an era. What had made crossing the Atlantic forty years earlier on the *Normandie* or the *Bremen* or the *Queen Mary* so unambiguously glamorous was that it was purely and simply the fastest way to reach Europe . . . period. In 1958, for the first time, more Americans flew to Europe than sailed.

I had come to New York on a special visa for intercompany transfers, yet my mindset was one of immigration. I arrived with seventeen suitcases on a freezing January 30 aboard the SS *Canberra*, the only liner crossing the Atlantic in the dead of that winter. In that 1973 cusp that was distinguish-ing the travel styles of the fifties from that of the eighties, the *Queen Eliza-beth 2* and her colleagues were already spending their winters cruising the Caribbean or the world.

The *Canberra* was British, one of the Peninsula and Orient (P&O) fleet of liners that since 1837 had been transporting colonials from the home-land to India, Malaya, Hong Kong, and Japan. (It was the abbreviation in P&O's intercompany telegraphs requesting cabins on the sides of the ship shaded from the sun—"Port Out, Starboard Home"—that gave birth to the acronym POSH and the subsequent adjective.) It was being repositioned to New York from its home base at Southampton for a winter cruising season that was to prove a commercial failure.

The crossing took a week; the weather was foul. I occupied a wood-paneled cabin that sat far enough above the waterline to be luxurious and near enough to the waves to be exciting, and it was divine. There was no communication with either shore. A thousand passengers spent seven days in utter limbo amid a not-entirely tuneful symphony of postwar British interior design that embraced hundreds of tons of Formica, consuming vast meals heavy on Yorkshire pudding, curries, and trifle; playing bingo; practicing the hokey-pokey; watching movies; and lying on the outer decks atop chaise longues and tucked beneath heavy blankets in order to gaze at gray skies, a gray horizon, and gray Atlantic swells.

It was an experience entirely from an earlier era. Apart from the fashions, it could have been 1913, 1923, 1933, or 1953. With one exception: the discotheque secreted down staircases in the plebian world of E Deck. There—amid psychedelic colors, flashing lights, groovy vibes, and booming rock music—one of my fellow passengers, a tall, thin young man, danced nightly with his monumentally attractive traveling companion in a kind of strutting, rhythmic coma. I don't remember ever seeing either of them in the day. They emerged solely at night, the tall, thin young man smeared with pancake makeup, his hair rainbow technicolored and hedgehog shorn. He wore three-inch glitter heels and sequined suits with exaggerated shoulders and stovepipe pants. His name, I learned, was David Bowie. Lurching across the Atlantic on the *Canberra* in that January of 1973 in the company of David Bowie was perhaps the most trenchant symbol possible of my traveling not merely between continents, or between phases of my own life, but from one epoch into another.

Nobody walks unannounced into a travel agency anymore and books a world cruise or a two-week tour of the Orient. But in 1973, that is precisely what New Yorkers did. Certainly, because it was Cook's, there was a vast amount of trust. It was the world's oldest travel agency, it was housed in that impressive space on Fifth Avenue, and the term "Cook's Tour" had long been part of the language. Thus it seemed not unreasonable for the public to place its reliance in so august a firm—particularly as there was no internet, of course, and few "how-to" travel media. Largely, it was we, along with Eugene Fodor and Arthur Frommer, who were the font of travel knowledge.

But there was more to it. The entire structure of the travel industry was simpler and less daunting. Unless one wanted to risk one's life on a charter flight aboard a lumbering, vibrating Constellation, the fares of every scheduled airline were identical, mandated by the International Air Transport Association. There were no deals, no angles, and—certainly at Cook's—no discounts. Four years earlier, Hollywood had released *If It's Tuesday, This Must Be Belgium*, a satire in which Suzanne Pleshette, Mildred Natwick, and Peggy Cass bus-toured through nine countries in eighteen days in the care of an erratic and randy tour escort, Ian McShane. Yes, it was satire, but it was also very real. Because while the movie's romantic undulations were a precursor to TV's *Love Boat*, the fact remained that nine countries in eighteen days—or five in nine, or seven in twelve—was precisely how tens of thousands of Americans, New Yorkers included, were still traveling to Europe.

Through the doors of 587 Fifth Avenue they would sweep, ladies usually in the morning and afternoons, men in hats at lunchtime. As each of us earned commission, there was more than a little competition for their custom. Whenever what seemed to be a likely prospect entered, we dropped what we were doing and stood perkily erect, all welcoming smiles, at the counter. If the entrant seemed of doubtful worth, phone receivers were lifted, faces were plunged deep into file drawers. And it was usually I, the greenhorn at the rear of the hall, who faced the prospect of wasting an hour on the sale of a one-way air ticket to Cleveland.

Yet appearances could be deceptive. A few months after my arrival, a meek and nondescript obese woman hesitantly entered. Suddenly, my colleagues became engaged in feigning weighty and urgent tasks and she was left to me. Forty minutes later, she was out the door having booked and paid for a three-week tour of the Orient that linked with a two-week tour of Europe. And she flew first class. My coworkers seethed.

After a year, Edward up at the front was transferred to Cook's in Boston, and, unexpectedly, I was appointed his successor as assistant manager. It peeved many, but there was also a grudging recognition that I was very good at the work. Partly it was that the English accent imparted a sense of authority. Partly it was that I knew how to charm, although it was not, I want to believe, the charm Anthony Blanche condemns in Evelyn Waugh's *Brideshead Revisited* as "the great English blight." Mostly, it was simply because since the age of six I had been strangely obsessed with the reading of timetables, hotel directories, travel guides, and atlases. I knew my stuff.

I was to spend a total of two years standing at attention at that counter, learning to divine New Yorkers' dreams. I learned what they wanted and expected from their travels; I learned what they knew and didn't know. I learned what they feared. And it was the fears that were the most palpable, and what drove them to us: fear of the unknown, fear of foreignness, fear of unintelligible languages, fear of unsafe water and peculiar foods, fear of advantage being taken. They would come to us reliant on our ability to wrap them in a cocoon of protection that would keep them safe and unabused in foreign climes.

In twenty-four months, I encountered every gradation of New York traveler: the highly experienced, the novice, the inquiring, the jaundiced, the bumptious, the shy, the extraordinarily knowledgeable, the paralyzingly ignorant. I met husbands who loathed their wives and were being bludgeoned into taking a trip they dreaded. I advised honeymooners expectant of romance, passion, daiquiris, and palm trees. I aided single travelers in search of company, or Mr. or Miss Right, or—on one occasion—both. There were the escapers from boredom, the yearners for discovery, the vacationers aching for excitement to wrench them out of the daily grind.

They all came. There was Park Avenue swirled in mink; there was Hackensack encased in polyester from Korvettes. There was Wall Street clothed at B. Altman; there was Forest Hills in Arnold Constable. There was the aging men's room attendant at the Waldorf who appeared weekly, bearing sacks of quarters to pay in installments for his cruise. There was the woman from Rhodesia whose return ocean voyage to Africa had been summarily canceled and who declared herself desperate for my "assistance with her back passage." There was the close-to-retirement bank clerk who returned from his first (and I suspect last) trip to Europe outraged at the shoddy maintenance of the Acropolis: "It was all in ruins."

Yet, through and above it all, as the months passed, an overarching epiphany slowly dawned. Wherever people were going or cruising or touring, I came to realize that there was a giant subconscious element to it all. In retrospect it seems idiotically simple, yet it was also deviously complex. The unvarnished fact was that everybody had a List. Usually, it was an invisible List pinned unobtrusively up in a lobe of the brain. Yet, on occasion, it was a List withdrawn from a purse and ceremonially unfolded. Sometimes the List was short; sometimes it covered pages. But whatever its length, it served to summarize all the places the bearer wanted or felt impelled to see before he or she died. So through the swing doors of Cook's they would come in a subliminal quest to place a check against one listed destination, or seven, or quite often as many as possible. Hence the attraction of nine countries in eighteen days: nine items on the List eliminated in a single swoop. Nowadays, the condition has a name: the "bucket list." But back then it was the "List That Had No Name."

But the concept of the List was even more intricate. I came to grasp that at least half of our "passengers" yearned less actually to see the sights than to *have* seen them. Their actual twenty minutes at Notre-Dame could never hope to compare either with the thrill of expectation prior to the trip or with the sense of accomplishment that accompanied the satisfaction that Notre-Dame was not merely seen and photographed but out of the way, finished, crossed off the List, and on to the next.

Fifty years on, that subconscious ingredient of traveling hasn't changed, even though the how and where of travel has been utterly and irreversibly transformed. How many of us go on safari twice? Or visit Nepal twice? Or Madagascar or Chile twice? We go, we see, we come back. We get it done. It's not that a second safari wouldn't be wonderful and that in Botswana rather than Kenya we might not see different, even better animals. It's not that we only saw a fraction of Nepal the first time around. It's not as if there isn't still much more to discover in Madagascar or Chile. It's just that for many, the List takes precedence.

The twenty-first-century version of five-countries-in-nine-days is the cruise. While cruising has been popular since the thirties, by 2020 it had reached an unprecedented and burgeoning zenith. But then along came the multiple horrors of the coronavirus. Thousands of passengers and crew were stranded for days, weeks, or months, some sequestered in their "inside" cabins, some infected with the virus and spreading it, while the captain searched for a port to accept them. Ever more immense cruise ships are on the drawing boards, the largest with a panoply of activities on board so grandiose—from Broadway musicals to climbing walls to ice skating— that the quick lurch ashore to snap a selfie, see a cathedral, and buy a T-shirt virtually takes on the character of an irksome chore. Three, four, five countries can be struck off the List in a week. And, unlike the bus tour of forty years earlier, there is no bothersome packing, unpacking, and repacking. But it is also possible that on the drawing boards these mammoths shall remain, the passion for giant-ship cruising dulled if not extinguished by the tragedies wrought by the virus.

In 2004, several careers on, I was invited to be guest lecturer aboard a luxury Baltic cruise. The passenger complement was entirely English-speaking, 90 percent American—of whom a goodly 75 percent hailed from "red states." I was to talk on the history of St. Petersburg, Copenhagen, and the Estonian capital of Tallin. Turnout at the lectures was feeble, not because I spoke poorly (one would at least have to attend to reach such a conclusion) but, I assume, because of disinterest. It was apparent that seeing, or having seen, the ports was the goal. Learning what made them what they were was an irrelevance.

It is, of course, no coincidence that the French word for "remember" is "*souvenir*." After their vacations, many of our passengers would return to share their experiences and their pictures. Standing at that counter on Fifth Avenue in the early 1970s, I grasped how a century and a quarter of tourism's development had coincided historically and technologically with that of photography: Nicéphore Niépce and Louis-Jacques-Mandé Daguerre had perfected photography by 1840; Thomas Cook led his first group excursion in 1841. This is not to say that each wouldn't have been invented without the other, but the interweaving and cross-pollination of their subsequent growth is so entwined as to be surely no accident. George Eastman introduced the Kodak Brownie in 1900. Tourism for the moneyed masses blossomed during the Belle Époque and surged after the Great War and Spanish flu ended. We have all seen the gaggles of tourists—ourselves included—who gather at the world's great monuments only to perceive them more through a viewfinder or iPhone than with the naked eye. It struck me then, and even more now, that in the final analysis many were traveling 3,500 miles to see Westminster Abbey less to inspect its gargoyles and to marvel at its flying buttresses than to be snapped for posterity in front of its bronze doors. Welcome to the "selfie stick."

In the early 1970s at 587 Fifth Avenue, the opportunity to book a passenger on a world cruise was considered the equivalent of hitting the jackpot in Las Vegas. So it was that one afternoon in early January 1975, a lady of a certain age entered Cook's and slowly approached the counter. She smiled, removed her coat, and arranged herself in front of me upon one of the tall stools. She took a deep breath and, from the depths of a tote bag, produced a folded, stained, crumpled brochure. "I want to book this," she said, stabbing a liver-spotted, perfectly manicured scarlet-nailed finger at one of the pages she was attempting to iron with the heel of her other hand. Despite the folds and dog-ears, I recognized the leaflet as that describing the hundred-plus-day 1975 world cruise of the MS *Gripsholm*, set to leave New York ten days hence. My heart bounded. The stateroom she wanted cost an astronomical $33,000—a sum not insignificant today, yet it would be the equivalent of an even more astronomical $170,000 in 2020. In a flash, I had the Swedish American Line on the phone. I learned that the ship was not full, but they could not immediately confirm her cabin. They would "get back to me."

Perplexed, I dialed upstairs for the assistance of Bill Plenge, the manager of another retail department at Cook's, a unit secreted in a sanctuary on the second floor and devoted to the booking of travel arrangements for the "privileged" rather than the hoi polloi that ambled in unannounced off Fifth Avenue. Bill, who booked people on world cruises as often as most of us brush our teeth, would know how to help. Out of the client's hearing, I explained the situation.

"I see," he said. "Would you come upstairs?"

I asked the prospective passenger to make herself comfortable and raced up to Bill's desk.

"What's her name?" Bill asked me, telephone receiver in hand.

"Mary Davidson," I responded.

"Mary Davidson," he intoned into the telephone. I realized that while I was bounding up the stairs, he must already have gotten Blanche to get Swedish American on the line. A distant voice spoke unintelligibly into Bill's ear. He looked up at me searchingly.

"Is she Jewish?" he asked.

"Huh?

"Do you know if she's Jewish?" he enunciated slowly, as if addressing a half-wit.

"I don't think so," I responded, too baffled even to think his question through.

"You sure?" he asked me.

"I'm sure she isn't," I responded, "but what on earth . . . ?"

He raised his hand, signaling me not to speak.

"She's OK," he said into the telephone. Another pause. He replaced the receiver.

"The cabin is confirmed," Bill said to me, waving me away and returning to the papers on his desk. Bewildered, I returned to the main floor. I told Mary Davidson all was well. I helped her complete a mound of forms. I fancy I bowed my head as I accepted her check for $33,000. I handwrote her ticket with its wad of different colored carbons and handed it to her along with a clutch of dazzling baggage tags. She stood, she thanked me, she shook my hand, I helped her with her coat, and out she sailed: to Fifth Avenue and the world.

I had just come face to face with the last gasp of a *Gentleman's Agreement* syndrome that would largely vanish with the introduction of reservations-by-computer and the demise, a few short years later, of the Swedish American Line itself. I suspected the policy on which I had chanced did not emanate in the line's headquarters in liberal Stockholm but was the devising of a narrow cabal in New York that oversaw the peopling of the *Gripsholm*'s annual world cruise. Yet it was a policy that was, I came to learn, not merely agreeable to the *Gripsholm*'s complement of repeat passengers but unmentioned and expected.

Four ships were to make world cruises that January 1975: one hundred or more days at sea in the company of the same mostly aged faces, roaming the farthest reaches of the planet, playing a thousand rubbers of bridge. Supposedly, the first month of a world cruise is a delight, the second month fractious, and during the third month barely anyone speaks to anyone else, the ship steaming on its course in a state of benumbed ill temper. Habitually, several aged passengers inevitably die during world cruises, and a supply of coffins is unobtrusively loaded aboard at the start of the voyage along with the All-Bran and the caviar. The captain officiates at funerals at sea that are performed at dawn. The widow or widower tearfully grasps the flag that had draped the casket before its discreet slide into the depths, and then repairs to breakfast.

The passenger profile of two of the ships that undertook the 1974 world cruises, the *France* and the *Queen Elizabeth 2*, certainly permitted the inclusion of passengers from the Five Towns and West End Avenue. And Norwegian America Line's *Sagafjord* admitted all of Park Avenue and those from Great Neck who could "pass." But, I learned, the passenger complement of the *Gripsholm* was purposefully decreed to be as restricted as could be managed.

Gregory Peck I was not, yet disgusted I was. More than that, I was deeply disappointed. I had come to America for a variety of reasons. But one was assuredly to escape Britain's antisemitism. I had been educated at a British "public school" for boys—that is, a private school for the sons of the privileged. I had witnessed or experienced all the "peculiarities" of the British public school that appall and fascinate Americans—from the teachers' intermittent fondling of their pupils' upper thighs to the bullying, the rules, the mercurial edicts and punishments meted out by prefects, the beneath-the-desk mutual groping during French class, the caning, the victimization . . . and the antisemitism. At the age of ten, I had arrived at the City of London School under the assumption that I was an Englishman who attended synagogue every now and then, only to learn I was considered by many a Jew who, by quirk of birth, had chanced upon the right to be a subject of Her Majesty.

During my first year at Thomas Cook in London, I had produced a quotation on the cost of two couples' trip to Italy—and, new to the job, had made a whopping mistake. I had calculated the published cost of a hotel night—per room rather than per person. The difference amounted to thousands of pounds, and Thomas Cook was being held to the quote, it was explained to me, "because the passengers were Jews." I wasn't penalized and my mistake didn't hurt my career. Yet, most incredibly of all, even knowing I was Jewish, there was not the slightest hesitation in explaining the passengers' insistence on taking the trip as quoted being as a result of their religion, just as, three years later in New York, Bill Plenge unabashedly clued me in to the unspoken attitudes of the Swedish American Line.

I had believed America would be different. I recall one evening in London being enchanted during the *Dick Van Dyke Show* that Rose Marie had mentioned Rosh Hashana. The mayor of New York was Jewish, as was the secretary of state. It had to be different. And, of course, in the general scheme of things, it was. Unlike England, where the antisemitism seemed ritually inherent, the antisemitism I encountered in New York in 1974 was so eclectic and arbitrary that it seemed to matter far more to those who practiced it than to those it was designed to exclude.

A few months later, I was to have another related encounter. An older gentleman had come to me to book a vacation in Europe. He was a bachelor, rather frail, courtly, and effete. His entire working life had been spent at Sloan's, a vaguely patrician, now defunct furniture store next to the now equally defunct Lord and Taylor. During one of his visits to discuss his trip, he delicately placed a pasty, hairless, and manicured hand atop mine. He wondered if I might join him for a cocktail one evening. I responded that it was a lovely idea, silently praying we could postpone the appointment for a decade or two. A moment later he paused, as if struck by a new thought. "Are you Jewish?" he asked. "Er, um, yes," I responded. There was an ever-so-slight curl of the lip. "Yes," he said as the pasty, hairless, manicured hand was gently withdrawn, "I can always tell." He did take the trip to Europe. We never did have that cocktail.

Just as those years at the counter at Thomas Cook were on the cusp of change of one era of tourism to another, and on the cusp of the final demise of restricted passenger lists, they were, unknowingly, at the cusp of yet another development, one that was monstrously more ominous. And it was a development that was embodied, literally, by Bill Plenge.

Despite our *Gripsholm* experience, I liked Bill. He was funny, flamboyant, theatrical, warm, and welcoming. He was passionate about ice skating and the opera. Each spring, he would lead groups of travelers to attend the World Figure Skating Championships. He was a devoté of the Metropolitan Opera, owning several subscriptions. Bill was, in the elegantly naive words of the adolescent Harvey Milk, one of the many attendees of the opera who were "men without wives."

It was in the summer of 1974 that Bill started getting sick. He would come down with inexplicable and peculiar complaints: odd skin lesions, breathing problems, gastrointestinal infections, a curious brand of pneumonia. And because he traveled the world incessantly, it was assumed he had inexorably acquired some obscure alien malady. Specialists in tropical medicine were consulted. He got better. He kept traveling. He kept going to the opera. He got sick again. He lost vast amounts of weight. He got well again and some of the weight came back. He got sick again, and well again, and on it went.

By 1981, when it was no longer dubbed GRID (gay-related immune deficiency) or the "gay cancer" but identified as HIV (the human immunodeficiency virus), the escorted bus tour was already in a rapid decline. The arranging of travel had been upturned and revolutionized by the computer. The Concorde had been flying to New York for five years. Both the Swedish American Line and Sloan's furniture store were out of business. B. Altman, Arnold Constable, and Korvettes were gone from Fifth Avenue, a street that now was home to Banana Republic, Barnes and Noble, and H. Stern. Raymond, with the pierced ear and the tours to the backrooms of Amsterdam and Hamburg, had succumbed very quickly as the epidemic washed over Manhattan. The two gentlemen whom I had helped change the Thomas Cook window display every other Wednesday evening were dead too. And I had attended a heartrending and aria-laced memorial service for Bill at the Church of St. John the Evangelist on First Avenue.

1949

I was born into a family of travelers at 6 a.m. on New Year's Eve 1949, the very last day of the 1940s, at the London Hospital in Whitechapel. Whitechapel, in London's East End, was far from our home in marginally fashionable Maida Vale. But it was the hospital with which my mother's obstetrician was affiliated, so there I was too, born precisely at the fulcrum of the century, in a neighborhood still scarred by the ravages of the blitz, a neighborhood sited within "the sound of the bells of Bow Church," a circumstance that is the sole criterion for a Londoner to be considered an authentic Cockney. Eight days after my birth, still ensconced in the London Hospital in Whitechapel, my bris was performed by the seventy-nine-year-old Reverend Doctor Jacob Snowman, who—my mother would forever broadcast widely—had, thirteen months earlier, circumcised Prince Charles at Buckingham Palace. Despite Dr. Snowman's unquestionable skill, my fourteen-year-old brother fainted as he watched.

Entering the world via "cockney" Whitechapel, heart of London's turn-of-the-century Jewish immigrant quarter, was a curiously paradoxical emblem of the two prime energies that galvanized my mother's theory of how I should be raised. First, she was possessed with the insistence that I must never look, seem, sound, dress, appear, or behave in any way she considered "Jewish." And, with an obsession even more relentless, I was to spend the first twelve or so years of my life engaged in the unceasing torture of vocal drills and the repetition of vowel sounds to ensure that I would never, ever utter a cockney-tinged vowel and, by extension, be considered "common." It was imperative that I speak "beautifully," as if I were a member of the royal family. No matter that I lisped and dropped my r's. Speech impediments didn't matter. The appearance of breeding did.

Quite where my father figured in all of this escapes me. He was certainly present at those endless meals of Irish stew or smoked haddock and poached eggs or liver and bacon, when my chatter was interrupted to have a mispronunciation mercilessly echoed and rectified. But as he was often away from Monday to Friday "on business"—only the lower orders referred to it as "work"—he inevitably missed much of the incessant forays into the world of Henry Higgins meets Fagin. Only decades later did I come to suspect that all that traveling may have been purposefully arranged to effect an escape.

Yet, even when he was around, I'm not sure how much time he devoted to my actual upbringing. The endeavors he did share with me are activities that stand out now as beacons of comfort and diversion precisely because they involved his and my being alone. And should I mistakenly let a vowel lapse, he would never tell. Actually, he would never notice.

He and I shared a passion for cars. At seven, I could and would and did name every car on the road—not only the manufacturer but also the model and year of production. Each year, he would take me to the motor show at Earl's Court so I could ogle and scrutinize and fondle every model, and collect reams of brochures proclaiming the wonders of the 1957 Ford Consul or Riley Pathfinder or Morris Oxford.

Sunday mornings were his and my special time. Together, we would drive up to Hampstead Heath. I, of course, sat blissfully untethered, as did all children in the 1950s. So I could see over the dashboard, my perch was a little red wooden stool with white painted prancing bunnies, perched perilously on the front bench seat. At the Heath, we would find branches,

Me, at age four. So angelic.
(Author collection)

snap off twigs to convert them into walking sticks, and go for "stick walks" through what was true countryside almost in the heart of London. We would stop at the White Stone Pond and he would buy me a pony ride and watch as I was walked sedately around Hampstead's bucolic, literate streets on my micro-steed.

Those Sunday mornings would usually climax on the terrace of the Blenheim pub in St. John's Wood, the only place, it seemed to me, in the London of the mid-1950s where one could consume warm orange squash and potato chips in an ambiance so cosmopolitan as to evoke an outdoor café. There, Pa and I would invariably be joined by my grandfather and by my brother, Anthony, as well as by Grandpa's dachshund, Rudi, who, though significantly shorter than I, was, at least, more or less my contemporary. And there, in the weak sunshine, we would perform what is now termed male bonding. Then home we would trundle—my father somewhat tipsily I suppose after several pints of Guinness—to Sunday lunch of roast beef and horseradish sauce and Yorkshire pudding and boiled cabbage, with my mother and grandmother; my young aunt Ann; and Grandpa's second wife, Bee, whom everybody except I seemed profoundly to loathe.

On some Sundays, and just sufficiently occasionally as to make it a legitimate adventure, Pa would sneak me out of the apartment early to drive to the heart of the City of London for breakfast at the ABC Tea Room. The ABC was cafeteria style, all Bakelite, Formica, and chrome, with black-and-white tile floors. At the age of six or seven, I chose to admire its spare, sans serif chromium-plated "ABC" logo set against a pale-lemon moderne background. We would devour poached eggs, sausages, watery bottled orange juice, hot-buttered toast, and marmalade. This was really living. Anyone could go out for lunch or for afternoon tea or for dinner. But to go out for breakfast felt so brazenly glamorous I could have burst. And thirty years later in New York when, early on Sunday mornings, I began to take my three-year-old son, Benjamin, out to the Greek coffee shop at 69th and Broadway, it was not only to re-create that time of father-son bonding but also to invite waves of warming nostalgia to wash over me.

But what made those Sunday mornings so singular came before the Heath, before the ABC Tea Rooms. It was bath time. I would bathe and Pa would shave, then he would bathe and I would keep him company. And we would chat about his chief passion: travel. He would regale me with detailed tales of his travels as a child, as an adult, and as Staff Sergeant Weill in His Majesty's Pioneer Corps. In my mind, each journey would take on almost a religious quality. Like a sponge, I greedily absorbed the minutiae. His passion for travel had nothing remotely to do with sightseeing or what we now define as tourism. It was all about the conveyances, the hotels, the routings, the intricate meshing of schedules, the itineraries . . . and the names that rolled seductively off his multilingual tongue: Imperial Airways, Fokker, Mitropa-Wagen, Rheingold, Frankfurter Hof, the Hook of Holland, the Amstel, the Flying Dutchman, the Metropole. We would talk about the ideal itinerary for a continental motoring holiday: "First night Reims, second night Dijon, third night Lausanne," etcetera. Each sound, each place, each idea, each Wagnerian reference, became like a sacred rosary, so much so that most nights even now, after I've turned and plumped and flattened my pillow to find that ideally cooling patch of linen, I recite mantras of routes flown or ships sailed in order to lull myself to sleep.

Perhaps the most celebrated of Pa's trips was that connected with his Bar Mitzvah in 1922. Pa had been born in London in 1909, but the event took place in Frankfurt so that most of his father's family could attend. (My grandfather had come from Germany to England in 1899 from Kippenheim, a small town not far from Alsace-Lorraine and the Black Forest.) It was at the height of the ruinous post–World War I inflation in Germany, when the savings of millions were wiped out overnight and a pound or a dollar was equivalent to millions, then billions, then wheelbarrows, then truckloads of marks. And it was the inflation that was key to the occasion's opulence: the entire extravaganza cost Grandpa about twenty-five pounds sterling—including a private Mitropa railway car attached to the Rheingold Express to speed the English friends and relatives in splendor from the Hook of Holland to Frankfurt, suites for all at the Hotel Frankfurter Hof, and a vast dinner for hundreds. The dinner's coda was a special memento of the evening: for the women, chocolates encased in a box whose candy wrappers sported my father's photograph; for the men, a box of ten Havana cigars with Pa's photo not only embossed in sepia, scarlet, and gold on the inside of the lid but also beaming from each red-and-gold cigar band.

What nobody had known on the morning of Saturday, June 24, 1922, as Pa stood chanting from the Torah in Frankfurt's Börneplatz Synagogue, was that 420 miles away in Berlin, ultra-right-wing nationalists had assassinated Weimar Germany's Jewish foreign minister, Walther Rathenau, as he drove to his office. So, a century later, how do I view all the Bar Mitzvah's splendor? Was Grandpa—the émigré who had made good—flaunting his

My grandparents, father, and Aunt Esmé, 1918. (Author collection)

wealth in the faces of his temporarily impoverished relatives? Or perhaps it really was as my cousin Ludwig described it to me sixty years later, a magnificent high point in the midst of their despair: a reminder that their fortunes could turn too. But I also wonder what all those waiters thought about during this extravaganza. Grateful for their jobs, of course, but knowing that outside the hotel's doors, crippled World War I veterans were limping as they pushed baby carriages brimming with worthless money to buy a loaf of bread, while a ballroom of Jews—some awarded the Iron Cross for their service in that same war—were swilling champagne. And we all know where those thoughts were to lead.

Another of Pa's journeys that fascinated me came in 1928, when he was eighteen, in the wake of his mother's death in Paderborn, Germany— a journey whose nuances became as familiar to me in 1958 as they still are now: the grief-laced telegram from his sister Esmé, the anxious telephone calls to align schedules, the wicker armchairs of the Imperial Airways biplane from London's Croydon aerodrome to Paris, the Air France plane onward to Brussels, the Sabena plane to Cologne, the train ride to Paderborn.

After our baths, Pa would sometimes share the secrets of his shrine: the map drawer. I would pore over the rows of neatly arranged road maps— organized by country—and, like a Hasidic father instructing his son in the intricacies of the Talmud, he would teach me how to discern, understand, and differentiate between the symbols describing hotels and inns and market days in country towns in the hotel and travel directory published by the Automobile Association. The near divinity of the symbol for a five-star hotel became imbedded in my psyche as I absorbed Pa's simple credo that however magnificent or tawdry a hotel was, he would not stay in it unless he were guaranteed a private bathroom—in itself a rich illustration of the times.

I used to love driving around London with Pa, particularly on those traffic-free Sunday mornings. And, as much of my care seems to have been delegated to my brother, Anthony, it was also he who, in his airless, Perspex-domed, three-wheeler Messerschmitt bubble car, took me on outings to St. Paul's Cathedral and the Monument to the Great Fire and the Tower of London—and even on journeys to Richmond Park, with its ferns and tame deer. I learned the city, its layout, its landmarks, and developed a keen and so far infallible sense of direction. Scraps of knowledge, of Blitz lore, seeped in and stuck. St. Paul's survival, while all around it burned,

caught my imagination. In our own street, one of the apartment buildings had been bombed then restored with impressive contemporary metal
windows, replacing the rotting Victorian wooden frames to which our un-
blitzed apartment remained depressingly condemned. The synagogue we
attended was in a temporary basement; the splendid Moorish-Gothic edi-
fice in which my parents had been married had been bombed in 1943.
And near our home, Pa used to show me where he had been brought as a
child during World War I to be awed at the crater of a house destroyed by
a zeppelin's bomb.

In the early 1950s, London remained scarred with thousands of World
War II bombsites. They were ubiquitous, not frightening, just omnipres-
ent—and I would wonder just how it was that so much of London had
survived the bombing rather than how much had been destroyed. One
of the sights that fascinated me most was the multitude of standing retain-
ing walls of sheared-off buildings, on which one could see the individually
decorated walls of stories of flats, like layers of a tall, multicolored cake. It
was as if the families whose homes these once were had only yesterday
had their walls blown away, leaving exposed, for all the world to see, the
duck-egg blue or fawn wallpaper of their living room, no longer hung with
pictures or rows of china ducks, now a memory-filled gash, still rudely
open a decade or more later.

The London in which I grew up was in tone, manner, and content a far
earlier London, a city of the 1920s or '30s. I assumed this was my personal
pretension until decades later in New York I saw the original movie of *The
Ladykillers*—not the vile remake with Tom Hanks, but the 1955 film starring Alec Guinness and Peter Sellers that portrays so Edwardian, even Victorian, a London that the contemporary cars seem totally incongruous.
But like my father's penchant for hotel rooms with a private bathroom,
that's precisely the London I inhabited as a child: a London of quietly dreary
streets whose gas lamps were kindled nightly by a ladder-toting lamp-lighter
on a bicycle, bomb sites, kettles boiling for tea, one-channel black-and-
white television, coal fires, coal-smoke blackened buildings, and fogs so
thick that once, at eleven, I had literally to grope my way home from the
tube station. It was a London of exquisite polity and belabored gentility, a
city full of Londoners who hadn't yet brought themselves to acknowledge
that the empire was gone and that we were no longer the greatest power
on Earth. It was a London where Victorian-Edwardian manners and styles
confronted the twentieth century, a clash so perfectly symbolized, it seemed

to me, by the image of Queen Mary at 1951's opening of the Festival of Britain, resplendent in an ankle-length outfit identical in cut to the one she had worn in 1910 at the funeral of her father-in-law, Edward VII.

Perhaps it was London's drabness and restraint that attached such extraordinary glamour to the tales of my parents' and grandparents' travels. Somehow I learned that the concept of traveling was assuredly the fastest route to a life that was more than merely "ordinary," a goal my mother insisted was paramount. It undoubtedly also fulfilled a neurotic, internal need to set me apart from my peers. I remember an English class at my very British public school when I was fifteen during which the teacher, one Roger Hadaway, was extolling the wonders of the Noh theater of Japan, which was on an unprecedented engagement in London and for which he was arranging tickets for the entire class. After all, he reasoned, "this is a once-in-a-lifetime opportunity. You'll never ever get to Japan." While my classmates were unmoved, or doodling, or diddling each other's groins beneath the desks, I was outraged by his presumption, by his imposition of limits. (And there was an unreasoned element to his setting for limits. For there was an oft-related feature of Mr. Hadaway's experience that inspired me. He had spent the previous year teaching at a suburban high school in Northern California. There, instead of the customary productions of Shakespeare or Marlowe or Shaw de rigueur at the City of London School, he had participated in the school's production of Meredith Wilson's *The Music Man*. I was mightily impressed that in America, schools did not look down snobbish noses at musicals.) In any event, I politely declined his tickets and six years later, on my first visit to Japan, I triumphantly directed a silent epithet in Mr. Hadaway's direction as I descended the flight stairs at Tokyo's Haneda Airport.

It wasn't just the notion of traveling that excited me; it was the notion of "abroad." I came to believe, at a ridiculously early age, that England equaled dreary, while abroad equaled exciting. Somehow, I had come to resent the claustrophobic reality and manners of both my parents and the sceptered isle and to believe that it was only periodic or—later—permanent excursions from it that could hope to make my life bearable.

1953

It wasn't just Pa who inspired my love affair with travel. My mother too was able to summon up and infuse me with the romance of event-filled journeys. She was a second-generation Australian, born—in 1909 like my father—three scant months after the marriage of her English-Moroccan-Jewish father, Bertie, to Kate Campbell, descendant of fiercely anti-Catholic Scottish Presbyterian and Irish Orangeman stock. Shockingly, the mixed marriage caused far less flack in either London or Melbourne than one might have expected. His fervently Sephardic Jewish parents were apparently less upset that Bertie had married a Christian than had he married an Ashkenazi Jew. And Kate's parents—doubtless aghast at her by now burgeoning condition—would have blessed any marriage she undertook—as long as the groom wasn't Catholic.

My mother first traveled in 1912 at the age of three, a long trip to England so she and her mother could be converted to Judaism by Dr. Moses Gaster, the Chief Sephardic Rabbi of the British Empire, confidant of Theodor Herzl and Arthur Balfour. The formal conversion was enacted in order to ensure my mother remained a beneficiary in Bertie's parents' will, a document of phenomenal complexity permitting legacies only to Jewish grandchildren. And her second trip, in 1918, was to bring her from Australia to England for good.

I would hear and demand repeated tales of these myth-like voyages and her earliest memories: at the age of three being terrified in a rickshaw in Colombo, and then the appalling heat of Aden. And she would share her far more detailed recollections of the voyage from Australia to England, when she was nine: the tearful parting from her doting grandparents (whom she was never to see again); the appalling seasickness crossing the Tasman Sea to New Zealand; the long haul across the Pacific; the bald, cut-down tree trunks sprouting from the waters of the recently completed Panama Canal; riding a trolley car in Newport News and being bought a stars-and-stripes pencil at the five-and-dime; seeing the capitol in Washington, DC; and, most vividly of all, a narrative repeated and repeated, the story of her arrival in England.

Their ship, the *Tainui*, had crossed the Atlantic from Virginia, one of a World War I convoy of merchant ships. Just six years after the *Titanic* had gone down, not only were additional lifeboats slung to the sides of the *Tainui*, but once in the Atlantic, the passengers were also required to carry life jackets at all times. Just before lunch on April 8, 1918, just three hundred miles from England, there came the dull thud of a German torpedo. The *Tainui* stopped dead in the water and, very quickly, collapsed into a dramatic list. Ma would relate the utter absence of hysteria, the clambering

up of now-vertical stairways, the un-panicked disembarkation into lifeboats, and the lifeboats' descent into the water—through it all, her rag doll
swinging in her hand. Then came ten interminable hours waiting in the
lifeboats while a destroyer—unable to stop and risk being targeted by yet
another torpedo—circled, its crew snatching one passenger up to the safety
of navy blankets and beef tea with each revolution. The ordeal continued
as the destroyer steamed to Falmouth in Cornwall, where—exhausted,
scared, and grimy—they entrained for the long ride to London and my
grandfather Bertie, who, incredibly but quite in character, reprimanded
my grandmother for the disheveled state in which they arrived. Ultimately,
the *Tainui* didn't sink. Its captain, one R. A. Kelly, and the crew reboarded
the ship and were able to steam—stern-first—to Falmouth. My mother and
grandmother received their waterlogged trunks some weeks later.

With each absorbed tale, my hunger to travel gently converted into lust,
an insatiable craving, and finally an addiction. Ever since adolescence, I have
experienced a sense of desolation, hopelessness, and panic if no trip is in
the planning. And, to assuage the pangs, or to give myself a quick travel
fix, I came to surround myself with guidebooks, maps, atlases, brochures,
timetables, schedules, and—my favorite palliative of all—those dozens of
red Michelin guides lined up along a long shelf describing in a parade of
miniature symbols and hieroglyphics not the sights but the attributes of the
hotels of France and Italy and Britain and Germany.

1954

In reality, it did all begin with hotels. At four, I developed a blend of revulsion-
enchantment with the aroma of the Metropole Hotel in Brighton, a fra-
grance that to this day stimulates reminiscence. What was it precisely?
Most probably a curiously British amalgam of lavender floor wax, brass
polish, roasting mutton, broiling kippers, pipe tobacco, chrysanthemums,
and toast . . . and, to be sure, most hotels in England seem to remain suffused to this day with a rendering of it. In 1971 I marched up the stairs of
the achingly colonial Repulse Bay Hotel on the southern coast of Hong
Kong Island, only to be assaulted by the identical aroma.

In the mid-fifties, the Metropole was the grandest hotel in Brighton, the
resort on the English Channel we visited often. Even though it was only
fifty-two miles from London, the drive through London's endless boroughs,
then towns, villages, and countryside was a complicated journey that took

up almost half a day. As we entered Preston Park on Brighton's outskirts, Pa would announce, "First one who sees the sea gets a penny!" and I would crane to catch that first glimpse of the churning gray Channel.

Until the day he died, Pa believed the cure for illness, mild or serious, was a "breath of sea air." Inevitably, after any of us had suffered a cold or flu, we would drive down to Brighton and stand on the elegant promenade with its fussy wrought iron railings and noble streetlamps to breathe in deep gulps of freezing, salty winter air as the waves crashed up the shingle beach. Sometimes it would be just a day trip, but more often than not we would take rooms at the Metropole, a giant red-brick Edwardian pile smack on the "front." Over the years, we stayed at other Brighton hotels too, each with its own slightly recast version of *le parfum du* Metropole: the Salisbury, the Royal Albion, Hockleys, Clarges—but never at the Grand, just next door to the Metropole, a place where, I somehow divined, "Metropole people" didn't stay. (It was at the Grand Hotel in 1984 that Margaret Thatcher was almost killed by an IRA bombing.)

I can close my eyes now and summon up the Metropole's thick floral carpets, its brass and oak revolving doors, its arching aspidistras in copper urns, its giant quadrangular stairwells lit by stained glass skylights, the white wicker furniture, and sea-spray splattered windows of the conservatory facing the sea. Best of all was that intoxicatingly coddled sensation of returning after supper to my bedroom, its curtains snugly drawn, its bedside light aglow, its bed invitingly turned down, pillows plumped, and a hot-water bottle tucked between crisp sheets.

It was a far simpler time. No glossy catalog of hotel services perched on the dresser. There was no television, only a radio tuned uncompromisingly and barely audibly to one station, the BBC's Home Service. No symbols of waiters, or maids with mops, or porters toting bags danced around the telephone dial . . . indeed the black telephone, with its twisted plaited-fabric cord, had no dial. One just lifted the receiver and waited for the operator, somewhere deep in the hotel's bowels, to respond. Similarly, there was no breakfast order form to hang on the doorknob before retiring. Yet, each day at seven thirty, a tray of "early morning" tea and the *Daily Telegraph* would be delivered to the room by a uniformed waiter.

I don't think it was as a result of my parent's particular quirky desire for privacy, but even at the age of five or six, I always occupied my own room. British hotels didn't have vast rooms with two queen beds and cots ubiquitous in the United States. No, I slept privately in my small room and my narrow bed, and no thought seems to have been given to the lurking dangers that could result from my isolation. And even though my parents insisted on having a private bathroom, my room usually didn't. It would have a sink and towels. A swing door in the front of the bedside table would open to reveal a porcelain chamber pot, the emptying and cleansing of which was the happy responsibility of the chambermaid. Lavatories, and separate bathrooms, were down the hall somewhere, so it was always necessary to travel with robe and slippers. I would bathe in a tub still wetly warm from its last occupant, then return to my room to dress or for bed. I didn't consciously realize it then, but there was inevitably something seductively provocative, a quality unfathomly risqué, about such an arrangement . . . quite apart from its extraordinary lack of hygiene, for these bathrooms only contained bathtubs, never ever a shower. As I write this in twenty-first-century New York, it seems preposterous that so antediluvian a circumstance could still have existed in the 1950s (and '60s and '70s), but just as I felt the London I knew was of a far earlier era, so was much of Britain's—and my—way of life.

Brighton also meant visiting Great-Aunt Vi, Grandpa Bertie's sister, my mother's aunt (after whom my mother, Violet, had been named). Vi, like Queen Mary, was another wisp of Edwardiana grafted—not in the least inappropriately it seemed to me—onto my vision of the 1950s. She had been raised in a vast house in Maida Vale—no more than two blocks from my own home—with her staggeringly elegant Anglo-Franco-Moroccan-Jewish parents, four siblings, and a coterie of servants. She reeked of the fin de siècle and lived—bereft, tubercular, and stooped—in an apartment carved out of an immense late-Victorian mansion, near the sea in the genteel neighborhood of Hove. Her colossal sitting room had thirteen-foot ceilings and was crammed with a suitably colossal polished sideboard, chaise longues, and ormolu screens, and everywhere, perched on every surface and atop protruding ornamental shelves, stood Gallé vases, Limoges boxes, Sèvres tableaux vivants, Meissen bowls, Staffordshire figurines, fulsome hydrangeas in wicker baskets, and gigantic gladioli soaring in violet and peach fan-shaped arrangements toward the carved cciling.

Aunt Vi's bedroom was capacious, but the grandeur of the two front rooms was in distinct contrast to the private quarters. The lavatory was a small room somehow slung on to the back of the house's main floor that, even in July and August, was freezing. Next door was the tiny kitchen, containing creaking cabinets, a deep square porcelain sink, an ancient two-burner gas stove, and a hot water tank suspended perilously midway up the wall from which golden blue flames would belch without warning. The claw-foot bathtub had a full-length, hinged lid that doubled as a scarlet Contact-papered countertop (the lid was raised only at bath time). There was no refrigerator—milk and other perishables were secreted in an alcove screened with wire mesh and open to the elements.

Nevertheless, Great-Aunt Vi somehow symbolized unfettered opulence. Not the kind of arriviste excess exhibited by many of my far-too-Jewish-for-my-mother school friends, but an honest-to-God grandeur born out of the immense wealth her father had amassed by 1900. She would serve gigantic platters of daintily constructed smoked salmon sandwiches; large orange-membraned smoked cod's roe; melons and peaches purchased inexplicably and extravagantly out of season; and Herend or Wedgwood bowls heaped with violet and rose cream-filled dark chocolates, each crowned with a corresponding crystallized flower petal.

Great-Aunt Vi was passionate about music and would tell me about "that night at the Royal Albert Hall" when, with Toscanini conducting, Sergei Rachmaninov had been the soloist for his own Second Piano Concerto. At the final chord, the entire audience had risen, tear-filled, to its feet to acknowledge the equally tear-filled conductor and composer. I learned only in my teens that the most searing of Vi's passions had resulted in her divorce in the 1920s: a scandalous affair with a married man, who died still married in 1949, causing her to immerse herself in a period of mourning so bottomless that she was said to have developed tuberculosis. During her last years, Great-Aunt Vi would spend each winter in a sanatorium for the tubercular in Sussex and my mother would address letters to her aunt "in care of Isolation Ward."

Mourning was an infinitely more theatrical pursuit in those days, for if we were visiting Great-Aunt Vi in the summer, I would be treated to a double dose of time warp as her sister, Florence, would be on an extended visit from Paris. In 1928 Great-Aunt Flo too had descended irretrievably into grief after the death of her adored son Raymond, also of tuberculosis. Until the day she died, Flo was never again to be seen in any color other than those permitted the Victorian mourner: black, gray, white, and lilac.

If Great-Aunt Vi merely reeked of the fin de siècle, it coursed liberally from Flo's every pore. Far shorter than Vi at four foot eleven, Flo had penetrating, slightly goitered eyes, a determined gait, and a closet-choking collection of chapeaux. She had lived in Paris since her marriage at the turn of the century. Then in her eighties, she would travel the Golden Arrow boat train from France to England to summer with Vi (during the intervening ten months of the year, they would exchange daily letters). The two would spend their summers gloriously, recounting old times, shopping, bickering, visiting us in London, and playing thousands of games of canasta and bridge with Vi's circle of equally aged and patrician friends—either at Great-Aunt Vi's home or on the porch of Cecily Oppenheimer's beach shack, or "chalet" (pronounced "chally," says Paul Theroux in his *Kingdom by the Sea*) on the seafront promenade. There, in a white-painted cocoon of refinement, they would spend languid afternoons perched on upright beach chairs, clad in layers of cardigans, protected from the Channel's gusts by the strategic positioning of the chally's doors, sipping milky tea poured from thermoses into bone china cups and saucers, their playing cards secured from the gale beneath the card table's elastic corner bands.

Flo's style of traveling seemed marvelous to me . . . and perfectly proper. She would not for a moment have considered flying from Paris, insisting on what was even by then the increasingly outmoded and complicated journey aboard three trains and a boat to reach Brighton. But that is how it ought to have been. The image of Flo on a plane would have been completely out of character: rather like those mortifying photos of the Duke and Duchess of Windsor doing the twist at El Morocco. Flo's English was perfect, as was her French, but her unique eccentricity of speech had to do with the fact that the languages were not to be mixed: words had to be pronounced in accordance with the language being spoken. If she was talking in English about France's second-largest city, Lyon, she would pronounce it "Lions." If she were referring to her Channel crossing from Dover, her destination, Calais, would be pronounced "Callous." A menu with a large choice of items was "on the card."

Flo and Vi brought a bygone era alive as they entertained me with tales of their, their singlings', and their parents' summers in Deauville, winters in Nice, springs in Paris, and autumns in Evian—with all the attendant packing of trunks, airing of rooms, advance dispatch of servants, and grand hotels with palm courts. Their father, Aaron Afriat, was born in 1850 in Oufran, a tiny oasis of palm trees and red mud houses in the Anti-Atlas region of southern Morocco, a vision straight off Cecil B. DeMille's back lot. Jews were said to have lived in Oufran for some 2,500 years, and when the news arrived in 70 AD that the Temple in Jerusalem had been destroyed, Oufran became known as the New Jerusalem. The Afriats were wealthy traders in an eclectic collection of commodities that included gold dust, ostrich feathers, and ivory transported by caravans of camels from Timbuktu, across the Sahara, to Oufran and eventually to Mogador, a port city on Morocco's Atlantic coast. When Aaron was a child, his father moved the family to Mogador—nowadays called Essaouira—then Morocco's chief trading port, a city whose population was more than 50 percent Jewish. Here, home was a whitewashed mansion with blue doors, similar to all the town's whitewashed, blue-doored houses, hovels, mosques, and synagogues—all protected from the Atlantic breakers by spectacular terracotta battlements and turrets built by the Portuguese. Aaron matured in a house that was nondescript outside and palatial within, sited in the heart of the town (his brother's house nearby was in the 1980s to become Essaouira's first boutique hotel). In 1873 wanderlust moved Aaron to London, where he opened a branch of the family import-export business and quickly developed it into the period's largest Anglo-Moroccan trading house. Now wealthy beyond his dreams, he sailed back to Morocco to wed Rahma Toledano of Tangier, a direct descendant of the Jewish elders of Toledo expelled from Spain in 1492, and brought her back to London. It was in London that their five children were born and from which they peregrinated to Deauville, Evian, the Cote d'Azur, and Paris, and where, despite Rahma's extravagance and Franco-Spanish-Arab hot temper, they lived more or less happily ever after.

Another guest at Auntie Vi's was sometimes that other of Aaron and Rahma's remaining offspring: Vi's brother, my grandfather Bertie. He lived in London but we saw him seldom, for he and my grandmother, who lived with us, had separated in the 1920s, and their relationship, if no longer rancorous was, well, at best awkward. He, like Vi and Flo, was exquisitely profligate, almost always with money he didn't have, and whenever he came to visit would arrive toting a vast and expensive cream gâteau packaged in the distinctive orange cardboard box of Maison Lyons at Marble Arch.

Bertie, like his sisters, had lived a colorful, travel-filled life, the components of which I was quick to digest. In 1906 his despairing father had packed his lazy and spendthrift son off to Australia, where he met, courted, impregnated, then married my grandmother. After the outbreak of World War I in 1914, he was one of the first 350 "Australians" to volunteer for the army and in 1915 sailed boisterously off with his brothers-in-law and the Australian Anzac troops to Egypt. Then they were shipped to Galipoli, where, unlike so many who were instantly slaughtered as they landed on the beaches, he was merely struck down by malaria and evacuated to Cairo. A year later, after recovering in England, he was back in uniform—no longer a lowly Australian private but an officer in the British army. At the battle of the Somme, he received a bullet in the side of his head and his "batman"—the archaic term for a British officer's "servant"—carried him over his shoulder from the front lines to the medical tents as blood poured from his bandaged skull. Grandpa's injury was so grievous that his convalescence took two years and was so unexpected and inventively achieved that it was detailed in the British *Lancet* medical journal. Picturesquely, the injury to his temple, while leaving his taste buds intact, had severed the nerves enabling the tongue and mouth to differentiate hot from cold. Even at the most elegant dinner, he needed to poke at his food with his finger to ensure he wouldn't be burned. After World War I, he became a part-time gambler, satyr, painter, and antique salesman, and because of his affinity for languages, he worked intermittently as a courier for the very same Thomas Cook & Son where my career began fifty years later. He would accompany groups of English travelers to the Continent, interpreting, troubleshooting, no doubt taking particularly good care of the single ladies, and developing the sightseeing dogma that I would eventually come to inherit, that "once you've seen ten churches, ten cathedrals, and ten museums, you've seen them all."

After one visit to Brighton, Ma and I returned alone to London by train, permitting me a glimpse of that fading era that Vi and Flo and Bertie epitomized. We came home on the Brighton Belle, a train made up entirely of brown-and-cream art deco Pullman cars (coaches that were mothballed in the 1960s and revived in the 1980s as part of the re-creation of the British segment of the Venice Simplon-Orient-Express). In each car, ranks of Queen Anne wing chairs, upholstered in mushroom Genoa velvet, faced each other across tables covered with starched white tablecloths. Stewards in frock coats served tea from silver pots and passed silver platters piled with toast drenched in melted salty butter. On each table, adjacent to windows framed by swooping, brown velvet drapes, there perched a small table lamp crowned with a cream-colored, brown-fringed shade. Those lamps helped exude so warm and cozy a glow that it filled not only the carriage but also me with a sense of butter-drenched well-being palpable to this day. The glow was reflected in the window as we rolled at sunset through Sussex, and weary travelers in their drab commuter trains would gaze back—enviously and wistfully, I fancied—at our coddled and romantic environment.

The Afriats, London, circa 1895. Back row (*l to r*): Great-Uncle Edward, Great-Grandfather Aaron, Great-Grandmother Rahma, Great-Uncle Frank; front row (*l to r*): Great-Aunt Flo, Great-Aunt Vi, Grandpa Bertie. (Author collection)

I never met another of Vi, Flo, and Bertie's siblings: Great-Uncle Edward. At the turn of the century, when he was nineteen, Edward contracted syphilis. Great-Grandpa Aaron expended a fortune relaying him from specialist to specialist to specialist in London, Paris, Switzerland, Vienna, Berlin, following every lead, pursuing every quack's theory, in an elusive search for a cure. I have a copy of Edward's elegantly bound journal describing his and his brother Frank's visit to Tangier, their mother's hometown, when he was eighteen. It details their adventures, their explorations, their meeting with the British consul, a Monsieur Hatchwell (a distant relative), all in innocently ardent cadences. Was it on this trip that in a chamber deep within the kasbah, aromatic with rose water, illuminated by ornate, hanging brass oil lamps, the floor warmed by handcrafted rugs and piled seductively with gilt-embroidered brocade pillows, the fatal spirochete was transmitted? (It could, of course, just as easily have been transmitted in London, for the Afriats' elegant home was not more than a five-minute stroll from Portsdown Road, notorious for its squadrons of prostitutes.) By the time of my parents' wedding in 1934, Edward was intermittently demented and his gait, aided by two malacca canes, had deteriorated into a gnarled, frenzied goose step. And by the end of the decade, when Alexander Fleming was scooping teaspoonfuls of penicillin from a grimy windowsill at St. Mary's Hospital in Paddington—no more than five minutes by taxicab from Edward's home—he was dead.

1957

At eight, I was as obsessed with other people's travels as much as I was preoccupied with my parents' or mine. I wanted the details. I wanted to hear the minutiae most people consider irrelevant. If they went to Rome, it was nice to see their small black-and-white snaps of the Vatican and the Forum, but I was far more interested to know what airline they had flown. It mattered to me to know at what hotel they had stayed and where they had eaten dinner. It amazed and frustrated me then, just as it amazes and frustrates me still, how at eleven I could ask Aunt Hilda on what kind of aircraft she had flown on her recent visit to Brussels and be met with a disconcerted "I haven't the slightest idea, darling."

Clearly, for almost everybody I knew, the plane or the boat or the train was merely the device to effect the reaching of their destination, just as their hotel was a place simply to sleep. I feel sorry for that vast majority who loathe airports. I feel sad for those who see a plane in the sky and don't ache to know what airline owns it, or what type of aircraft it is or where it's going or coming from. I feel distanced from the people who say to me—in regard to a hotel in, say, Florence, "What does it matter what it's like? We just sleep there." While all the while there is this part of me that seems to feel that all the sightseeing that must inescapably be performed on a first visit to Budapest or Madrid or Delhi—activities that I really do treasure to varying extents—are pastimes somehow required to fill the day in between the enjoyments of the hotel. It is as if the tours of the Taj Mahal or the hours at the Prado are the price to be paid for the "hotel pleasure."

Because "hotel pleasure" is exactly what it is. Had Freud identified it, it would be part of our language—*Hotelvergnügung*—up there alongside Schadenfreude and Weltanschauung. I cannot help but note the tiniest details: from the cut of the concierge's jacket to the timbre of the service to the typeface of the room service menu to the display of amenities on the bathroom counter to the arching of a vaulted marble lobby. That unfathomable glimmer of the erotic that as a small boy I somehow derived from bathing in a tub warmed by a previous guest's bathwater at Brighton's Hotel Metropole has not as an adult diminished. Indeed, it has ripened.

Ultimately, perhaps it is the awareness that a hotel embodies a series of enclosures in which more than one hundred strangers are cavorting privately, unfettered by the strictures of their regular lives. Those benign corridors of benign doors are like masks that conceal the bathers, the lovers, the sleepers, the insomniacs, the writers, the readers, the thieves, the tricksters, the disguised, the porn watchers, the rope-bound masochists, the naked promenaders, the sad, the happy, the benumbed, the suicidal— each separated from me by no more than an inch or two of lumber.

Every Do Not Disturb sign challenges me with the silent question: "Why?" The opening of every door augurs a seductive array of opportunity. A knock or a press of the bell heralds countless possibilities: the arrival of a hamburger accompanied by ketchup in an endearing miniature Heinz jar; a fax in a giant envelope with an elaborate clasp; a trolley bearing foie gras, slices of toast enshrouded in a linen napkin, and a bottle of Veuve Clicquot; a vase of roses with the warmest greetings of the general manager—the signature forged by his secretary on her daily pile of such cards or, better yet, just printed in blue to contrast with the letter's black. The knock could announce the entry to one's private lair of that

busty maid with the legs that go on forever, or that adorable room service waiter with the bubble butt and yard-long eyelashes, that delicious
little laundress with the bewitching dimple, that hunky technician reeking
faintly of sweat summoned perhaps just a little too often to reconnect a
laptop to the internet. Perhaps it is simply that the wanton opportunities
proffered by a hotel—real, imagined, fantasized, realized, unrealized—are
infinite.

Yet the love affair with hotels that began at the Metropole in Brighton
was not one to which I—through no fault of my own—was to be permanently faithful. Because circumstances both familial and financial ordered
that there was in my early years a great deal of staying at the homes of
relatives—and, far more than that, a great many relatives staying with us.
As a child, I particularly enjoyed the latter. The arrival of guests—often
for a week or more—brought a welcome break from the habitual, with its
rearranging of sleeping arrangements, the crowds at breakfast, the tumult,
the secrets, and in those exhausting days appended to puberty, the not-so-
occasional frisson of sex.

With shoals of relatives of my mother periodically appearing from Australia, with my father's sister in America, with Aunt Flo in Paris, Aunt
Vi in Brighton, and Aunt Olga in South Africa, we became the London
base of operation to many. My most favorite guests came from Paris: my
mother's cousins Henri (Aunt Flo's son—pronounced "On-rrri") and Joyce,
and their son, Raymond—pronounced with a rolled "r" and a silent "d"—
who was gossipy, Brylcreemed, charming, exasperatingly handsome, and
thoroughly engaging. Henri was thoughtful, quiet, and amiable, with dimples and smiling eyes that could light up a room. Joyce was bossy, gregarious,
witty, and just a touch manly. She exuded colossal charisma. While most
of us merely walked, Joyce marched. She was London-born, the daughter
of Frank, yet another of Flo's and my grandfather's siblings I never knew.
For Henri and Joyce were both married and first cousins, a circumstance I
had no idea at the time was something many people considered, shall we
say, unusual.

Raymond and my closeness was remarkable, although understandable,
for he in Paris and I in London had grown up in similarly claustrophobic
Edwardian environments, with two forty-something parents and a grandmother whose heyday was the turn of the twentieth century. We shared
common interests: stamp collecting, music, the mysteries of sex, admiring antiques, rearranging the furniture, and playing canasta—the latter

three pursuits, even in 1958, not entirely customary for the average male eight-year-old.

Henri, Joyce, and Raymond's annual visits to London embodied an array of traveling styles. Their spending was modest—not, my mother impugned, because they were particularly reduced in circumstances but because they were chronically frugal. Their journeys from Paris to London and back were never a simple plane flight, nor even the stylish Golden Arrow train that Flo would board for her annual visits to play bridge and bicker in Brighton. No, their journey was usually achieved aboard something called Silver Arrow—a three-stage journey that was curious, endless, and cheap . . . the Ryanair of the 1950s. A bus ride would take them from the center of Paris to the town of Beauvais in northern France (whose airfield to this day the no-frills Ryanair terms "Paris"), on the lawns of whose windy aerodrome they would board an ancient Elizabethan airplane. Next would come the ear-shattering, piston-driven thirty-minute flight to Lydd, not far from the English side of the channel. There they would disembark, clear immigration and customs, and then clamber aboard yet another bus for the ride to Victoria Coach Station in London.

Joyce and Henri didn't believe in hotels either. For their month in England, they arranged a complex schedule of stays with arrays of relatives and friends—three days here, five or seven days there, etcetera—and their frugality, if that is what it was, would be mitigated by their arrival on the threshold shouldering a vast gâteau in a box, or an immense basket of exotic fruit. I think my mother was being uncharitable, a sentiment she managed often easily to radiate. I think Joyce and Henri probably did have to watch their expenses. But I also believe they enjoyed the bonhomie and camaraderie of being houseguests. They liked helping burn the toast at breakfast and sharing bathrooms and making beds and the chaos, endless chatter, reminiscences, and anecdotes. I liked it too.

Our apartment was large, on the second floor of a red-brick Victorian block of genteel "mansion flats" at the corner of Lauderdale and Ashworth Roads in Maida Vale—a neighborhood perfectly middle class in 1960, and quite ritzy now. The building overlooked the red-brick copper-domed Spanish and Portuguese synagogue whose erection in 1896 Raymond's and my great-grandfather had helped fund. The entrance to our "block of flats" was flanked by black marble columns, the entry hall was black-and-white tile, and the apartment itself was surrounded by balconies. There were four bedrooms. The dining room—with mock-Tudor table and

chairs as well as armchairs and the one-channel black-and-white television—
was where we lived day to day. Here we dined, watched the news, played
canasta, did puzzles, and battled over Monopoly. It was where I did much
of my homework. It was where the invitations, the charts, the table plans,
and the thank-you notes for my Bar Mitzvah were to devolve into a project
so gargantuan and fractious that it surpassed in complexity the planning
of the landings in Anzio. And it was from the dining room's mock-Tudor
sideboard that my father took to pouring himself the generous gins and
tonics of the fifties, the Camparis and soda and Pernods and water of the
sixties, and the chain-drinking shots of scotch from nine thirty in the morning until bedtime of the seventies and eighties.

At the apex of the apartment there was a stately sitting room, full of
books, excellent antiques, and velvet couches. It was a room used only
when we were entertaining and where Ma would arrange spectacular tall
displays of flowers in a fan-shaped vase. There was a big family kitchen
with a stove from Dickens and a laundry rack suspended from the ceiling.
This device was raised and lowered by rope pulleys so that family suppers
of kedgeree or kidneys and bacon were habitually experienced beneath a
canopy of my mother's drying corsets and my father's bizarrely capacious
woolen underpants. At the rear of the kitchen, a window was opened
once daily so that trash could be placed onto a tiny goods elevator operated by "the porter" standing two floors down at the base of the air shaft.
His readiness to collect the garbage was signaled by his blowing air into
a mouthpiece in the basement that, after passing through fifty feet of lead
piping, emerged piercingly through the holes of a whistle secured into
our kitchen wall. On the other side of the kitchen, a door led to the pantry
where tiled shelves abutted a window left permanently ajar so cold air could
circulate. Here was where eggs, butter, cheese, vegetables, fruit, joints of
lamb, and crocks of beef drippings sat atop the tiles that were certainly
cool enough for much of the year, but clearly not in the summer. I will
never forget wiping a glob of Camembert onto a slice of toast only to realize, before it reached my lips, that the glob was wriggling. Yes, there was
a refrigerator, with Raymond Lowy curves and no shelves in the door,
where milk was kept. Beyond the kitchen was the former maid's room—
which was where my grandmother lived. Hers was the only part of the
apartment that remained immune to the addition of mattresses and sleeping cots when guests came to stay. The maid's tiny washroom and toilet
had been shortsightedly converted years before into a large murky storage

Lauderdale Mansions, Maida Vale. Our flat wrapped around much of the second floor. (Author collection)

closet piled high with luggage and impossible-to-find ephemera, old clothes, and junk.

My parents' bedroom, with its twin walnut beds placed together, was a symphony of mauve, lilac, and lavender, the favored color palette of my mother, Violet. Flowery curtains (purple, violet, and gray) covered the bay windows. Two oval gilt frames on the wall contained toddler photographs of Anthony and me. Ma's art deco dressing table was covered with art deco silver brushes and mirrors that sat atop lace doilies. Anthony's bedroom was near the flat's entrance, boyish with gray diamond wallpaper, and my bedroom—attached to my parents'—was originally the master bedroom's dressing room: small and square and unexceptional.

Yet with all this space in the flat, there was but one bathroom and one toilet. It never occurred to me until I was grown that in a home with four or five permanent residents, and with intermittent battalions of house-guests, this was not entirely convenient. More than that, there was no central heating. In winter, the sitting and dining rooms were feebly heated by coal fires, with buckets of grimy, dusty coal hauled from the basement by the porter or my father. Eventually, they and the bedrooms were warmed by gas fires. The kitchen was heated by lighting the oven and leaving the stove door open. Our cat liked to nap in the bottom of the warm oven. The bathroom and toilet were not heated at all.

Yet to a little boy who was by no means incurious about matters erotic, the paucity of bathrooms had a definite magnetism. For there was—particularly when Henri, Joyce, and Raymond came to stay—a seductively locker-room quality to the daily ablutions. In a space of no more that sixty square feet, including the bathtub, my father would bathe, Henri would shave, Raymond and I would chatter and spectate, then Henri would bathe and Pa would shave, then Raymond and I would bathe. Conversation was effected in a manner no different than had, say, Henri been seated on a brocade armchair munching a cucumber sandwich rather than toweling his crotch. For a somewhat troubled small boy, it was difficult to concentrate on social banter and the pros and cons of the Suez Crisis, the newest Jaguars, or the lunch menu amid the flaunting of so much brazen naked-ness. The extravagantly in-your-face (literally) soaping, rinsing, stretching, and drying of so assorted a variety of genitalia was at the same time mesmerizing, embarrassing, intriguing, and intimidating.

As with every aspect of my life, my mother had a set of rules—in this case "visitor rules" to be employed both by guests in our home as well as

My Parisian cousin,
Raymond, and me,
circa 1959. (Author
collection)

to be followed when we stayed at the homes of others. For instance, it was
an unstated requirement that the guests were to arrive with a gift. Depend-
ing on the time of day of the guests' arrival, beds were either made up
with fresh sheets, or sheets, blankets, and pillows were prepared in neat
piles to be applied to cots and the sitting room sofa at bedtime. The towel
racks in that solitary bathroom were rearranged, with space made for
towels (large, small, and face) for each guest. Even though we had a daily
maid—"the daily," as she was known in the London of 1957—guests were
expected to make their own beds and neaten their "space." Meals were
always prepared en famille, consumed en famille, cleared away en famille,
the dishes washed and dried en famille. Seventy percent through the stay,
it was customary for the guests to arrive home from the day's peregrina-
tions bearing a second gift—preferably something for the house. On the
penultimate or final night of the visit, it was expected that the guests take
the hosts to a restaurant for dinner. And on the final morning of the visit, the
guests would strip their beds, placing their sheets, pillowcases, and towels
in the laundry hamper and, generally, leaving the place as they found it.

When I was twelve, an aged first cousin of my grandmother named Nell Campbell came from Australia to stay with us, accompanied by her even more aged husband, Herb. Nell had been a middle-aged spinster when she married Herb Baker, a man from the outback, rather rough at the edges, whom my mother adored. For her, he represented the real Australia. He had a fiercely broad Australian accent; he was courtly, yet his demeanor was rough and outdoorsy. He had made a lot of money—I have no idea at what. They stayed with us for a very long time and made their presence felt by never considering it necessary to lock either the bathroom or the lavatory door. Their house gift was to take us to see Lionel Bart's new musical *Blitz*, whose story revolved around a Jewish and a Christian family in London's East End during "the War" (the universal way to which World War II was, and to me still is, referred), and the forbidden love of the Jewish son for the Christian daughter. The scenes of the air raids were brilliantly conceived, and I was thrilled by the scene set in the air raid shelter on the platform of the London Underground—when the passing of a tube train was dazzlingly conveyed by sound and flickering lights.

Yet the part of Nell and Herb's stay that engaged me the most was their departure. We drove them to Liverpool Street Station to see them onto the boat train to east London's Tilbury docks, from which they would sail back to Sydney. Their voyage of six weeks would take them in first class aboard a bilious green Shaw Savill liner through the Bay of Biscay, the Straits of Gibraltar, the Mediterranean, the Suez Canal, the Red Sea, the Gulf of Aden, the Arabian and Andaman seas, and the Indian Ocean. Herb allowed me to help him complete the stickers and labels for their copious suitcases. And he honored me by letting me lick the backs of the gummed labels and plaster them on the sides of the bags. "They must always be stuck on at an angle," he instructed, "never straight. That way, the porters can see them."

There was a simplicity to Nell and Herb. They were good people, upstanding, courteous, interested—but there was a bluntness to Herb that revealed his lack of formal education. Like Americans and all good "colonials," he eschewed the homeland's exaggerated politesse. Nell and he also radiated a sense of the puritanical that symbolized the stark difference between my mother's mother's Christian side of the family and that of her and my father's Jewish sides. When Toby, Pa's Jewish high school friend who had moved to Australia in the 1930s, came to London with his wife, Joyce, they did not stay with us. They stayed at the Connaught. They shopped at Fortnum and Mason, Joyce wore floor-length mink, and they invited us to dinner at the Mirabelle—at the time London's finest French restaurant, now the location of the Caprice, grimly and permanently shuttered by COVID-19.

1958

While it was customary for Aunt Flo and for Henri, Joyce, and Raymond to come from Paris to stay with us every summer, it was not until I was eight, in the late spring of 1958, that we returned the favor.

"You're going to get killed!" my schoolmates taunted me prior to the trip. "You're going to get blown up."

No, this was not Charlie Hebdo and 2015. That May 1958, the news reports from Paris were indeed alarming. Frenchmen, infuriated by President Charles de Gaulle's intention to give up France's possession of Algeria, were bombing the streets of Paris, and on our one-channel black-and-white television we saw demonstrations, mayhem, and even tanks on the Champs-Elysées. France was awash in terrorism.

No matter, we were going. We were to ride the boat train from London's Victoria Station to Paris's Gare du Nord—an eight-hour journey, and, needless to say, I was to worship every moment. As had by now become customary, the details were observed and preserved in my memory. A particular favorite was—after the train ride from London to Dover and the springtime crossing of the English Channel—the dark-green French train. It seemed trenchantly exotic. Unlike the brown train cars in England, with their rectangular windows and copious doors, the windows of the French train were strangely oval. I considered this outstanding. And there was an interior corridor on one side of each coach that opened into individual compartments . . . again, exceptional. Boarding the train, we were immersed in a fog of Gitanes smoke so entirely French and so utterly different from the English tobacco stinks to which I was accustomed. I sat at the train's window as it raced through Picardy, noting—and marveling at—how dissimilar from England were the architecture of the houses, the shape of the haystacks, the girth of the cows, the structure of the churches. The cars we passed were entirely different too: racy black Citroëns with running boards and the seemingly flimsy and ubiquitous Deux Chevaux—their arching carapaces, curved like those of the train's windows, bespeaking a palpable sense of the alien.

It wasn't just the smells and views that were different but also the tastes. Ham baguettes and sweet orange soda were purchased from a man pushing a cart the length of the train. I was familiar with the "French bread" Ma bought from Grodzinki's Bakery in Elgin Avenue, but that bore not the slightest resemblance to the wax-paper-wrapped sandwich that was thrust into my hands. How could something as pedestrian as a ham sandwich, something so simple, taste so delicious? The bread was crisp on the outside, yet its core was chewy. The butter was thickly wiped and unsalted. There was an earthy crispness to the lettuce; the ham was moist and succulent and plentiful. It was not the gummy single-slice, single-taste Wonderloaf ham sandwich of England. Here, every element of the combination of flavors was discernible. The orange soda was my first ever carbonated drink. The bubbles went up my nose.

Paris was an apprentice cosmopolitan's dream and, apart from the occasional police van's siren, in five days we witnessed not a hint of the threatened havoc. While Ma, Pa, and Anthony were to sleep at a small hotel on the Boulevard de Courcelles, I was to stay around the corner with Flo, Joyce, Henri, and Raymond. Their apartment was classic Paris, located in the aristocratic 17th arrondissement, a ten-minute walk from the Arc de Triomphe. A vast doorway on the narrow side street swung open to reveal a fat cat, an aging concierge shuffling in furry carpet slippers and, beyond them, an oval art nouveau iron-and-glass elevator that sat within the swirl of a graceful fin-de-siècle marble and bronze staircase. The elevator car was tiny—with room for one. It rose at a pace so painfully slow that it was quicker to walk up the four flights to the apartment.

The flat was simultaneously cavernous, elegant, and just a touch decrepit. Double entry doors led into a gracious, wide gallery with stucco ceilings, intermittently frayed Persian rugs, crystal chandeliers, mirrors, and occasionally peeling paint. To the right, the gallery led to both the dining and drawing rooms, each with marble fireplaces and French windows looking onto Rue Théodule Ribot. The two rooms were divided by elaborately Napoleonic wrought iron and bronze gates on which—to Flo's fury—Raymond and I liked to swing. The living room furniture was Louis XV and paralyzingly formal. At the end of the gallery, double doors led to a small square hall that led on to Flo's grand bedroom—also facing the street—and the vast apartment's only bathroom.

An almost invisible door in the left wall of the entrance gallery opened to reveal a small corridor that led to the kitchen, a room that faced the interior stairwell. Here, the Belle Époque instantly evaporated into the set for *Les Misérables*. The walls were dun colored. Inexplicable thrusts and parries of pipes brought water lurching through the cold-water faucet into the deep, cracked porcelain sink. A lightbulb hung bare. The stove was pre–Joan of Arc. A checkered oilcloth covered the table. A back door led out to another stairwell, with stairs up to the unused servants' garret and down to garbage cans and the tradesmen's entrance. There was no sign of a refrigerator: in comfortably middle-class Paris of 1958, food shopping was performed twice, three times, a day. Beyond the small square hall that gave onto Flo's bedroom and the bathroom, another small door opened into a winding narrow corridor that led to Henri and Joyce's phenomenally cluttered bedroom and ultimately to Raymond's room, where I was to sleep on a cot.

The layout of the apartment bespoke the relationship of the four people for whom it was home: the grandmother—both aunt and mother-in-law to her son's wife—ensconced in the front of the apartment, with everyone else in the back. In alternating waves of emotion, Flo loved Joyce, her niece, and loathed Joyce, her daughter-in-law. And Joyce despised and adored her right back. They both doted on Henri, who spent his life trying to placate the two of them. He exuded a frail bonhomie that bespoke not only a sense of silent martyrdom but also utter frustration that his placating could never succeed. Raymond was ensnared in constant conspiracy, privy to his mother's and grandmother's secrets and their vicious denigrations of the other. Through diplomacy, guile, manipulation, and charm, he accomplished walking the emotional tightrope between the two. The ultimately poisonous ingredient was that Flo had lived in the apartment since World War II and considered everyone else her guest. Her clinging on to the grand bedroom, with her son and daughter-in-law / niece condemned to much smaller and peculiarly shaped quarters in the apartment's interior, was an act of bizarre selfishness, perhaps her way of reminding all of the pecking order.

When I first arrived at that apartment in the spring of 1958, it all seemed intoxicatingly chic. Yet there was certainly something both remarkable and discomfiting in the grandeur of the front of the flat in contrast with the drabness of its rear. The first impediment I had to overcome was the bathroom. An immense porcelain tub perched atop gilded claw feet, surrounded by ominous pipes and racks atop which an array of elasticated caps and baffling pink rubber tubes were drying. There was a large oval sink atop a pedestal. And there was an oddly shaped, very low toilet that, instead of a flush, was equipped with two porcelain faucets, a small spray nozzle akin to the top of a pepper shaker, and a drain. I recognized that I could pee in it, but how could I do anything else? I was panicked. It wasn't for hours that I discovered that behind a door far down the peculiarly shaped back hallway was a tiny dank room containing a recognizable toilet—and that the contraption in the bathroom was called a bidet, a continental contrivance, my mother straight-facedly explained, that existed for the purpose of washing the feet.

Each morning, Raymond and I would wake early, quickly dress, and run down the stairs to the corner to buy baguettes still warm from the oven, and fresh, unpasteurized milk. We returned to an apartment in the throes of the ablutions du jour. Because the heating of Parisian water was, it was explained, astronomically expensive, bathwater was shared: first Henri, then me, then Raymond, each cavorting and toweling in front of the other naked and steeping in each other's bathwater. It was the London bathroom-locker-room phenomenon again, yet this time with the addition of Joyce's weaving in and out, her robe never quite closed, giving an eight-year-old boy intriguing glimpses of pendulous breasts and a baffling triangle of black hair.

Flo rose later for a separate bath in fresh water. She appeared after nine and would emerge from her room shrouded in a floor-length dressing gown and turban, bearing a white porcelain chamber pot with a gilt porcelain handle—daintily covered with a cloth—that she would walk to the lavatory. Over breakfast, Flo spoke of the trauma of her first son's death from tuberculosis in 1928. And she spoke of the days after the German invasion in 1940 when she and her second husband, Georges, fled to the unoccupied zone of France but then inexplicably returned later that year to their twelve-room apartment on the Rue du Faubourg Saint-Honoré. One day in 1941, a German officer appeared at the apartment's door and, at gunpoint, robbed them of silver, jewelry, and anything portable; he left saying, "I'll be back." As a result, they decided to decamp to a less conspicuously prosperous apartment and moved to the flat in which I stayed in 1958, still affluent but certainly one that spoke less of extravagance and wealth than their earlier home. They dutifully wore their yellow stars, miraculously escaped the *"rafles"* (the roundups of Jews), and survived.

Ma, Pa, Anthony, and I toured Paris with Raymond in tow. We rode the elevator to the top of the Arc de Triomphe and the Eiffel Tower. We visited Notre-Dame and Sacré-Coeur. We toured the Conciergerie, where I cried uncontrollably as my mother, in the freezing dungeon in which the incarcerated Marie-Antoinette had given birth to the Dauphin, graphically described how the guards must have derided her in her birth agony and then shipped her off to the guillotine.

Paris was also an introduction to new delicious foodstuffs well beyond the railroad's ham baguette. There were omelets that dissolved in the mouth. Eggs mayonnaise. Escargots in their metallic pools of butter and garlic. Some evenings we strolled the ten minutes from the apartment up Avenue Wagram—with its towering side view of the Arc de Triomphe—to La Pergola on the Champs-Élysées, a family-style restaurant with crepe-paper table covers, steak-frites and poulet-frites. (Eight-year-old children of my acquaintance were not taken to the Tour d'Argent.) I had grown up in a land where "chips" were a slightly soggy accompaniment to slightly soggy fried fish—and now I discovered the joy of authentically French french fries. And then we would stroll home in the still light evening, through the Places des Ternes, where Flo would sneer as we passed Chez Dupont, a restaurant that, from 1940 until the liberation just fourteen years earlier, sported a sign in the window declaring "Interdit aux Chiens et aux Juifs" (Off-limits to dogs and Jews).

One evening at the apartment, an elegant dinner produced by Joyce included a gigantic and sumptuous platter of perfectly cooked asparagus drizzled with melted butter—my first encounter with what remains my favorite vegetable. I learned to eat it—as I still eat it—the French way: with the fingers. To this day, a taste of asparagus rockets me back to that flat in Paris. And, to be totally honest, it also rockets me to my reading of the second volume of novelist Nicholas Monsarrat's autobiography, *Life Is a Four Letter Word: Breaking Out* (1970), in which he tells us of a brass sign in the men's cloakroom of London's aristocratic Athenaeum Club that read "Gentlemen are requested not to urinate in the umbrella stand during the asparagus season."

But the Paris that thrilled me most was the Paris of transportation. We rode in low-slung black Citroën taxis with running boards. We rode the Metro that, in 1958, still had first- and second-class carriages and signs instructing travelers to give up their seats to *mutilés de la guerre*. We rode the funicular to Montmartre. And, my favorite of all, we rode the dark-green and-cream buses that sported a rear, open balcony where the ride could be enjoyed in fresh air separated from the Gauloises-choked interior. One afternoon, emerging from the Invalides after viewing the imposing marble tomb of Napoleon, we spied a parked Citroën DS19—Europe's hottest car of the moment, an aerodynamic wonder that still, sixty years later, appears futuristic. It was known for the unprecedentedly comfortable ride it owed to its revolutionary technology of springs. Even an eight-year-old could and did stand at the back of the car and gently press it down. Its secret air cushioning would slowly and gently raise it back up. I had to be dragged away from continuous experiment.

Unlike London, Paris had not of course been bombed. And even though our visit was before the colossal cleaning project that Paris's buildings were to undergo in the sixties, this eight-year-old recognized that it was magnificent and it was grand. It fascinated me that we drove on the right. It fascinated me that the avenues and boulevards were cobblestoned and lined with sidewalk cafés. It fascinated me that everything seemed so wide and so grown up, that it all seemed so gay and lavish and generous, so very different from the dour, ordered, and parsimonious postwar London that was my home.

That visit to Paris represented a triangle of experience: sightseeing, family, discovery. Aesthetically, the grandeur of the Arc de Triomphe seemed to speak to me more persuasively than the soaring thrust of the Eiffel Tower. The trauma of the Conciergerie affected me far more viscerally than did the nave of Sacré-Coeur. The family encounter was immensely engaging at the same time it was so utterly fraught with emotional dangers. Silently, I was required to accompany Raymond in his daily navigation of the bizarre tightrope of loyalties that was his life. Yet I could also stand back and observe as he wheedled favors from Flo, imparted forbidden secrets to Joyce, and—with the raising of an eyebrow, the shrug of a shoulder, the shaking of a head—shared with his father their unspoken, unconscious, unadmitted sense of mutual discomfort. I allowed myself to indulge in a precocious Schadenfreude as I both participated in the family machinations and simultaneously watched them, undamaged, from the periphery. In any event, I had my own familial emotional morass to navigate.

But it was the third apex of the experiential triangle, the "discovery," that spoke to me with the greatest impact. It was to cement within me the notion of why travel was so immensely satisfying. Far more interesting to me than Paris's actual monuments was the web of spectacle, dress, behavior, aspect, food, and unabashed abroadness that made Paris, a mere 197 miles distant, so radically and exotically dissimilar from London. The warm baguettes; the ludicrous elevator; the stark comparison between the backstage of the flat and the front; Raymond's oddly feminine school tunic—de rigeur for every Parisian schoolboy; the breadth of the boulevards; the sidewalk cafés; the ovoid Deux Chevaux cars; the waiters dressed in black that was swirled beneath vast, tight white aprons; the *citrons pressés*; the buses with balconies; the aroma of French tobacco; the unfawning yet gracious service all spoke to me. And it was with alacrity that I joined the conversation.

A tiny black-and-white photograph bespeaks that 1958 family vacation. My parents and I are seated at a sidewalk café in Montmartre's Place du Tertre. Pa is wearing an elegant suit, white shirt, and tie. Ma is wearing a suit and a fetching hat. They are both smoking. I am wearing shorts, a white shirt, and a perfectly knotted tie. A camera is strapped around my neck. I am drinking a *citron pressé*. My head is thrown back and I am laughing. I am in abroad heaven.

1954

In 1954, when I was four, Anthony, who was eighteen years old and on his way to becoming an Olympics-standard swimmer, had become very ill. They called it pleurisy, and all I knew was that he was taken away to a hospital to which I was admitted entry just once. It was a menacing Victorian

Ma, Pa, and moi. Montmartre, Paris, 1958. (Author collection)

red-brick building. The ward in which he lay was immense with a glass conservatory-style roof. There were beds everywhere, perhaps twenty or thirty, each tightly made with starched linen, most with a table displaying a bowl of fruit, vases of daisies, and boxes of chocolates. (In my Edwardian London of the 1950s, the appropriate gift to bring on a hospital visit was always some little luxury: a box of chocolates, flowers, or—most often—a bunch of grapes. Grapes, plump and pit-filled, were very much considered a treat in the London of 1954.)

Anthony's bed abutted a column at the room's center, and only as an adult do I realize how frightened he must have been. At the time, I imagined the whole matter an adventure, a concept confirmed by the paper model of London Bridge (the London Bridge before the Great Fire of 1666 that resembled Florence's Ponte Vecchio) on which, propped up in bed, he was working, proof positive that this was not much more than an extravagantly complex, phlegm-filled playdate. He was in the hospital for a month and then at home, confined to bed for a further eight months, and he missed a year of school. A nurse came to the house daily to give him injections, and his bed was relocated into our sun-filled sitting room, where a second one-channel black-and-white television set was installed. With his illness came the realization that his hopes of swimming in the 1956 Olympic Games in Melbourne were dashed. It was only as an adult that I learned what pleurisy was and that Anthony's particular version of it was tubercular.

I also learned that illness was a totally mercurial, cause-and-effect phenomenon. A year earlier Pa had been bringing coal from the basement coal bunker up to fill the scuttles of our flat's coal fires when our obese, black-and-white, and bipolar cat, Teetoe, chose to scratch his coal-dusted hand. Days later, the hand had become infected and Pa was given a shot of penicillin—then still quite new. Within hours, he developed septicemia, his entire body a mass of seeping sores. Quite why I was allowed to see him in that condition makes me wonder still, but I did, and I recall our family physician, Dr. Whig, marching down the long, narrow hall into our sitting room, where Pa was standing naked, blood and ooze seeping from every pore. He took one look, barked "Jesus Christ," and called for an ambulance. Years later, I would learn that Pa did almost die. Dr. Whig had told my mother, in his peremptory military way, "to steel herself."

In my parents' medical galaxy, everything had to have a source, a reason. Rather like how the Black Death or Germany's defeat in World War I had to be blamed on the Jews, my mother and father were possessed of a medieval attitude to calamity that required some abstruse but identifiable source to bear responsibility. So just as I almost lost my father because of a cat scratch, my brother's pleurisy needed an explanation. Pa determined that its genesis was Anthony's sleeping out all night in front of the gates of Buckingham Palace in order to nab a prime spot to watch the coronation parade of Queen Elizabeth II. It would never have occurred to Pa to do such a thing. But because Ma supported the scheme and because it poured with rain throughout that coronation eve in June 1953, Anthony's pleurisy of 1954 became enshrined in family lore as "my mother's fault."

With Anthony's 1956 Olympics hopes shattered by pleurisy, Ma took it upon herself to seek some kind of solace for him. And that solace came in the form of Ma's discovery of a place called Israel. Imagine if you will, my mother, this Margaret Rutherford sound-and-look-alike who, on the one hand, loathed any gesture, sound, or characteristic she classed as Jewish, yet who, on the other, was fanatically offended by the merest hint of anti-semitism. She discovered something called the Maccabiah Games, a qua-drennial gathering of Jewish athletes at a massive sporting convocation in the Promised Land. First mounted in 1932 in Tel Aviv, the Maccabiah Games really found its legs in 1935, bringing more than one thousand Jew-ish athletes to Palestine—many from Germany, who stayed behind after the games rather than return to the Nazis. In 1950 the Maccabiah Games—complete with the sobriquet "Jewish Olympics"—were restored and in 1953 began their every-four-years cycle that continues to this day. Well, not quite: Covid-19 forced the postponement of the 2021 games to 2022.

Perhaps Ma could have saved the effort, for Anthony quite possibly did it alone. After winning a race and breaking a record at a swimming match in 1956, he received a telephone call one evening at home. The caller con-gratulated him on his win. Then he paused.

"May I ask you a question?" said the caller with hesitation in his voice.

"Of course," Anthony responded.

"Are you, er, by any chance, er, um, Jewish?"

Thus, Anthony was signed up to swim for Britain at the Fifth Maccabiah Games, a year after the Melbourne Olympics, set for July 1957 in Tel Aviv.

1957

The departure of the British Maccabiah team for Israel took place in July 1957 outside a travel agency behind Selfridges department store, where the group of some forty athletes was photographed for posterity and by excited mums and dads. The athletes were decked out in snazzy uniforms, provided courtesy of Marks and Spencer. Since the arrival of Anthony's big box of clothing, we had spent days photographing him in his uniform: blue blazer, white shirt and pants, striped tie, and straw hat. He looked good, particularly with the swim team built-for-speed crew cut that made him more hip, so different from his usual upper-class parted shock of floppy hair.

The team's images were captured in front of the bus that was to take them to Northolt aerodrome. The lumbering motorcoach sported moderne swirls and sweeping curls on its side in an effort to imply an aerodynamic message of speed. Theirs was to be a long journey to the Holy Land. I had, of course, become enmeshed in the minutiae of the travel arrangements. The flight from Northolt was aboard a chartered two-engined unpressurized DC-3, first to Nice for refueling and then to Brindisi in the heel of Italy, where the team and flight crew would sleep overnight in a hotel. The next day they would fly onward to Athens to take on more fuel, and then finally head to the far end of the Mediterranean, and Lydda Airport near Tel Aviv.

"Shhhhh," my father snapped irritably two weeks later as we clustered around the big prewar radio in the sitting room, craning to hear transmission of the games on shortwave. It was one of those large prewar radios, all fabric speaker covers, chunky Bakelite knobs, and a backlit window revealing the names of exotic radio stations around the globe. Beyond crackles and buzzes and white noise, we heard little as Pa delicately swiveled the tuning knob, his ear to the fabric-covered loudspeaker as if he were cracking a safe. Finally, honing in on the "Voice of Israel," a faint English-language voice reported no scores but that one of the British swim team had been hospitalized with sunstroke. Beyond this alarming nugget, we learned nothing. And in that era before automatic leaps to the phone to call another continent were de rigueur, not to mention simple taps on WhatsApp, my parents remained frantic until days later we learned that the stricken swimmer was not Anthony. We also learned that the sun had played a starring role in his not earning the gold medal he had been favored to win. During the climactic race, he had turned to see how far ahead he was, only to be blinded—and disoriented—by the July Middle Eastern sun. He came in fourth.

But if he had lost the race, he had won a new goal in life. Within the time span of three weeks, Anthony had fallen in love . . . both with Israel and with a sixteen-year-old Israeli girl named Ariela. After the games, he came back home to England; he stayed seven months and returned to Israel—this time for good. And it was this departure that gave my parents the impetus to change our apartment's sleeping arrangements . . . and my equilibrium.

Prior to his leaving, maps spread on the sitting room floor foretold the measures of his long journey. For me, each element of the trip was more engorged with romance than its predecessor: the boat train from London to Dover, the cross-channel ferry to France, the train onward from Calais to Paris and eventually Marseille, where he would board the Israeli Zim line vessel SS *Artza* for Haifa.

For days I had been saddened by his leaving. It was an event whose enormity I couldn't quite divine, but even at eight, I sensed this was a pivotal moment. We said good-bye beneath the soaring iron-and-glass canopy of Victoria Station. My mother, in a quest both to hide her tears and to ensure there was not the remotest possibility anyone could avoid knowing she was crying—wore oversized wraparound sunglasses. The atmosphere was one of stiff-upper-lipped gloom masked by faked chirpiness. We stood in the murk on the platform as the engine blew billows of steam into the air and around our feet. It was all very *Anna Karenina*. There was the carrying of bags into the railway car, there was the slamming of train doors, there were clinging hugs. And there were tears, because even though Anthony's stay on a kibbutz in Israel was to be "a mere" six to twelve months, my parents sensed it had all the potential to be much longer. Inevitably, in my mothers' eyes, it must have been a replay of her and her mother's departure from Melbourne in 1918—exactly forty years earlier—under similarly portentous and tearful circumstances.

Yet for me, the most harrowing part of that day took place not at Victoria Station but when we arrived back home. Within minutes of our return—and without the merest hint of premonition, warning, or preparation—I was moved lock, stock, clothes, toys, and barrel out of my little bedroom and into Anthony's far grander room on the far side of the flat. Some of his larger possessions were piled away in a trunk and out-of-reach closets and, without ceremony, Anthony's room became Geoffrey's. Boom. Simultaneously, my father moved out of the nuptial bedroom into the adjacent "dressing room" that, until moments earlier, had been my bedroom. It was connected to my parents' (now my mother's) room by a small private door. The given explanation for the game of musical bedrooms was that my mother stayed up late, snored, slept fitfully, read books, and chomped apples at 3 a.m., while Pa liked to retire no later than nine and found it impossible to sleep to the accompaniment of snores and the crunching of fruit, nor in the glow of a bedside light draped funereally in velvet in an unsuccessful effort to reduce glare. At eight years old, I divined no other reasons for the new sleeping arrangements.

With my twenty-two-year-old brother gone not only from his country and his home but also eerily deleted from his room, I became an only child. The redrawing of ownership of the bedrooms was to affect me for years and decades to come. I had been propelled into Anthony's room in a lurch of removal so secretive, so rapid, so redolent of Jacob and Esau and messes of pottage that its only possible outcome could be the inevitable eventual fury of the displaced sibling. He was surely coming back to reclaim it, wasn't he? And when he did come back, where would I be now that my old room was Pa's?

There was an unspoken ominousness to it all. Anthony's bed became mine, his desk became mine, his closet became mine, the possessions he left and were not packed away by him or my parents—knickknacks, pictures, records—became mine. His bookcase became mine too. Its bottom shelf contained a neat row of *National Geographic* magazines sent to him by Aunt Esmé in New Jersey from about 1948 through 1956. In the ensuing weeks then months and years, I took to sitting on the floor for hours to pore through them. Doubtless I was trying to flee the peculiarities of what had occurred to me after waving Anthony off at Victoria Station. The orgasm of moving rooms had been so violent and sudden that I fancy I saw myself as Jacob impelled by mercilessly devious parents to rob his first-born sibling of his birthright. I certainly liked the bigger and better room—but I was so wracked with conflicted emotions that I was hard pressed to enjoy it. I took to having extravagant nightmares and macabre middle-of-the-night fears that my mother had died in her sleep, that the gas fire was leaking, or that planes screeching overhead on approach to Heathrow Airport were really Russian bombers.

What added to the humiliation and torment was that after my brother left for Israel, or maybe even before, my father took only rarely to calling him Anthony, but—wait for it—he called him "My Real Son," with the stress on the "real." It became a family fixture. Its nexus had, I think, to do with the witty notion that, unlike Anthony, I was delivered by the stork, but the sobriquet stuck. In the London of the 1960s, mailmen would climb flights of stairs three or four times a day to insert letters in the slit in each apartment's door. I would hear the plop of envelopes dropping through the letter box onto the hallway carpet, race to the door, and if there was a letter from Anthony, I would excitedly shout out, "A letter from your real son!" and I did it without a hint of conscious fury. But what did it mean? As a child, I didn't know, and as an adult I still don't. But "the real son"— a name that was supposedly some kind of macabre example of Pa's epic sense of humor, had an effect both on my conscious and my subsconsious that was simply calamitous.

The pages of the *National Geographic* magazines seemed a worthy refuge. My poring through their pages was extremely particular. Unlike my contemporaries who, on playdates, would search feverishly through *National Geographic* hoping to spy the naked breasts, willy, or bum of the members of some New Guinea tribe, my interest was restricted virtually entirely to what came before and after those world-explicating articles of discovery: the advertisements. To an eight-year-old in postwar London, with its bomb sites and one-channel television, living in a four-bedroom apartment with one bathroom, a flat heated by coal fires with a gas stove dating from the year the *Titanic* sailed, and a refrigerator so pitiable it could not keep ice cream hard, the advertisements in the *National Geographic* magazines were an escape hatch into a fantasy world of American order and lavish well-being.

It was not merely the products being sold that were so seductive. It was the images of Eisenhowerish solidity and abundance in which they were presented. The cars were extraordinary. Long, wide, strong, and sturdy, these were cars that attested not merely to a phenomenally higher standard of living but to a vision of suburban modernity, calm, and security. Cadillacs and Buicks with bulbous chrome and two-tone color schemes were usually pictured not on a city avenue but outside a ranch home surrounded by a suave father smoking a pipe, a mother in an A-line skirt, and two cute-as-a-button children cavorting with a cheery dog. There were ads for mysterious products called Postum and Sanka. There were full-page ads for giant air-conditioning units whose necessity was unknown to me. There were fantastic advertisements for chairlifts that could transport the infirm up a staircase. There were advertisements for Sheaffer, Esterbrook, and Parker 61 pens that exuded a profound sense of wealth and status. There were ads for Princess phones that—with their pastel colors, backlit dials, and twisted plastic cords—seemed so futuristic in comparison to the clunky, black Bakelite model with the tin dial and plaited fabric cord that sat on a butler's table in our drawing room.

There were kitchens whose modernity was simply unfathomable to this eight-year-old Londoner, with their curved counters that swept around corners, their uniform cabinetry, their wondrous Formica, their double-door refrigerators that were more spacious than the armoire known as a "compactum" where my father hung his suits. There were even devices into which dirty dishes could be stacked in order to be mechanically scrubbed and dried. I yearned for the day I might know what it was like to live in a home whose kitchen had a sweeping Formica counter, a refrigerator with two doors, a wall with two ovens, and a double sink. It was the unlimited-ness of it all for which I yearned, the generosity of installing two of every-thing. I wanted to be in a home where I could climb onto a chrome-legged stool topped with scarlet vinyl, chat to my friends on my Princess phone, write my homework essays with a Parker 61—all the while sipping Postum, whatever that was, served by a mother in an A-line skirt . . . a home where my brother wouldn't hate me for stealing his room.

I wanted the televisions too. Giant contraptions they were, on slanted legs, with concertina doors and screens whose sides were strangely elliptical. I admired the capacious hi-fi units that promised the latest developments in sound and contained phonographs whose 45 rpm records were piled atop a wide column. That column inspired a sense of American solidity, so unlike the wobbly spindle atop which my 45s would sit in Anthony's portable red-and-beige Dansette gramophone that of course had now be-come mine. It was the sturdiness of the column holding those records that seemed, somehow, to be symbolic of the sense of well-being conveyed by those big, rich cars and those massive refrigerators in kitchens with continuous Formica counters in spacious ranch homes that spelled Amer-ica. But I also knew that the sense of security could be fleeting. For each magazine's back cover was home to advertisements for the Metropolitan Life insurance company whose images depicted the horrors of that ranch house up in flames, with Mom, Dad, the cute-as-a-button kids in robes and pajamas, and the dog cowering wistfully next to the fire truck yet relieved by the knowledge that a check would shortly be in the mail.

Yet all these images were reduced to insignificance when compared with the advertisements that spoke to me the most intensely: the ads for travel. Like their counterparts, these images also spoke to a uniquely Eisenhower-era sense of confidence, solidity, and plenty. The planes they depicted spoke of reliability—with none of the fears associated with air transport in the 1950s. TWA's Constellations with curvy fuselages, triple tails, and four engines sat atop gangly legs, as women dressed in the New Look and tall men with hats climbed stairs to enter them, turning to wave to envious well-wishers. Pan American's Stratocruisers invited passengers to sweep seductively down a spiral staircase from the main cabin to the lounge in order to perch on a moderne banquette and imbibe a highball (what the hell was a highball anyway?). The blandness of the design of the DC-7 was offset by visions of planes sweeping through a sky high above the Arc de Triomphe or Sugar Loaf Mountain or the Grand Canyon. The interiors of the planes promised elegance, comfort, and panoramic vistas through giant windows. Air hostesses took passengers' coats; served extravagant luncheons from shiny trolleys; or tucked Mom, a little girl, and a teddy bear into a sleeping compartment.

Then there were the trains. Vistadomes promised fellowship and wondrous views as the very same women in the New Look and husbands in suits and ties snaked relaxedly in aluminum-reinforced splendor through the Rockies. In one ad, a black conductor welcomed his white passengers aboard—an image that exuded all the fuzzy warmth of the Confederacy. In another, a woman with her aerodynamic train case and a daughter with a doll sat snugly on a cushioned bench as they admired the Grand Tetons from giant windows.

The Cunard advertisements told me what I actually already suspected when they proclaimed that "getting there is half the fun." This time, the women with hips and flared skirts played decktop shuffleboard with the same men now in sport shirts and sharply creased pants as the *Queen Elizabeth* and *Queen Mary* churned them through the blue Atlantic. The advertisements for the French Line were somehow more sophisticated. The images they chose to project of the *Ile de France* and the *Liberté* were usually night scenes of those very same women and men—he in a dashing tuxedo, and she in a gown whose tight bodice gave the merest suggestion of breasts and descended to a cinched waist and a skirt fashioned from dozens of yards of organza.

What conspired to add romance and style to these advertisements was that—whether for cars, pens, kitchens, trains, or planes—most were illustrated not with photographs but with paintings. Madison Avenue, in the days before airbrushing and Photoshop, knew that to convey the perfect and idealized message the camera wouldn't lie . . . but a paintbrush could be made to tell just the tiniest fib.

Perhaps the most revealing of the travel ads to this eight-year-old were those that were not just for the conveyances that could take one places but for the actual destinations themselves. I came to recognize the Eiffel Tower and Neuschwanstein, the Colosseum and the Sydney Harbor Bridge. But I was most intrigued by the advertisements for the London I knew, illustrated with images I did not. Courtly bobbies stooped to chat with Mrs. A-Line and Mr. Hat-and-Sharply-Creased-Pants with a bonhomie I couldn't recognize. Cotswold villages promised cream teas and tweeness in a style that seemed to me utterly artificial. The London they depicted was grand, gracious, generous, gay, blue-skied, un-bombed, free of coal smoke and fogs. I recognized that it was London, but it was a London over which a wash of faux warmth and grandeur had been splashed. It was a London without grayness, a London without the Blitz or rationing, postwar austerity or pettiness.

Subconsciously, I suppose, I may have wondered that if these messages could present the London I knew with such intelligent and seductive artifice, perhaps the ads for ships and boats and trains—and refrigerators and Oldsmobiles—contained their own exaggerations too. It certainly didn't annoy me. It didn't confuse me, it didn't deflect me, it didn't alter my fascination for the images. Quite the opposite: I believe it spoke to the kind of Weltanschauung I had been taught to adopt: that appearances were everything, that manners were paramount, that there must always be smiles and charm—no matter that deep inside there might be roiling insecurity, panic, confusion, and pain.

1958

At the Christmas that followed Anthony's departure, I was given a toy theater. I had apparently been asking for one for months, and my mother had discovered an obscure shop in an attic in Bloomsbury where an elderly man created model theaters. My Christmas gift comprised a proscenium arch in maroon Bakelite onto which was glued a vision of mid-Victorian theatrical gilt and red velvet. The stage itself sat on feet. The curved wooden front had its own mid-Victorian overlay—of musicians and a conductor. Above the stage were wooden slots through which one could lower backdrops and wings. Overhead lights and footlights with 3-watt bulbs were attached to a cumbersome transformer that was attached to batteries. Colored gels slid in and out of the overhead lights to enable nine-year-old impresarios to change the mood on stage. From the front—the audience saw elegance and glamour. From backstage, it was bare Bakelite and wooden struts. Again, it was like the ethos Ma evangelized: smiles and charm to the audience.

The toy theater came with booklets of plays and the appropriate scenery and characters that were to be cut from the pages and glued onto cardboard. The character pieces slotted into long wire holders so that—from backstage at the side—little hands could move them as little voices read the fractured scripts of *Bluebeard* and *Aladdin*. The grandfather of the gentleman in Bloomsbury had been a man named Benjamin Pollock, who, from a small factory in Hoxton in the grimy depths of the East End, had sold these booklets of plays, scenery, and characters in costume to nineteenth-century bourgeois parents for the price of one penny (printed in black and white) and two pence (water-colored by hand), giving birth to the expression "penny plain, tuppence coloured" that lasted well into twentieth-century Britain. But I wasn't interested in the purchased plays, and I was completely uninterested in performing them. Instead, I wanted to design and create my own scenery. I would come home from a Christmas pantomime or my first outings to real theater and redesign the sets. I didn't copy what I had seen: I created my own "improved" designs.

It was a few weeks after Anthony's departure to the Levant that I was taken in my gray flannel suit with short pants, white shirt, tartan tie, long socks, and lace-up shoes to London's grandest theater, Drury Lane. We were to see a show that I had assumed from its name would have something to do with the collapse of London Bridge but which turned out to chronicle the successful attempt by a martinet named Henry Higgins to convert a woman named Eliza Doolittle from a common flower girl into a duchess.

As I sat in the eighth row of the orchestra and watched the developments of the plot, I was awash in familiarity. Henry Higgins aka Rex Harrison wore the identical beige Cox Moore cardigan sweaters my father favored. His constant haranguing of Eliza aka Julie Andrews to bludgeon her into correcting her vowels was an echo of my mother's identical harangues designed to ensure I spoke the Queen's English. Mrs. Higgins, Henry's mother, was an Edwardian amalgam of Aunt Vi in Brighton and Aunt Flo in Paris, each of whom well into the 1960s were living lives of Edwardian pomp—even if, in Vi's case particularly, it was pomp now vaguely impoverished and patched with scarlet Contact paper. Lisson Grove, where Eliza lived in a damp basement, remained déclassé and was ten minutes from our flat. It was where my mother bought us fish and chips in newspaper.

My Fair Lady was London, yes. It was England, yes. But to me it was an appealingly faux, entirely enhanced London created with the identical sense of bold American romance and blinkeredness that had spoken to me from the advertisements in the *National Geographic* magazines. It was a theatrical London. And so I came to understand that one could create theater not only on a stage. "Theater" could also encompass the creation of a seductive image to speak from the pages of a magazine or from the walls of a travel agency.

The day after the performance, I set about re-creating the scenery for *My Fair Lady*. I had Pa drill a small hole in the wooden floor of the stage. I took a 45 rpm record as a template for cutting a circle of cardboard and, with a nail inserted through its center and the hole in the stage floor, I had a revolving stage. I corralled my mother into attaching a remnant of red velvet onto another piece of cardboard and sewing, at its base, nine inches of gold lampshade fringe. Presto, I had a real curtain. And I drew and painted and built my version of the scenery for *My Fair Lady*, complete with staircases, doll's house furniture, backdrops, and wings. I would play the record of the cast recording and change the scenes to match the songs. This was not a few minutes' work. This was a monumental project that absorbed me for hours and days and weeks and months as I worked, all the while admiring the cover of the record. I recognized how contemporary was the setting of the typeface that read "Rex Harrison," "Julie Andrews," and "My Fair Lady." I studied the Hirschfeld caricature that had God pulling the strings that made Harrison and Andrews move. It would be years before I understood that the picture's puppet master was not God but George Bernard Shaw. And it would be twenty more years before I understood that the show's title was Alan Jay Lerner's dazzling pun that connected the old English folk song about London Bridge falling down with how the cockney Eliza would have pronounced "Mayfair," the fashionable London neighborhood close to the home of Henry Higgins.

Thus it was that I came to my private and subconscious understanding that the two most fervent of my youthful passions—theater and travel—were very much interwoven. I saw that by the artful creation of an image—be it on a record cover or the stage at Drury Lane or in an advertisement in the *National Geographic* magazine—idealistic likenesses could be created of the city I knew so well. They were likenesses that certainly spoke of London. But they spoke of it with a creativity and frisson of seductive untruth that was designed purposefully—and, I determined, harmlessly—to hoodwink.

I was sold.

1956

I don't remember precisely how and when I acquired my first travel poster, which is sort of sad because I am now considered a collector. I suppose I must have been about twelve. But the enthusiasm for the graphics of tourism promotion had been born earlier as I sat on the floor exploring those *National Geographic* issues, and, on one special occasion in the summer of 1956, when I was six. In my personal chronology, 1956 is not the year I started attending Hereward House, an eccentric private preparatory school for boys aged six to thirteen that occupied a rambling Edwardian mansion in Hampstead. No, 1956 was the year it was decided that we—Pa, Ma, Anthony, and I—would go "abroad" by car.

From the moment I was first apprised of the trip, I was in a state of feverish expectation. "We're going to the Continent," I would shout to friends and announce to passersby, jumping up and down with glee. "We're going to the Continent!" I quickly composed my first travel mantra, "Franceitalygermanyswitzerlandliechtenstein," representing the five countries we were to visit. I would recite it and repeat it a thousand times until it had merged into a single, thirteen-syllable utterance that stills effortlessly trips off my tongue.

For the trip, I had been given a small brown cardboard suitcase in which to keep my favorite toy cars and crayons that would entertain me in the long summer evenings in Franceitalygermanyswitzerlandliechtenstein. It was the only piece of baggage for which I was required to maintain responsibility. My jobs were to ensure that my "valuables" were collected together and packed and to supervise the case's placement in the car as we left each hotel. As the trip through Franceitalygermanyswitzerlandliechtenstein was beginning, we stayed overnight in Reims in northern France. In the morning, as we were waiting in the lobby while Pa paid the bill, the concierge, complete with frock coat and striped pants, walked solemnly over to me. He stopped. He dropped into a crouch and, from behind his back, produced a luggage label to which his tongue gave a giant lick and which he then pasted onto the side of my brown cardboard suitcase. The label was an oval of green, red, and pink. "Hôtel de l'Univers," it announced, in bold art deco letters curving around a relief of the hotel facade. Had he presented me with a massive toy or an ice cream or a thousand francs, I couldn't have been more excited. It was as if I had been given an award.

For hours, as we drove onward deeper into France, I admired the label's lines, its typeface, its rendition of the hotel's triangular architecture. The presentation of this label somehow seemed to imply enormous portent. I had been given an imprimatur. My small brown cardboard suitcase was no longer a receptacle for toys: it had been deemed luggage. And I was no longer a small boy toting cars and crayons: I was a traveler.

1965

I have another photograph taken in my bedroom—when I was about fifteen. In the foreground are Herbert, a man my father had befriended in the army, and his daughter, Irene. Herbert was born in Hamburg and he would tell me that as a young businessman in the late 1920s and early 1930s, he had often needed to come to England. A devoté of ships, he would schedule his visits to London to enable him not to travel the traditional way—by the pedestrian overnight ferry from Hamburg or the Hook of Holland to Harwich—but amid the transatlantic glamour of the *Bremen* and *Europa* on the first or last legs of their voyages between Hamburg and New York. In 1933 Herbert prophetically elected not to return to Germany, changed his name from Süsskind to Sutton, and eventually acquired the best English accent of any German I had ever encountered. In 1940 he, along with thousands of young German Jewish men in Britain, was interned on the Isle of Man and then deported to Australia aboard a ship called the *Dunera*. That six-week voyage was to become the stuff of legend in Australia —with books and a television documentary recalling how the British and Australian crew tormented their young Jewish passengers physically and mentally. After a year in Australia, Herbert returned to Britain, joined Her Majesty's Pioneer Corps, and met my father. After the war, he married the anorexic, neurotic, doubtless Holocaust-guilt-scarred, slender Detta—also a refugee from Germany. Their daughter, Irene, was born in 1948.

Herbert was caring, overbearing, and bossy; Detta was phobic and entirely in his thrall. Irene evolved from a shy, immensely troubled girl into a shy and immensely troubled teenager into a shy and immensely troubled adult. She was tall and thin, with mousy looks, a pasty pallor, and short straight black hair. She was painfully introverted, needy, and brilliant. When Irene was about twelve, in the tradition of his love of ships, Herbert bought a motor yacht that was moored near Henley on the River Thames. Herbert would play captain, Detta would play seasick, and Irene would sit inside to escape the anemic English sun and to read. After graduating from Cambridge, Irene became a librarian. She lived with a female friend in what I hope in retrospect was a lesbian relationship—but I will surely never know. In 1977 my wife and I arrived in Southampton from New York aboard the *Queen Elizabeth 2*. My parents met us off the boat train at London's Waterloo Station, and when we arrived at the apartment in which I had grown up, the telephone was ringing. It was Herbert asking my father to meet him at a police station. Irene had been found dead in a cubicle in the ladies' room of the Charing Cross Hotel. She had slashed her wrists. In blood, on the cubicle door, she had written, "Don't blame yourselves." Would this nightmare have had less drama had we not just arrived on a steamship in England or had Irene not chosen a hotel bathroom in which to end her life? Possibly not. But it was yet another traumatic episode in my life that was inevitably linked to the world of traveling.

In that photograph taken in my bedroom, behind Herbert and Irene, there are three posters on the wall. One is an impressionistic travel poster of Jerusalem. One is for a musical called *Maggie May* and another is for a musical called *Divorce Me Darling*, both of which were playing in London in 1965. I clearly, at fifteen, had an excellent eye for color: the posters are prominently gray and violet and purple—their pastel hues working well with the room's geometric gray wallpaper.

Divorce Me Darling was not a major smash, but it spoke to me. It was self-effacing; it was tuneful; it was elegant; it did the Charleston—which was and remains my favorite form of exercise. It was a musical about travel and it was what we would now call camp. It was the not terribly successful sequel to the 1953 musical called *The Boy Friend* that on Broadway had starred an unknown British actress named Julie Andrews. Like its predecessor, *Divorce Me Darling* had a vacuous plot devoted to the tale of a string of upper-class Englishwomen who had been immured in a finishing school on the French Riviera and whose marriages—ten years after meeting their husbands in *The Boy Friend*—were exhausted.

In the first tuneful scene, after the customary Charlestoned introduction, Polly (the Julie Andrews part) strides into the small hotel (the Villa Caprice, "where we were finished," scream the other wives in upper-class tones) and announces to nobody in particular, "If I don't like my room, I'm going straight to the Negresco!" The audience at London's Globe Theatre loved that line. I did too . . . because at fifteen I already knew the Negresco was the best hotel in Nice and I was proud of my precocious understanding of the joke.

Of course, I knew the Negresco was the best hotel in Nice because of my father's bathtime instruction. Pa also used to sing to me. He idolized Louis Armstrong and syncopation. His voice was not as fine as my mother's, but he could certainly hold a tune, and he would back it with perfectly rhythmic foot tapping and trombone toots. One of his favorites was "Someday I'll Find You," written in 1930 by Noël Coward for *Private Lives*. My father explained the plot to me: the chance meeting on adjacent balconies of a luxurious French resort hotel of an ex-husband and an ex-wife, each newly wed and on their honeymoons. It wasn't the Negresco, but it certainly could have been. (Indeed, in revivals of the play in London and on Broadway, *Private Lives* is always "set on the Riviera," while Coward had originally set it in fashionable Deauville on the northern coast of France, a place perhaps too obscure and passé for it to speak to turn-of-the-twenty-first-century audiences.) *Private Lives* became iconic for me, just as would Neil Simon's *Plaza Suite* and *California Suite* years later: three dramas in which the elegant hotel is not merely the setting but integral to the plot. And Coward's quasi-autobiographical "coming out" final play, *A Song at Twilight*, is also set in a hotel suite—this time in Switzerland.

Coward had written *Private Lives* in a suite at the Cathay Hotel in Shanghai while nursing influenza. How could one help but picture Coward wrapped in a Chinese silk robe, coughing and sneezing into linen handkerchiefs and sipping chicken broth as he completed in ten days one of the wittiest scripts ever composed. Many decades later I would stay at the Cathay Hotel—now the Fairmont Peace Hotel, beautifully restored to art deco splendor after years of Communist neglect—and if I strained hard or used an ear trumpet (never travel without one), I could imagine Coward coughing in the next room.

That poster for *Divorce Me Darling* thus amalgamated theater and travel—and beatified for me that short era, from 1920 until 1939, when travel was at the pinnacle of chic, romance, and glamour. What is so extraordinary is how so many of that period's most elegant and idealistic images of travel were laid atop what was unarguably building up to the most ugly, frightening, chaotic, and turmoil-filled period of the twentieth century. Or perhaps that is why producing those escapist images was so potent. Hitler was marching into the Rhineland, Vienna, and Prague. Stukas were bombing Guernica. The Japanese were raping Nanking. Americans were wandering through dust bowls to the bread lines. German Jews were being stripped of their rights and pleading for passage to Palestine or America or Shanghai or Havana or Hampstead or wherever the hell would take them. And yet no travel image was more powerful then, or still, than one created in 1935—the same year as the enactment of the Nuremburg Laws—by Adolphe Jean-Marie Mouron, a Russian-born Frenchman known as A. M. Cassandre. Cassandre had begun his career in the 1920s. He was awarded first prize at Paris's Exposition Internationale des Arts Décoratifs, the exhibition whose abbreviated title gave birth to the term "art deco." His long career (he died in 1968) produced classic images such as the 1929 poster for the *Nord-Express* train. But the most famous of his images is that produced for the French Line's launch of its superliner *Normandie*. Instead of depicting the *Normandie*'s profile or its on-board chic, he depicted its height. Cassandre portrayed the ship's giant looming bow, with its superstructure of cabins and funnels somehow diminutively positioned above. There is no additional artwork, other than some seagulls whose tininess only accentuates the ship's enormity. The rest of the poster's cleverness is type, with giant moderne letters spelling "Normandie" or, in some versions, "New York." It is a poster that has been reproduced a million times on posters, coffee mugs, and T-shirts and aped on behalf of a dozen other lesser ships—but its majesty has never been equaled.

As the *Canberra* had steamed me up the Hudson that frigid morning in January 1973, my thoughts had drifted back to a similarly frigid morning in New York Harbor forty-one years earlier. The *Normandie* had been berthed on the West Side of Manhattan since the 1939 outbreak of war. After Pearl Harbor and America's entry into the war, it was commandeered by the U.S. Navy and during its conversion into the troopship *Lafayette*, the *Normandie*—moored at its pier at Fifty-Second Street and the Hudson—caught fire. Workmen removing the towering art deco floor lamps from the first-class

Normandie, 1935. Adolphe Mouron Cassandre, artist (1905–68). Compagnie
Générale Transatlantique.

lounge had produced sparks that became flames that spread to the carpets and drapes. The resulting fire was eventually stanched by the New York City Fire Department hosing so much river water into the ship that the giant vessel creaked into a list then collapsed onto its side, like an executed elephant. The photographs of the giant liner foundering are heartbreaking, doubly so because that soaring vertical bow that Cassandre had so powerfully depicted was now horizontal, half-submerged, awash with murky river water. The navy and the city of New York hastily built barriers to block New Yorkers' view of the stricken *Normandie*, hoping to conceal the fact that just sixty-four days after Pearl Harbor, the mismanagement of a simple electrical fire was declaring to an already demoralized nation that its navy could not even keep the world's most famous ship afloat in the secure confines of New York Harbor.

(1925)

Cassandre's idealization of travel at the same time the Europe he was romanticizing was falling apart underscores how the heyday of the travel poster was all about benign deception. It was a harmless game, one that was perhaps even understood by the intended traveler—just as I, sitting on the floor leafing through *National Geographic* issues, understood that London, and doubtless elsewhere, was being presented through rose-colored glasses.

The romanticizing was encouraged by those who commissioned the posters. Most travel posters of the 1920–60 period were produced under the auspices of official bodies: government tourist boards; local regions; local municipalities; and railway, shipping, and airline companies that were nominally private but largely state-sponsored or so vast as to be above reproach. Thus was added to the posters' ambition the aim not merely to encourage business but also to promote an often not entirely honest self-image. The poster could be used to improve morale. It could promote a fantasy that would endear itself to its own constituency just as much as it might claim to promote travel by outsiders.

Just such a poster hangs in my living room today fifteen minutes from the Hudson River, where the *Normandie* capsized and the *Canberra* deposited me thirty-one years later. It is a poster issued by the Dutch railways just after the close of World War II. It promotes riding the Pullman train between Amsterdam and Brussels. The names of cities en route race across the poster in type that bespeaks speed. But largely it is an image not of smoking locomotives or windmills, tulips, or costumed ladies embroidering lace—but of food. Brussels was liberated by the Allies in September 1944 but Amsterdam had to wait until May 1945. So what is so curious and so endearing is that this poster was issued before 1945 was even done. A coterie of railway bureaucrats had found the time and inclination to commission, publish, print, and distribute this image in a country that was in the earliest throes of recovering from occupation, terror, deportations, destruction, and shortages. Thus it becomes evident that the poster's aim was to speak to a yearning for the calm, the elegance, the gentility—and the plenty—of the days before the arrival of the Germans in May 1940.

The poster's painted illustration is a close-up of the interior of a Pullman compartment. Its focus is the window and the table beneath it. No dykes, ladies in clogs, or Flanders fields are visible through the window—just clouds and bluish sky. The focal point of the poster's seduction is the table that is covered with a crisp white cloth. Atop perch a table lamp with a fringed maroon shade, a silver coffee pot, a porcelain cup and saucer with the art deco Wagons-Lits logo, and—at the focal point of this focal point—a silver salver bears three crusty sliced rolls interwoven with thick slices of pink ham. It is 1945, the war is won, and this poster for a train ride is designed specifically to speak to an audience that yearns for a tranquil corner framed by an elegant table lamp atop starched white linen; an audience whose taste buds have been paralyzed by five years of rationing and acorn coffee, whose stomachs and palates yearn for the hearty simplicity of fresh rolls spread with creamy butter and topped with slices of the juiciest ham. I empathize with that yearning: those crusty ham rolls appear similar to that whose deliciousness captivated me when I was eight, seated next to an identical train window, as my parents, brother, and I journeyed by train not from Brussels to Amsterdam but less than a hundred miles south, from Calais to Paris.

Another poster in my collection, which hangs in the guest bathroom, is designed with a similar goal of post–World War II seduction. Published by the newly nationalized British Railways, it was one of a massive series of posters designed to lure British visitors to dozens of England's seaside resorts. The series' images speak of warm summers. Women are in bathing suits, arms outstretched to welcome the sunshine; children play with pails and shovels (buckets and spades in British parlance) in the acres of sand. The realities of sheets of rain and windswept strands are disregarded

De Pullman Rijdt Weer (*The Pullman Rides Again*), 1945. Fedde Widma, artist (1915–2000). Afd Propaganda Nederlandse Spoorwagen. Printed by Ned. Rotogravure Mij., Leiden. (Author collection)

in this poster series whose intent was to draw Britons to the country's beach resorts. This was a time when traveling to the Continent or beyond was simply impossible for most Britons because of the currency restrictions imposed by the postwar Labour government—just as vacationing outside Britain or Ireland seventy-five years later in the summer of 2020 was made impossible by the coronavirus. In the late 1940s, no more than ten pounds per person could be legally taken out of Britain on a vacation trip to a non-Commonwealth destination. So that unless one had relatives in France or Italy who could cover the costs, or unless one vacationed in a British colony, the options were to risk discovery and prosecution for secreting wads of crinkly parchment-style five-pound notes in one's underwear . . . or to vacation in the British Isles.

My poster from the series is for the resort town of Torquay, in Devonshire. The town was to enter an immortality of sorts in the 1970s when the BBC produced a comedy series in which John Cleese and Prunella Scales portrayed Basil and Sybil Fawlty, who owned a small and frumpy hotel in that very town. *Fawlty Towers* has become somewhat of a cult series, partly because of its excellent writing, its slapstick, and its true wit but also for its curiously surgical commentary on British behavior, on British attitudes to life in general and to travel and tourists in particular. The Fawltys' Britain is on the cusp of becoming European—a transition that allows plentiful humor to be derived from the lead characters' inherent pettiness as they confront a changing world.

Torquay is Britain's southernmost resort. It is warm enough for palm trees to flourish, giving the town an entirely un-British caste. At first glance, the poster seems as if it must be depicting a resort on the Mediterranean rather than on the north coast of the English Channel. Painted in fulsome watercolor, it portrays a harbor full of yachts; a "Grand hotel" on the promenade; ranks of parked cars; manicured lawns; and flower beds, sunshine, and a distant beach—all framed by a giant palm tree. It is odd, for instance, that parked cars should be part of a travel poster; in the twenty-first century, we consider parking lots an eyesore, but in 1947, rows of parked cars perhaps imbued a sense of elusive prosperity. Overall, there is a deliberate playfulness to the poster. It depicts an England that is romantic and balmy. With its patrician houses on a rise overlooking the yacht-crammed harbor, with its blue sky and its palm tree suggesting a sense of the subtropical, it is as if it is deliberately seeking to mount a challenge to Monte Carlo.

1959

Even though the draconian currency restrictions were lifted by the early fifties, when I was a small boy we vacationed every August in England, usually in a house rented for a month on a beach on the English Channel. (The one exception was the journey that had heralded the ceremonial affixing of the luggage label to my cardboard suitcase.) None of my school friends' parents seemed to ascribe to the notion of renting a house by the sea and as none of them appeared to have relatives in Paris, they didn't venture there either. In the late fifties and early sixties, just as the Jews of New York were beginning to abandon the Catskills for the greater charms of Florida, the Jewish middle class of northwest London were losing interest in the drizzle and boredom of Brighton, Bournemouth, and—yes—Torquay. Each summer instead, my closest school chums—Stephen, Richard, and Roger—were whisked away on midnight charter flights for two-week stays at resorts on the Italian Riviera or one of Spain's "Costas." Stephen Gilchrist was my closest friend, and I was, I think, envious of his exotic vacations, although—as children are wont to do—I was able to argue internally that while our vacation spot, Shoreham-On-Sea, certainly wanted desperately for the lure of the Mediterranean, at least I got to spend a whole month there.

The Gilchrists seemed to have a great deal more money than we. "Gilchrist" was the anglicized version of "Glicklach" scrawled by a tetchy immigration officer on Stephen's grandfather's turn-of-the-century entry documents at the port of London. Born in Lithuania, the grandfather was to open a dress business in the West End, not caring that the Yiddish-tainted "Glicklach" had been transformed into something so palpably Christian. Stephen's father, Hyman, and his mother, Annette, exuded both richesse and glamour—particularly Annette, whose hair was always perfectly frosted and coiffed and her eyebrows dramatically arched above sparkly butterfly-shaped glasses. They lived in an apartment not far from ours. Their downstairs neighbor was comedian Benny Hill.

Unlike my mother and I—whose skins were freckled and fair and required repeated lashings of Cooltan, a loathsome, sticky unguent squeezed from a tube and designed to protect us from the searing English sun—the Gilchrists would return from the Adriatic or Mediterranean deep chestnut brown. The names of their vacation destinations rolled off Annette's tongue in vowels unmistakably English-Jewish-Cockney. The Gilchrists' 1960 summer holiday was spent in Riccione ("Ritch-ee-ow-nee") on the Adriatic; 1961 was in Torremolinos ("Torry-malleeee-noss"); 1963 was in Lido di Iesolo ("Leedow di Jezelow"). Perhaps Annette's massacring of the names served to diminish both their allure and my envy.

The currency restrictions were to be brought back by the Labour government of Harold Wilson in 1964. This time, the limit was twenty-five pounds per traveler, again dashing the plans of the majority of Britons uninterested in restricting their vacations to the homeland or to destinations in the "Sterling Area" that included Bermuda; the British Caribbean; and esoteric places like Gibraltar, Malta, and, oddly and irritatingly, in Israel's neighboring enemy, Jordan. The week after the currency restrictions were finally lifted a few years later, the Carlton Hotel in Cannes—a traditional, pre-restriction favorite of the wealthier stratum of British Jewry—placed a full-page advertisement in the *Jewish Chronicle*, the weekly newspaper that touted itself then as "the organ of British Jewry." The advertisement was a full-page photograph of the hotel and the foreshore and jetty that fronted its access to the Mediterranean. The advertisement contained two words: no logos, no signatures, no addresses, no telephone numbers, and, of course, websites had yet to be dreamed of. Nor even did the advertisement identify itself as having being placed by the Carlton Hotel in Cannes—so recognizable was its facade. The two words, in large type dropped out of the photograph, were "Welcome Home." Somehow, I found this advertisement profoundly moving. I admired its graphic simplicity. I admired the intelligence it presumed of its readers. I admired its creativity. I admired its ability to speak directly to a specific audience with a message so subtle that it could not be mistaken for anything but what it was.

Three of my summers were spent in Shoreham-by-Sea, in the county of Sussex, a half hour west of Brighton and Hove, home of Aunt Vi. Here we rented a house that rejoiced in the name "Artists' Retreat." The house was not much: a big living room, three or four bedrooms, one bathroom, and—at the front of the house—a glassed-in porch that fronted the entire width of the lot, in which we spent 90 percent of our waking hours. A lawn reached to the front gate that reached to the road that reached to the shingle beach that reached down to the waters of the English Channel. The lawn was bordered by rose bushes, whose fat and fulsome blooms were cut and placed in vases around the house. At the back was a greenhouse full of tomato plants. As the door of the greenhouse opened, the pungent smell of ripe tomatoes was overpowering. To this day, when I sniff the

"tomatoes on the vine" at Whole Foods, my brain instantly catapults me
back to that Shoreham greenhouse.

My parents had been visiting Shoreham since the 1920s. Pa's parents
would customarily rent a house there every summer. Most of the original
Shoreham beach houses were of a unique design: two disused railway cars
were hauled to the beach and set down parallel about twenty-five feet
apart and at a ninety-degree angle to the waves. The compartments of the
railway cars—or carriages, as they were called—became the bedrooms, and
a living room, dining room, kitchen, and bathroom were constructed and
roofed over between the two. The final touch was a glassed-in porch that
fronted the entire house on the side facing the sea. By the late 1950s, many
of these houses had been replaced by more traditional homes, but not all.
Even Artists' Retreat, though not built from railway cars, maintained the
front porch as its central element.

Days were spent eating, swimming, and playing canasta; eating, swimming, and playing canasta. There was no television. Various friends would
come and go in succession, staying for a few days or a week, usually haul-
ing along a son of my approximate age who would share my room, with its
bunk beds and sweeping view of the tomato greenhouse. The shingle beach
was a font of treasure. Inexplicably, a few inches under the pebbles, there
was an endless supply of pieces of broken china plates, cups, saucers, vegetable bowls, and sauceboats. Raymond and I, and then my friend Nicholas
and I, would spend hour upon hour upon hour in the pursuit of dozens,
hundreds of pieces of china that we would collect in our beach pails and try
to amass into sets—blue willow pattern, red flowers, yellow flowers, boring
plain white. We would arrange our archaeological finds into a giant display
on the lawn of Artists' Retreat—a presentation of museum-like complexity,
complete with sign cards describing the design of the items on exhibition.

Nicholas, the son of my mother's oldest and dearest friend, Hilda, was
three years my senior. It was he who, when I was nine, explained to me what
were then still quaintly known as "the facts of life." In turn, I explained
them to Raymond, who, although nine months older than I, seemed considerably less sexually precocious. Which didn't stop him and me—at
eleven—one day stuffing socks into our Speedos and sunbathing, crotch-
thrustingly spread-eagled, on the lawn. Our sunbath was interrupted by
the next-door neighbor appalled at our appearance as she watered her rose
bushes. Aghast, she summoned my mother and Joyce, who surely found
our prank more amusing than abysmal, insisted—after the socks' removal—

on Raymond and my sitting at the dining table to write the neighbor letters of apology. I cannot begin to imagine what we wrote.

Those Augusts by the sea were indeed happy and carefree for me,
although with endless housework and cooking I assume for my mother, but
with lots of company, entertaining, playing with Teetoe the cat, and with
bracing lifeguard-free swims in the waves of the 65-degree-Fahrenheit English Channel, a temperature I thought was normal. There had been other
summers on the English Channel. The summer of 1954 was Rustington-
on-Sea, in a faux-Tudor house on the shore, outside which a man with a
hand-hauled refrigerator on wheels sold popsicles: Pa arranged a charge
account with him for me. The summer of 1955 was spent at Middleton-
on-Sea in a house owned by a famous British actor of the era named Richard Murdoch. This home was far more impressive than Artists' Retreat. It
was white Bauhaus moderne, with a sweeping curved balcony. My "girlfriend" of the moment, Susan, daughter of a London neighbor who was
a single mother of dubious reputation, joined us, and I recall one evening
creeping along the balcony through shimmering drapes into her bedroom
and embracing her. The summer of 1957 saw my mother and I staying
alone—I wonder why—in a depressing small hotel in the depressing resort
of Felpham-by-Sea where depressing people ate three depressing meals
a day and sunbathed on the depressing all-pebble beach. Felpham's and
neighboring Middleton's only escape was the nearby resort of Bognor-
Regis, where I was taken to see a summer variety show called "Dazzle."
I enjoyed it and even came home to re-create the scenery, but it was
doubtless ghastly. It is said that on his deathbed in 1936, King George V was
reminded by Queen Mary—in an apparent attempt to cheer him into
recuperation—that they were soon to have a holiday in Bognor. "Bugger
Bognor," His Majesty is said to have exclaimed and then promptly expired.
On the day I too am faced with the choice of death or a vacation in Bognor,
I might make a similar decision.

1959

The spring after Anthony left, my grandmother and I vacationed alone in
Bournemouth, another resort on the English Channel, one substantially
further from London than Brighton and Bognor and generally considered
more refined. It was also, parenthetically, a smaller English version of New
York State's Catskills, a place where British Jews went for summer vacations

and to celebrate Passover. (Chanukah in the Britain of 1959 had not yet become the American-made Jewish Christmas: at my home, we just lit candles and sang a song and then, because my mother wouldn't have recognized a latke if she had tripped over one, we ate shepherds' pie for supper.)

Downtown Bournemouth is flanked by two cliffs, East and West, each rather like the cliff portrayed in the "Torquay" poster. The "Jewish" cliff was the East Cliff, where many of my school friends would spend, if not summers, long weekends at the sprawling Green Park, Cumberland, or Majestic Hotels, the British equivalent of Catskill Grossingers or Kutshers. My parents, and particularly my mother, would have happily died rather than enter one of them. Our Bournemouth forays took us to the gentile gentility of the West Cliff, where we stayed in Christian refinement at an assortment of small and large hotels as the years passed. I wonder now if the Jewish hotels were pervaded with the Metropole aroma. Probably not: I'm sure bacon was a pivotal ingredient in the perfume's recipe.

I remain haunted by that spring stay in Bournemouth alone with the grandmother who had sailed from Melbourne to England with my mother in 1912 and again in 1918. Her name was Kate, but as a toddler my brother had dubbed her "Marmi" (Mar-My), and the name stuck. We stayed in what was called then a "private" hotel—the curiously British appellation describing an establishment that had no liquor license. It was a sleepy place, and in the late winter or spring I cannot begin to imagine what we did all day. The beach was too cold, I was too young for movies, there was no television, and Bournemouth out of season was as exciting as a nursing home. I'm sure I was the only guest at our hotel younger than seventy. The entire coterie of enfeebled residents would, in the fifteen minutes prior to each meal, congregate outside the dining room awaiting the waitress's strike of the gong announcing the repast's readiness. Meals were dreary and silent. Floury cream soups tasted of nothing. Slices of overcooked meat were surrounded by overcooked vegetables and smothered by globular gravy. Apple crumble was submerged beneath England's ubiquitous Bird's Custard, yellow as the sun. Marmi and I shared a twin-bedded room and, halfway into our stay, I awoke in the middle of the night to hear her wheezing and coughing, unable to sleep and in considerable distress. She must somehow have contacted my parents, who soon after breakfast appeared and drove us home to London, where she was diagnosed with pneumonia.

But another significant event transpired during that trip to Bournemouth. One morning before my grandmother became ill, I awoke to discover my teddy bear was missing. Marmi pointed to the window, which was ajar, and explained, "During the night the fairies had come and taken Teddy away, but"—she countered with a dramatic flourish that turned my attention to the bedside table—"they left you this red rose in exchange." Incredibly, I believed every word.

1956

There was a book on my parents' sitting room bookshelves that intrigued me. It was one of my mother's favorites, the biography of César Ritz, *Host to the World*, penned by his widow, Marie-Louise, and published in 1938. The book had my mother's name signed inside the front cover, but the inside rear cover revealed a petty felony. Ma had withdrawn it on October 2, 1943, from "Boots' Booklovers' Library" and never returned it. Perhaps the branch of Boots from which it had been withdrawn was subsequently bombed, enabling my mother to reason that the book's retention was permissible.

Parenthetically, I have had an obsessive dread of library books ever since my childhood in the 1950s. Why? Because when books were returned to our local library on Sutherland Avenue, they were immediately placed in a fumigation chamber. The argument was that people with colds, coughs, flu, and TB sat in their beds reading, coughing, spluttering, wiping their noses or even more questionable body parts, and then turning the page. Six decades later I continue to shun all contact with a library book, and the coronavirus pandemic certainly underscored the validity of that strange 1950s custom.

The César Ritz book is rather drearily written, awash with uncritical adoration. Yet it is a fascinating tale and I absorbed every facet of how a simple, ambitious Swiss boy came to create what is arguably still the world's finest hotel, how he discovered an obscure French cook named Auguste Escoffier, and how his career was to give birth to both an adjective and a song to which Fred Astaire could tap.

Another book on those shelves was the *Traveller's Manual of Conversation* published by Karl Baedeker in Leipzig in 1875. It is a glossary and phrase book that translates thousands of words and sentences into English, French, German, and Italian. I would pour over it for hours. It exudes a fabulous sense of the archaic. It tells the traveler how to say—in four languages— "Porter, if you damage my portmanteau I shall immediately summon the British Consul." It enables the traveler to tell the landlord of an inn, "My boots are quite wet, will you have them thoroughly dried up for me by

tomorrow morning; for I catch a cold always, if they are at all damp."
It provides translations of unforgettable demands such as "Will you have
this chest of drawers wiped out, it is quite dirty" and "Will you send for
the washer-woman directly, as I want my linen washed and my stay here
is short."

How could anyone, let alone an already travel-obsessed and totally
eccentric adolescent, not be charmed by a book that provides translations
to phrases such as "What is it usual to give to the servant per month?"
or "I wish to see a medical man, I am unwell" or "At what o'clock does
the diligence set off?" It was not just the fabulous pomposity and arro-
gance of the phrases. I also enjoyed imagining a traveler in a dire situation
thumbing feverishly through the book in order to locate the urgent and
suitable translation for a phrase such as "Steward, will you assist this lady
to go on deck, she is very unwell" or "I want some medicine . . . Have you
fresh leeches? These do not bite. Please to change them for others," and,
my favorite of all, the wonderful "Let us go and see the king."

And then there was the illustrated history of the Folies Bergère. I
ignored the two hundred or so pages of prose and concentrated on the
black-and-white photographs. Josephine Baker cavorted on stage sporting
nothing more than bananas, her breasts so pert and modestly sized that it
seemed incredible that they had scandalized St. Louis and New York. Parades
of statuesque women strolled languidly up ramps and down staircases,
also bare-breasted yet in a chaste sort of way, escorted by tepidly muscular
chorus boys wearing bulging thongs and the feathers of an Indian chief.

The Folies Bergère's parades of Amazonian women were a reminder
of Nan, the six-foot-two-inch-tall friend of my grandmother from their
girlhood in Australia, who had moved to New York. Nan's letters would
drop with a thud through our letter box. She wrote in a script that appeared
almost like Chinese—each word a boxy mass of florid squiggles so un-
readable that I continue to question how the mailman could possibly have
deciphered our address. Each missive from Nan contained six or seven
sheets of thick vellum carpeted in hieroglyphics that bespoke tallness, self-
assurance, and wealth. Before Wall Street crashed, Nan had been traveling through the United States and, so I was told, walked into the Casino
in Central Park and was spotted by Florenz Ziegfeld. He hired her on the
spot to become one of the women whose occupation was merely to saunter
elegantly around the stage of the New Amsterdam Theatre during elaborate first- and secon- act finales of the Ziegfeld Follies. Nan went on to marry

a member of the Italian aristocracy and to live in glamour in a large suite at the Ambassador Hotel on Park Avenue.

Clearly, my grandmother must have been important enough to Nan for her to have arranged a meeting for us with her husband's brother in Milan during our automobile trip to Franceitalygermanyswitzerlandliechtenstein in 1956. Indeed, specifically because of this meeting Pa had creatively slung netting across our car's ceiling, into which my mother's navy straw picture hat was inserted, and it accompanied us as we drove through five countries. Pa, Anthony, and I wore suits and ties, and my mother the straw picture hat and long white gloves, to lunch with Nan's brother-in-law at Gianino. It was quite the most elegant restaurant I had ever experienced, complete with my first fish tank with live fish waiting to be eaten. I remember nothing about Nan's aristocratic relative except that he was a "society" jeweler, ferociously charming, and he carried a silver-tipped cane. Which is quite a lot, I suppose, for a six-year-old to remember for more than six decades.

1958

In the fall of 1958, soon after my brother's permanent departure for Israel, and a year after Sputnik was launched, Britain became preoccupied with the nearest thing possible to the space race: the Anglo-American contest that would determine whether Britain's Comet 4 or America's Boeing 707 would be the first pure jet to enter sustained service cross the Atlantic. Seen from the distance of decades, it was a ridiculous competition: the 707 was vastly superior. But in 1958—only two years after Suez, when the English en masse remained secure in the belief that the world had four super-powers and Britain was one of them—it all seemed very real. British Over-seas Airways Corporation's Comet did, in fact, win, reaching New York a few days before Pan American was able to begin 707 flights across the Atlantic. Not that winning mattered: within a year the smaller and less efficient Comets were transferred to less prestigious routes, and BOAC was flying its own 707s—albeit powered by commendibly British Rolls-Royce engines—to New York.

To turn the excitement of the race into an educational exercise, my third-grade class was taken on an excursion to London Airport to glimpse the new planes. In 1958 London's Heathrow Airport was in transition. The "North Terminal" was a series of enlarged World War II Nissen huts that still served as Britain's base for long-distance flights. "Heathrow Central" had recently been opened for shorter-range flights and was reached through a reinforced concrete tunnel that ran beneath one of the main runways. (Sixty years later, the very same tunnel remains the only way to reach two of the airport's terminals.) It was at Heathrow Central that my friends Stephen, Richard, Roger, and I stood on the viewing terrace of the airport's new red-brick Queen's Building and marveled at the sights. The three of them had all flown. I had not and it was clear that I was the most excited as I identified curvy Constellations atop their awkward undercarriages, lackluster DC-6s and DC-7s, lumbering Stratocruisers, dozens of graceful British European Airways Viscounts with their giant oval windows, and a BOAC Britannia. Suddenly, a deafening roar heralded the arrival of a giant silver, white, and blue aircraft.

"Geoffrey, look, it's a Boeing 707!" Stephen yelled over the noise.

And indeed it was. We gaped at a vision of swept-back wings, sleek underslung engines free of clunky propellers, and the space-age Pan Am logo emblazoned on its tail. As we plugged our ears and snapped pictures with our Brownies, it was if I was somehow gazing into an all-powerful, all-American future, one that before long would enshroud not only the planet but me too.

In 1955 Juan Trippe, founder of Pan American, had set the aviation world aghast by ordering twenty Boeing 707s and twenty-five Douglas DC-8 jetliners. (Trippe would repeat the challenge a decade later when Pan Am became the launch purchaser of the Boeing 747, an airplane he helped design.) Due for delivery in 1958, the airlines of the world knew that from the moment the jets went into service, all their non-jet aircraft would be out of date. Airline executives from five continents embarked on an almost vulgar rush to the West Coast—to Boeing in Seattle, to Douglas in Long Beach—to get in line for the earliest delivery of the jets that were almost twice as fast and thrice as reliable as their existing propeller-driven fleets. Boeing was producing its 707 and Douglas its DC-8, and with few exceptions the airlines that had operated DC-7s remained with Douglas, while the Constellation operators plumped for Boeing. But what to do in the interim? Saddled with dozens of state-of-the-fifties-art propeller-driven air-liners that, without the arrival of jets, should have given five or ten years of solid frontline service, the airlines looked for ways to depict their spanking new pre-jet equipment as the best, the fastest, the most advanced in the world . . . which, briefly, it was. One way was to make posters. I have four of this genre on display, each designed to seduce and to speak to what were both the heyday and the last desperate gasp of the propeller airliner.

My TWA poster from this period is a close-up painting of the nose, wings, and engines of a Lockheed Constellation. (Transcontinental & Western Air morphed into Trans World Airlines in the mid-1930s.) The massiveness of the image transmits a sense of strength and reliability. The plane flies to the right, across clouds and a blue sky that rise up to a dark-blue stratosphere. *"Chaque année, un million de passagers,"* it proclaims—as I have the poster's French version. It makes no mention that to reach New York from London or Paris it would have to stop at least once to refuel. The poster's glory is how it exudes a sense of reliability, success, and resource.

A Swissair poster I hang in the same group dates from 1956 and touts the virtues of the airline's new Douglas DC-7C, known, cleverly, as the "Seven Seas." It proclaims that this is the fastest airliner in the world. The designer of the poster presumably understood that its wall-life would be fleeting: the Douglas DC-8 that would make it obsolete in two years was already in production. Yet the poster proclaims the DC-7C's state-of-the-art modernity in a design that itself reeks of modernity. It is spare, it makes use of modernistic type, and it radiates the future in a way that makes the illustration of the actual aircraft seem an anachronism, just as cars from the 1920s seem so out of place in photographs of Bauhaus apartment houses in Berlin. The red-and-white propeller-driven DC-7C, with its signature red tailplane with a white Swiss cross, feels out of place in a graphic setting that seems far more suited to jets.

A third poster seeks magically to evoke that romantic swansong of the propeller-powered superliner. Also issued by Swissair, it depicts a group of passengers ascending the rear stairs of a Douglas DC-6B airliner (on propeller planes, the choice seats and first class were at the back of the plane, where it was quieter than the front). In the foreground, the pretty face of a Swissair flight attendant smiles at the viewer. The passengers on the stairs are in classic 1950s attire. A mother with small daughter wearing white ankle socks and Mary Janes is being greeted by a flight attendant. The men are in suits and hats. They're all cousins of the passengers in the pages of *National Geographic* playing shuffleboard on the deck of the *Queen Elizabeth* or riding through the Rockies aboard a Vistadome.

The fourth poster dates from 1958 and is the most unusual of them all. It's little more than a sky-blue background with, center left, the nose of a Bristol Britannia aircraft peeking into the foreground. No airline name

Swissair, 1953. Hans Looser, artist (1897–1984). Printed by Eidenbentz & Co., St. Gallen, Switzerland. (Author collection)

or logo appears, merely the words "Every day to everywhere" in Hebrew. This poster, you see, dates from the nine months between December 1957 and October 1958 when Britain's BOAC and Israel's El Al had the commercial advantage of being the only operators of the world's fastest airliner, the jet-prop Britannia. It should have been in service in 1956, but engine development snags delayed it till December 1957. When El Al introduced the Britannia, it transformed its image from that of an ethnic, Third World airline into that of the big league. El Al was Marlon Brando, the bruised-up unimportant airline that was now a contender. An advertisement in the *New York Times* that declared, "From December 22, 1957, the Atlantic will be 20 percent smaller," won awards for audacity and creativity. The "20 percent smaller" message was transmitted graphically with dazzling minimalism, merely a full-page black-and-white photograph of the churning ocean, with a fifth of it torn away. It was the brainchild of Bill Bernbach, a man whose creativity and gutsiness would not only transform the image of El Al but would also convert the geeky Volkswagen Beetle from being seen as a weird Nazi anachronism into a car that would cause Americans to flood VW dealerships. Bernbach came from the "Welcome-Home-Carlton-in-Cannes" school of advertising where less is more, that a few uncomplicated, luminous words could do more than paragraphs of prose. Another of his advertisements for El Al when it introduced the Britannia sported the headline "No Goose, No Gander." It spoke to the reality that the Britannia could fly from London to New York and back without the bothersome and time-wasting refueling stops at the Canadian airports of Goose Bay and Gander, stops that remained virtually obligatory for the slower Constellations and DC-7s. Little did anyone dream that forty-three years later, dozens of the latest transatlantic jets would land and remain for days at Gander in Newfoundland, while panicked Americans repaired their psyches in the wake of 9/11—an adventure eventually memorialized in a smash Broadway musical.

When Pan American's Boeing 707 took off for Paris from New York's Idlewild Airport in October 1958, it marked what was to become a landmark in human development. Ever since the invention of the wheel, man has been obsessed with the concept of increasing speed. During the nineteenth century, trains and ships were exhorted to travel faster and faster. The race for swiftness intensified in the years 1890–1904 with the development of the automobile and the invention of the airplane. Man strove for haste. In 1910 the *Mauretania* seared through the Atlantic in eight days.

S.S. *United States*, 1951. United States Lines. (Author collection)

In 1936 the *Normandie* and the *Queen Mary* made it in five. And in 1953, the SS *United States* did it in three days, ten hours, and forty minutes. Similarly with flight: in 1950 it took a Pan Am Stratocruiser fourteen vibration-wracked hours to reach London from New York. By 1956 the latest TWA Constellations had knocked it down to eleven, and in 1957 BOAC's and El Al's Britannias reduced it to nine. A year later, the 707 reduced it to six hours and thirty minutes. And, with the one twenty-five-year exception of the Concorde, an aircraft available only to the mega-mega-rich, there it has remained. Long before it was fashionable to do so, man decided that the threats to the environment were just too great to go faster. So while the comforts and the efficiency of aircraft have been improved and updated, fifty years later, the journey between New York and London still—unless there are remarkable tail winds—takes six and a half hours.

1961

Another poster hanging in my home was issued by Israel's Zim passenger shipping line circa 1961. It is titled "Off to Israel" and is charming because it is utterly unreal. It portrays an image of traveling to Israel that was then—and is even now—entirely incongruous. The heart of the poster's image is a photograph of a collection of good quality suitcases, each appropriately tagged with a Zim baggage label. Next to the suitcases is a pair of flippers, a snorkel, a tennis racket, a beach bag, and a giant golf bag from whose opening sprout several golf clubs. And next to all of it sits a large boxer dog, its eyes facing the camera, a Zim baggage tag rakishly tied around its neck. A wealthy American couple—or family—with Fido in tow are "off to Israel." It is valiant in its conceit, in its self-deception. It's a poster that speaks to how Israelis wanted to project their self-image and has very little to do with the realities of a vacation—certainly a vacation in the early 1960s in what was still an austere and wildly unsophisticated country. Just as the seductive advertising of postwar London in *National Geographic* conveyed utter unreality to this Londoner, this poster for travel to Israel hanging in my home office portrays the unreal land its designers wished it had been or might, perhaps, one day become—as indeed it has.

Not far from this poster hangs another. Produced by the fledgling El Al in 1951, it was designed by "Israel's Cassandre," Franz Krausz—to whose work the Tel Aviv Museum devoted a retrospective exhibit in 1981. A noted poster designer in Vienna, Berlin, and Barcelona, Krausz fled Germany for

Palestine in 1934. His work became legendary, creating images of strong, socialist Zionists—images that somehow did not seem anachronistic even though their goal was utterly capitalist: to sell cigarettes, washing powder, and—in 1951—the Jewish state's new airline. The poster charms because the colors are elegant and because it exudes stability and strength of purpose. Its central image is a watercolor cluster of edifices emblematic of the cities to which the fledgling El Al flew: the Eiffel Tower, the Colosseum, Big Ben, the Statue of Liberty, the Empire State Building, all wrapped into a single unit atop a plinth that represents Jerusalem's ancient Citadel. At the top, the poster entreats "Fly Constellation" and next to the entreaty is a small painting of a blue-and-white plane. At the bottom it reads, "El Al Israel Airlines."

This is not the poster one could begin to expect from a country that had just fought a war for its birth and survival, a country that had seen hundreds of thousands of Arabs fleeing or evicted, a country that was trying to absorb a million refugees from fifty countries, many with tattoos on their arms and nightly nightmares. The grandeur of the images and the confidence with which they're projected do not seem quite appropriate to a fledgling airline that was founded with donated money, whose airplanes were held together with duct tape and prayers, whose first DC-4 aircraft was furnished with a three-seater velveteen couch bolted to the floor and whose flight attendants were only days before waiting tables at outdoor cafés on Tel Aviv's Dizengoff Street. No, this is a poster that speaks of boldness and stability and experience. This is a poster that Franz Krausz would have created—had he been asked—for Air France or Pan Am. Just like the Zim poster with the dog and the golf club, it reeks of wannabe, of elegant and daring conceit. And because it just had to impart worldly sophistication, it rolled off the presses in Vienna rather than in the then less advanced printing houses of Tel Aviv.

It was in December 1961 that my parents and I took an El Al plane from London to Tel Aviv to visit Anthony. It was ten years after Krausz's poster had been produced and several years, no doubt, after most copies of it had become torn, ragged, Scotch-taped, and finally scraped off travel agency walls and thrown in the trash. That is indeed a part of my attraction for these posters: they were created to inspire, to be hung, displayed, admired, regarded, discarded, and replaced. Thus only a fraction of the hundreds or thousands printed ever managed to survive longer than their useful wall-life.

Fly Constellation to Four Continents: El Al Israel Airlines, 1951. Franz Krausz, artist (1905–98). Printed by Brüder Rosenbaum, Vienna. (Author collection)

We did not fly on a Constellation but on a spanking-new Boeing 707—
one just like the Pan Am plane I had seen three years earlier, except that
El Al's version, like those of BOAC, was powered by aristocratically British Rolls-Royce engines. Pa bought us new luggage for the trip. Each was
"state-of-the-art" molded fiberglass, his and mine both in tobacco brown,
my mother's in powder blue, each with a contrasting plaid lining. As this
was still eons before one would ever consider traveling in sneakers, jogging
pants, and a sweatshirt, we dressed carefully for the almost six-hour journey.
Pa and I were in suits, white shirts, ties, and serious lace-up shoes, and my
mother traveled in a fitted costume accented by medium heels, gloves, and
I think, but am not sure, an honest-to-God chapeau from an honest-to-God
milliner, complete with net veil.

Ever since its creation, El Al had managed to radiate a larger-than-life
quality, one to which the 1951 Franz Krausz poster deftly attests. The reality was that in 1961 El Al was still a tiny airline whose budget, fleet, and
resources were stretched to the limit, yet it chose to overlook these draw-
backs by emanating savoir faire and creativity. Within the plane's interior, instead of the plain pastel walls chosen by every other airline, El
Al had commissioned Israeli artist Jean David to create subtle tableaux of
Tel Aviv to surround each window. The scenes are captured from above, a
cubist mass of Tel Aviv's Bauhaus buildings clustered to the left of each of
the 707's windows—with the windows themselves becoming an element
of the artwork by playing the role of the Mediterranean. The colors were
pale and unobtrusive. It was not merely unique; it was tasteful and refined
and it transformed an otherwise bland tube of fiberglass-lined aluminum
into an expression of the airline's raison d'être.

The identical Jean David cubist image of that massing of Bauhaus struc-
tures clustered on the Mediterranean shore is the central image of a poster
that hangs in my home's guest room. The poster's background is lemon
yellow; the buildings' cubes are blue and gray and white. The Mediterranean has a frothy white foreshore: the sea itself is a pool of dark and paler
blue stripes. The poster exhorts, "See Tel Aviv and Fly There with El Al"
and had been issued two years before our flight to celebrate the fiftieth
anniversary of the city's founding in 1909—the same year my parents were
born. This is a travel poster that presents a modernist artistic take on what
had been known in the thirties as the "White City"—yet it is not a poster
that seeks to mislead. The artist's use of cubism is less of a device of the
brush and more the quest to characterize on paper the aura of a city that

See Tel-Aviv and Fly There with El Al, Israel Airlines, 1959. Jean David, artist (1908–93). Published by Tel Aviv Municipality and the Government Tourism Corporation, Jerusalem (overprinted by El Al Israel Airlines). Printed by E. Lewin-Epstein, Tel Aviv. (Author collection)

then—and now—is home to more Bauhaus architecture than any other on earth.

The flight to Israel in 1961 was not my first flight. My parents and I had flown to Paris and back in August 1960 on another of those excursions that involved both the City of Light and visiting Raymond, Joyce, and Henri. Our flight from London to Tel Aviv was part of a journey that had begun in New York, and it also stopped en route in Paris. On the London-to-Paris leg, I was seated apart from my parents next to two young Yugoslav women who were flying from New York, via Paris, to Belgrade. As it was December, they were curious to know if I celebrated Christmas, and my innocent and truthful acknowledgment that indeed I did must have frustrated their earnest attempt to ascertain how Jews were different in ways other than operating an airline where milk could not be added to coffee after a steak dinner. The Yugoslav ladies said good-bye at Orly Airport, and after a bus trip to the terminal and back to a freshened plane, my parents and I sat together for the four-hour leg to Tel Aviv.

There was something remarkably glamorous to be flying aboard a jet. In 1961 very few people I knew had done it. It was if we had stepped into the space age. The lavish booklet in the seat pocket explained the facets of jet travel. Its shiny white cover was imprinted with the identical Jean David images of cubist Tel Aviv. Its pages were many, each designed both to educate novice jet travelers and to forewarn and elegantly calm nervous flyers such as my mother. It spoke at length of the various noises the jet engines would make as the captain adjusted thrust after takeoff, after the climb, and at the beginning of the descent. It warned of the steep angle at which the plane would ascend, of the roar of the reverse thrust upon landing, and of the sounds that would be made by the landing gear closing after takeoff and opening before touchdown. The booklet devoted several pages to extolling the attributes of Boeing's trademarked Passenger Service Unit—the aerodynamic boxlike structure that sat above each row of seats. It explained by means of numbered diagrams and copious text that it featured individual reading lights; individual outlets for ventilation that could be opened and closed at the passenger's discretion; a "hostess call button"; signs whose illumination would instruct travelers when to fasten seat belts and when to stop smoking; and, lastly, a flap that in the case of emergency would miraculously open and out would fall four oxygen masks. Seen from the distance of sixty years, the booklet seems quaint, simplistic, and fabulously anachronistic. At the time, it was an introduction to the twenty-eighth century.

This was how one dressed to go sightseeing in January 1962 in the ancient port of Jaffa (*l to r*): Pa, Ma, Me, and the gorgeous Ariela.

I sat next to the window . . . or, to be precise, windows. One of the advances promoted by the Boeing 707 was the provision of an endless row of windows along the length of the airplane. Previously, aircraft designers had placed a large window next to each row of seats. But the mid-1950s designers at Boeing in Seattle were prophetic enough to recognize that their buyers might rearrange the initial seating arrangement and that the solution would be to puncture the fuselage with an unlimited number of windows. In technical terms, it was hardly worth noting. But in terms of passenger comfort, it was a tremendous step forward. It was the one major difference between the 707 and Douglas's DC-8 that was designed with the one-window-per-row concept. (Douglas realized its mistake and with the DC-9 aped Boeing's "endless windows," as has every airplane ever since.)

Dusk eventually fell and, as warned, the engine noise changed as the plane tilted downward for the descent. There was a hush in the cabin as we flew low over the city of Tel Aviv; it did sort of look like a nighttime version of the artwork that surrounded the windows. Designed to play to the emotions of passengers making their first visit to the thirteen-year-old Jewish State, the traditional Israeli melody "Hevenu Shalom Aleichem" played from the loudspeakers and moist-eyed arrivees clapped along as we overflew the twinkling lights of the "White City." We touched down gently, the engines' reverse thrust roared, we taxied, and we descended stairs into a warm night.

When it was built by the British in 1936, the terminal at Lydda Airport outside Tel Aviv was the largest airline terminal in the world, a record it retained until 1939, when an even larger terminal building was opened at Newark. The cleanliness of its Bauhaus lines contrasted with the moderne curves of the control tower. Inside, it was all very *Casablanca*—except with signs in Hebrew. Fans swirled, clerks stamped passports, luggage was hauled into the customs hall on a trailer. After embraces and tears and the introduction to my brother's wife of three months, Ariela—a Sophia Loren lookalike—we piled into a lumbering 1940s Packard for the nighttime ride through the Judean Hills up to Jerusalem. The driver twisted and curved us up into the mountains, and by the time we reached Jerusalem, it was close to midnight. The city was at rest, the streets empty. Tired but with adrenalin pumping, I noted the limestone Bauhaus buildings with their curved moderne balconies. It was exotic, it was foreign, yet it was also somehow calming. The Packard swung to the left into the driveway of the King David Hotel.

The arrangements for our trip to Israel had been made by Pa, with me in tow, with a Mr. Richtiger, a crusty, elderly gentleman with an impenetrable Central European accent at the Soho offices of Isratours. My mother was never included in such negotiations, nor my grandmother who, at seventy-six, would not come with us but would remain at home. Pa and I made several visits to Mr. Richtiger. The making of the bookings was painstaking, and I involved myself in every detail. I breathed in the ambience of his frowsy and untidy office with its piles of timetables, posters, brochures, and baggage tags. No longer just guiding me through the Talmud of his map drawer, here my father was instructing me in the nuances of putting his Talmud into practice. We were to fly to Israel on El Al, we were to fly home seventeen days later on British European Airways (BEA), and we would stay at the King David Hotel in Jerusalem and at the Dan Hotel in Tel Aviv. It really wasn't terribly complicated—but the busyness of the hand-writing of the tickets, the procurement of visas, the mounds of baggage tags, the inscribing of hotel vouchers, the placing of the documents in cardboard ticket wallets all held for me the magic of an intricate religious rite.

The King David Hotel was the most glamorous hotel in which I had ever stayed—reeking of luxury. It did not reek in the slightest of the Metropole aroma—yet another confirmation that it's bacon-based. Because Anthony seemed to know somebody who knew somebody—in Israel it's called "protexia"—we were ensconced in a corner suite complete with bedroom and parlor. Pa looked at the tariff card behind the door and became pale. My brother assured him all was taken care of and not to worry. Our suite opened onto tiny balconies that faced a dark and impenetrable Old City. No more than fifty yards from the hotel garden, tank traps and barbed wire denoted the frontier between Israel's Jerusalem and the no-man's-land that stretched to the ancient walls where Jordanian Jerusalem began.

I slept soundly that first night, but long before dawn, my mother apparently awoke to the noises of what she determined was a squadron of infiltrators muttering in Arabic. It was a constant sound of Arabic cadences with which she proclaimed herself familiar as her Moroccan-born grandparents had—between themselves—conversed in Arabic. Alarmed and scared, she opened the door, and the muttering seemed louder. She donned a robe and crept into the hall to alert the staff to the imminent incursion. She tiptoed along the wide corridor and down the grand staircase. With each step, the muttering becoming louder and increasingly menacing.

She peeked around the corner of the staircase into the giant lobby with its Herodian friezes and throne-like armchairs and came face to face with the source of the Arabic muttering: a tired old gentleman vacuuming the rugs. It was the engine of the Hoover Upright that emitted a tone that to my mother had seemed indubitably to be a throng of Arabs with scimitars intent on evil. Abashed, she returned to bed.

I still have an early framed graphic from the King David Hotel. It's not a poster, exactly, but an information sheet to be posted on the back of each guest room's door, outlining the hotel's services and regulations. The King David had been built in 1930 by Egyptian Jews who also owned Shepheard's and Mena House in Cairo, the Cataract Hotel in Aswan, and the Winter Palace in Luxor. The poster speaks volumes in characterizing a hotel stay in the 1930s in the British Empire. "No shopkeeper, dragoman, or store-boy will be allowed in the hotel unless at the special desire of visitors who should inform the Hall Porter," it announces, with its implicit warning of robbery and suggestion of buggery. There is an imperious, imperial imperative to its tone: "Visitors who wish to be 'en pension' will kindly make arrangements at the Reception Office." It also recalls a moment in time when Jerusalem was connected by rail to Cairo and Beirut: "Visitors are requested to kindly notify the time of departure before noon or the previous evening if leaving by the early train."

Forty years later, I was to hear a charming anecdote about the King David from a friend of my brother. She was the daughter of a Chicago Jewish hotel magnate who, in 1950, owned both the city's Palmer House Hotel and the Willard Hotel in Washington. They visited Israel soon after the state was founded in 1948 and were taken to Jerusalem. They were shown the King David Hotel, its southwest wing blown off in a terrorist attack by the right-wing Etzel organization in 1946. They toured through the cavern-ous halls and empty rooms. The Israel government offered them the King David Hotel for the price of the hotel's linens and silverware. They turned the offer down. Big mistake. Huge.

We spent two weeks in Israel, becoming acquainted with Ariela's alarm-ingly Orthodox family and experiencing the frissons of dread and excite-ment of the barbed wire and concrete barriers that divided Jewish from Arab Jerusalem. We visited the so-called tomb of King David, and at Mount Zion's Chamber of the Holocaust, I remained outside with Ariela while my parents toured the grisly exhibition that apparently included lampshades made from human skin.

I think I only stayed that first night at the King David and then moved into Anthony and Ariela's apartment, where I slept on the living room sofa. The flat was quite large and one of its bedrooms was rented to a colleague of Anthony's by the name of Danny Ben Yaacov. Danny had been born in Berlin and, as an adolescent, had been tearfully placed by his parents on one of the last Kindertransport trains to freedom in England. Eventually, he came to Palestine as a teenager and fought in the War of Independence. His room was full of books and stacks of untidy papers. His one passion, or so it seemed, was his handlebar mustache, for which my parents had been deputized into bringing to Israel a jar of costly mustache pommade from a patrician store on Bond Street named Truefitt and Hill. Danny's English—like that of Pa's friend Herbert Sutton—was archly and exaggeratedly British, its vowels overenunciated and pedantic. He was charming, hypercritical, unpredictable, and wracked with eccentricity. One evening, he babysat me while my parents, Anthony, and Ariela went out for dinner. Danny put me to bed, a process that involved him giving me a mustachioed kiss good night on the lips and giving my nether regions a couple of gentle strokes. While it certainly made me somehow uncomfortable, I won't pretend it was entirely unpleasant. On another night, on my way to the bathroom in the dark, strange noises emanated from Anthony and Ariela's bedroom. I opened the door to make sure they were all right and found them sitting facing each other naked on the bed. I closed the door quickly and returned to my own bed. I realized at twelve that they were having sex, but it was a novelty to me that this could be performed in any way other than lying down.

Sexual frissons aside, ultimately, one of the two lasting leitmotifs of the trip—although I was only vaguely aware of it at the time—was the virtually instantaneous mutual loathing that was to consume my mother and Ariela for decades. The other leitmotif was the trip's agonizing and catastrophic ending, a small precursor of which took place soon after our arrival in Israel. We were already in Jerusalem when, on December 21, 1961, a British European Airways Comet 4B, registration number G-ARJM, slammed into a mountain outside Ankara while on the approach for an en route landing on its way to Tel Aviv. All on board were killed instantly. This was precisely the kind of plane on which we were booked to fly home. Ignoring the "lightning never strikes twice" rule, my mother insisted we change our flight arrangements back to London. Frantic cables were exchanged with Mr. Richtiger back in Soho and ultimately we were switched to fly home a

day later than planned, on El Al. Another telegram was sent to my grandmother, alerting her to the change.

Our last days in Israel were spent in Tel Aviv. We rode the train from
Jerusalem, almost a two-hour ride to cover forty miles, winding down to
the Mediterranean through the Judean Mountains. This was the same
route Theodor Herzl, Zionism's founder, had ridden on his way to meet
the Kaiser in 1898. We stayed at the oceanfront Dan Hotel. While the King
David had exuded colonial grandeur, the Dan was America. Sleek and
modern and bold of design, it simply made our postwar British mouths
drop open. Its giant lobby lounge seemed to be suspended above a pond
full of lilies, fountains, and sculptures. The furniture was Danish modern. This was the first time I encountered what I would learn was a "standard" modern hotel room, but at the time I was entranced: open the door
and find a closet with sliding doors on the right, bathroom on the left,
then on into the bedroom, bed on the left wall, dresser-desk on the right,
curtained windows in front. Yes, it was Israel, but it was also taking me
a step closer to the insides of an advertisement in *National Geographic*
magazine.

1962

On January 8, 1962, we clambered into another giant old American car, a
1939 Buick, for the ride back to Lydda Airport. The good-byes were tearful and I was so upset at leaving Ariela—whom I had come to adore—that
I was to throw up for the first part of the flight. The journey home was
aboard one of those El Al Britannias that in 1957 had made the Atlantic 20
percent smaller. After my retching, I napped and awoke to the vista of giant
plates of scrambled eggs. I retched again and went back to sleep. Eventually I felt better and sat glued to the giant oval windows for eight hours,
peering at the propellers and the jet exhausts, as we throbbed our way first
to Rome, where we admired the ultramodern Leonardo da Vinci air terminal at Fiumicino Airport, and then on across the Alps and the English
Channel to London.

We were driven home by my Uncle Angus, and while he and my parents busied themselves with the luggage, I raced upstairs to our flat and
my grandmother's embrace. I rang the bell repeatedly, hopping up and
down in excitement and impatience. Nobody answered and, disappointed,
I assumed she must have gone to the shops at the corner. Pa finally opened

the door. The apartment was warm, coal fires were lit, Christmas presents from my grandmother neatly arranged on the dining room table.

It was Pa who found her motionless on the floor in her bedroom. I gasped when I saw her from a distance, the gasp grabbing my mother's attention. Ma raced to her mother's side and I heard the plaintive wails of "Wake up Mummy, wake up Mummy" as my father dialed for an ambulance. My grandmother was warm to the touch, it seemed, but I was too terrified to approach. Within minutes, plans were made for Pa to drive me to my godparents, Hilda and Ferdy, while my mother would travel in the ambulance with Marmi.

Some hours later, Pa came to pick me up and bring me home. There were whispered exchanges with Hilda and Ferdy and in the car Pa explained to me that Marmi was very, very ill and we would know more in the morning. My mother was in the dining room when we returned, seated at the

Kate Campbell Afriat, my grandmother (1885–1962), two weeks before her death. (Author collection)

table still piled with our unwrapped Christmas presents. Tears were rolling down her cheeks. She was reading the accumulated mail and Christmas cards. I put my arms around her and assured her that Marmi would be all right. I was convinced of it. She seemed distracted and indifferent to my assurances. I crept into bed.

In the morning, Pa came into my room, sat on the bed, and told me Marmi was dead. She had suffered a massive heart attack called a coronary thrombosis, and she hadn't suffered. It would be years before I learned that she was already dead when he found her, and that the maintenance of hope until the morning was devised to protect me from learning the bad news at night rather than in daylight.

I did not attend my grandmother's funeral. Perhaps in the London of 1962 it was deemed inappropriate for twelve-year-olds to attend funerals. It took place at Golder's Green Crematorium while I was at school, and I returned home to a house full of family and friends having afternoon tea. It seemed oddly celebratory and I felt uneasy. I don't believe I had connected my frantic ringing of the doorbell with Marmi's heart attack. But, remember, I lived in a family where my mother's permitting Anthony to sleep outside in the streets in anticipation of the coronation of Elizabeth II had resulted in tubercular pleurisy. So it was in response to the inevitable inquiries that my mother, in relating the circumstances of Marmi's sudden death to friends and family, would explain that "Geoffrey's repeated ringing of the doorbell must have caused her to have a heart attack." "Her hair was not done," she would add, "so she must have been upset to realize we were already home, and the shock killed her."

Did she mean to blame me? We talked about it decades later and she denied it, explaining that she was merely describing what had happened. But in a child's mind, the lines between cause and effect, responsibility and blame are, at best, blurry. At twelve, I certainly believed I was guilty of killing my grandmother, and I would go on to spend my teenage years engaged in a paroxysm of sickeningly fawning behavior in an attempt to win my mother's forgiveness. I would dread the anniversaries of Marmi's birth and death, when Ma would be inconsolably tearful, each of her sobs reminding me of my misdemeanor. It was not until twelve years later in New York that the psychiatrist I had consulted responded, on hearing my tale, that "people don't die from doorbells." His words palpated the sense of guilt as if lifting a dark velvet curtain from my psyche. At the same time, it unleashed a wellspring of fury at my mother for allowing me to believe I had been responsible, a fury that, in retrospect, would partly explain my need to leave London and that flat. Half a lifetime is a very long time to be convinced of having committed manslaughter of one's grandmother. To this day, on her birthday, I persuade myself that a woman born in 1885 would—by 1985, or 1995, and certainly by now—most assuredly have expired without my assistance.

In the days and weeks and months after Marmi's death, yet another myth was born as the events were endlessly examined, rehearsed, and chewed over. The resulting fable was that had we not changed our flight home from Israel because of the BEA crash, none of this would have happened. It would take me years to be able to make a change in my travel schedule without the premonition it would lead to some unfathomable disaster.

A few weeks after my grandmother died, Ma and I were sitting in the car en route to visit her father. We stopped a long while at a traffic light, and she began noiselessly to cry. Apart from my mother's years at boarding school and the first eleven years of my parents' marriage, Ma had lived her entire life with her mother. They had been devoted friends. They would talk endlessly, they would gossip, they would laugh, and only occasionally would they disagree about anything. Every tear my mother shed, every sob of anguish that emanated from her chest, felt to me like an arrow of accusation. My wanton behavior had brought the world down around my mother, and there was not a thing I could do to make it up to her. Her sobs and tears were expressed in utter silence. Had she thrown herself on the floor, pummeled the carpets with her fists, and wailed inconsolably, it might have been easier for me to deal with, at least at the beginning. But the decorum of her grief, the sinister silence of her mourning, seemed somehow to augment my guilt with the further weight of her martyrdom.

As we sat at that traffic light, I put my hand on my mother's arm and said, "Perhaps it's for the best, she would have died one day, and we are getting the grief out now instead of later." It was a pathetic, desperate attempt to shake loose from my shoulders the crushing weight of blame. But my mother was incensed. The light changed, she slammed the car into gear, and off we drove in raucous silence along Sussex Gardens.

We were driving to a dank basement flat near Baker Street from which we were to assist my grandfather move. After separating from my grandmother in the 1920s, his homes had been a succession of rented rooms in once patrician houses. He was relocating to another similarly dreary basement in a comparable house a few streets away. We helped him carry his suitcases, his pictures, his boxes of mementoes. He was seventy-nine and he wasn't well. He had a racking cough, and he was wearing woolen gloves without fingers to keep his hands warm. It was February, it was cold, and the basement room in which we unpacked his belongings smelled of mildew and damp. He would pause every now and again and with an anguished sigh proclaim that he wanted "to be with Katie" (Marmi's real name). My mother made sure he had sufficient shilling coins for the gas meter, and we walked to the car and drove home. I don't know if it occurred to her to insist he come home with us and stay, if only for a while, in my grandmother's now empty room. Of course, it should have occurred to her. It seems outrageous that it didn't, but perhaps she was so consumed with grief or anger or both that she could think neither rationally nor charitably. A week later, Ma visited him at St. Mary's Hospital, and he died there a few days later. My father's father had died the previous April, so within ten months I had lost all of my living grandparents. Within a space of six weeks, my mother had lost both her parents and arranged for their corpses to be cremated. My grandfather's death was a sadly pathetic post-script to my grandmother's death. But at least nobody could blame that one on me.

The only solution to the emotional quagmire in which I now writhed was to fulminate with anger at the one being who could, from my viewpoint, have turned things around. On the night we had come home from Israel, I had given Him ample opportunity. I had promised God that if he made Marmi well, I would cease masturbation. He chose not to accept my offer and I retaliated extravagantly. Masturbating became an act of addiction performed over and over. I would masturbate till my wrists and elbows hurt—in my bed, in the bathroom, in the lavatory. I would secrete dozens of linen handkerchiefs crisp with dried semen in the folds of sheets and towels at the bottom of the laundry basket. I would jerk off at school, on the subway, upstairs on double-decker buses, in the park, in the shower after sports, in the changing room at Selfridges, and—more than once—on the couch at the home of my Bar Mitzvah teacher, Mr. Moser, when he went down the hall to answer the telephone.

I had begun Bar Mitzvah lessons two months after we returned from Israel. Mr. Moser was the chazan (cantor) at our synagogue, the man who sang each week's Torah portion in a grating, nasal voice. He was a widower who lived alone in a mansion flat near Tottenham Court Road whose windows were rarely opened. His breath smelled faintly of sardines and he employed a buxom Eastern European housekeeper whom he eventually married. I would take the Underground twice a week from my school to Mr. Moser's flat, where he would coach me in the monumentally long portion he had selected for me to chant. In fact, because my pitch was so perfect, I was to substitute for him as chazan for part of the service. One afternoon, toward the end of my lesson, the doorbell rang and Mr. Moser went to answer it. I could hear my father's voice, and then a lot of whispering. Pa came into the room and listened to me sing and then we bade farewell to Mr. Moser. In the metal cage of the lift that conveyed us downstairs, Pa told me why he had come to get me. Uncle Jack was dead, and his widow, Auntie Raie, would be at home when we got there.

Jack and Raie were not really my aunt and uncle: every adult friend of my parents was given that sobriquet, although there was a smattering of a relationship—Raie's sister, Stella, had been briefly and miserably married to Pa's mother's brother, Uncle Gerald, a man noted for his phenomenal stinginess. I loved Jack and Raie. They made me laugh. Jack had the most vulgar sense of humor I had ever encountered and Raie was warm, excitable, vivacious, poorly spoken, and considered common by both my parents, who had a prodigal facility of adoring yet simultaneously trashing all their friends. When we arrived home, I heard Raie wailing from the sitting room, "It must have been his illness." Some years before, one of Jack's kidneys had been removed and he was, I had always been told, living on borrowed time. Unlike Marmi's death, Jack's seemed to me to be "natural." In the 1920s, Jack and Raie had immigrated to America but had returned disillusioned to England after the Wall Street crash. I was to learn later that Jack had spent part of the 1950s in one of Her Majesty's prisons convicted of some financial misdeed, which explained why my father had been deputized to give their daughter, Shirley, away at her wedding in 1954 that I attended in a white shirt and scarlet satin shorts.

It was Nicholas, the son of godparents Hilda and Ferdy, who unwittingly told me the truth a few weeks later as we rode home on the Underground from the school we both attended. Uncle Jack's death had not been "natural" at all. He had locked himself in the kitchen of the small apartment in the suburb of Collindale that he shared with Raie. He had taped the frames of the door and windows, and he had knelt in front of the stove, laid his head on a pillow placed in the oven, and turned on the gas. I had lost three people I considered dear, each in baffling circumstances, within five months.

1962

In 1928 the Belgian National Railways produced a poster touting the ferry crossing of the English Channel: "Dover-Ostend; 3 Hours Sea Passage." Painted by Belgian Leo Marfurt, the poster is full of color and geometric angles. In the background a Channel steamer with two tall funnels sits at the dock. A gangplank leads up to the promenade deck. At the base of the gangplank stands a uniformed sailor. Other gentlemen in uniform escort passengers, most of whom are tall, svelte women in long, shapeless, Chanel-inspired dresses with cloche hats. Pastel shades, calm, and order emanate from the poster.

Six months after Marmi's death, my parents and I rode that Dover-Ostend steamer to vacation in Belgium and Holland. Our car was also aboard—a 1961 Vauxhall Cresta, a vehicle built by General Motor's British subsidiary that was a smaller, anglicized version of the 1958 Chevrolet Bel-Air. It had a wraparound windscreen and rear window and tail fins, it was dual-colored—Havana brown and clotted cream with white wall tires—and I thought it was the most stylish car in the world. Throughout our holiday there was the blatant yet unmentioned presence of my dead grandmother. My mother continued her intermittent noiseless weeping, and when she wasn't actually sobbing, she stared moist-eyed and silent into space. The more she cried the more my guilt was intensified. My escape was to read Leon Uris's *Exodus* with fervor and repetition. Incredibly, in 1962 only an expurgated version of it was available in England because of the intensity of its anti-British sentiment, but Aunt Esmé had sent us a copy of the real thing from America. Unable to quell my mother's grief, I would lock myself in my hotel room, reading and rereading the passages I regarded as erotic in frenzies of daytime and nighttime masturbation.

After a few days at a dreary two-star hotel in the ailing Belgian North Sea resort of Knokke, we journeyed on to Amsterdam to visit my father's aunt Bertha, who, at eighty-seven, resided in a nursing home in the pastoral suburb of Bussum. Bertha was wizened, white-haired, and tiny. She had been born, like my grandfather, in rural Kippenheim and had married Karl Goldberg, a physician; he was the doctor who took care of my grandmother at their home in the German city of Paderborn until her death in 1928—the same year the Dover-Ostend poster was published. Bertha was noted for her puckish sense of humor. When she was ready for dinner guests to leave, she would ostentatiously ring for the maid and inform her it was time to turn the beds down. On a visit to London when I was a small boy, she described the pneumonia she had recently suffered as "not single, not double, but triple." Tiny Bertha had before World War II been a tall, strapping woman. In 1935 Karl, no longer permitted to practice medicine, emigrated from Germany with Bertha and their son, Siegfried (Siggi), to Glasgow—where Karl was unable to master sufficient English to practice medicine. They moved to Amsterdam in 1938. In 1940 the Germans they had fled Paderborn to escape occupied Holland.

In freezing January 1944, Karl and Bertha were deported not to Auschwitz but to the Theresienstadt Ghetto, the Nazis' "model" concentration camp in Bohemia. Even the Nazis reserved a modicum of respect for those, such as Karl, who had been awarded the Iron Cross in the Kaiser's army in World War I. When the deportations had begun in Amsterdam, Siggi went into hiding. He was romantically involved with a German woman named Alice Koppel, who hid him in a closet behind the false back of an armoire in her apartment's bedroom. The closet was also used by the Resistance to store arms and a radio. To deflect suspicion, the comely Alice carried on an affair with a senior member of the Gestapo, who fucked her on the couch a few yards away from the hidden Siggi. Days after Amsterdam was liberated on May 4, 1945, Alice was declared an honorary citizen of Holland. Five days later, Soviet troops liberated Theresienstadt, and the painfully thin and aged Karl and Bertha made their way back to Amsterdam to be reunited with their son.

In 1947 my parents and Anthony sailed to Holland to celebrate Karl and Bertha's golden anniversary in a vastly elegant party at what was then Amsterdam's finest hotel, the Amstel. This was Anthony's first venture abroad—just two years after the war. To this day he still marvels at the incredible array of hams and cheese and cakes and delicacies at the breakfast buffet, a sight (and taste) beyond the imagination of an English eleven-year-old who had only ever known wartime and rationing and even grimmer postwar austerity. He was famous for rhapsodizing a wartime meal of "whale steak followed by tinned peaches with real mock cream."

Siggi married Alice and went on to become the managing director of De Bijenkorf, Amsterdam's largest department store. They remained close to their resistance friends but, as was not uncommon in the era before stents and shunts and bypasses, Siggi died suddenly of a heart attack in 1959. Fourteen years after World War II, Great-Aunt Bertha had survived the Nazis, Theresienstadt Ghetto, the death of her husband, and the death of her son. She died, aged eighty-eight, in 1963.

The Alice we visited had been a widow for three years. She remained in the elegant apartment she and Siggi had shared, where I was billeted while my parents stayed at the snazzy new Apollo Hotel. At fifty, she had a round face, large round eyes, a round hairstyle, and a plummy voice emerging from a round, heavily lipsticked mouth. She was not thin, and she had legs that were so shapeless, like two tree trunks, that passersby turned to stare. Yet she exuded the most extraordinary sexuality. It seeped from every pore. Men fawned over her. One afternoon, she took a nap and as I was tiptoeing to my room past her open door, she motioned me to come into her Louis XV–styled bedroom. She patted the duvet next to her and bade me sit. As we chatted, she absently stroked my knee with her scarlet fingernails. I was possibly too exhausted from the activities attached to the erotic passages of *Exodus* to respond—even had I realized what was afoot—which I actually hadn't. Alice, I suppose, eventually realized that I was, after all was said and done, a mere twelve, and our moment passed.

During that trip, I marveled at how everyone in Holland seemed to speak perfect English, and I became more and more obsessed with my *need* to speak languages. Perhaps I saw it as another aide to escape. At Hereward House, we had begun French at six and Latin at seven. So I already spoke some French, and I had been coached in basic Hebrew before our visit to Israel. My father spoke fluent German and Dutch, and I loved the latter's guttural throat clearings. And I also loved his ability to make himself understood and, for instance, to castigate—in Flemish—a harridan in a shop in Knokke who was irritated by my browsing and not buying. I determined I needed that facility too. He taught me several phrases, which I aped to perfection. He taught me to recite Alice's telephone number—a succession of phlegm-producing guttural barks with an industrial lilt. We took to eating one of his favorite Dutch fast foods—a slice of fresh bread and butter topped with either roast beef or ham and then two fried eggs. An *uitsmijter,*" he called it, and taught me how to pronounce the "uit"—a sound that doesn't exist in English.

Pa's facility with languages was diametrically opposed to my mother's, whose total inability to speak anything beyond the Queen's English was the stuff of family legend. At restaurants, she would mouth every foreign word on a menu with upper-class British vowels, causing waiters to mask smiles and dinner companions to wince. But her pièce de resistance was the performance of the obscure Eastern European version of the Hebrew alphabet she had been taught parrot-fashion at boarding school in 1925, which she would reel off very fast, complete with a series of bizarre grammatical inclusions—a piece of cabaret that would, in the 1970s and 1980s, send her Israeli grandchildren into paroxysms of mirth and writhing on tile floors.

And so I began to learn that one of the keys to successful traveling is to learn at least "hello," "good-bye," and "thank you" in the language of every country visited—which does much to break the ice. My musical ear has enabled me to mimic the words of a tongue I don't understand to the extent that native speakers assume I speak their language. It can be extremely irritating.

1960

At the age of ten, I had been enrolled in the City of London School, the same school Anthony had attended and from which he had graduated six years earlier, aged eighteen. Nicholas, three years my senior, went there too. It was a public school (i.e., private)—but it was a public school with two differences. Unlike the public schools recurringly celebrated in the vast, tortured oeuvre of two centuries of English literature, it was not a boarding school. There were no freezing dormitories, no fags (the name for younger boys who acted as "servants" to their older peers), and barely any buggery. Yet there were prefects who were permitted to cane miscreant small boys and from the ages of ten through nineteen, we swam stark naked in the school's swimming pool—a process that, as we roiled our way through puberty, made discovering each other's attributes no less interesting than perfecting the crawl or the backstroke.

Thus, because it was a day school, the classic sexual and sadomasochistic excesses of the classic English public school, while certainly not entirely eliminated, were considerably reduced in scale. The school's other difference was that unlike every other public school in England, the City of London maintained no "Jewish quota." Whereas Eton and Harrow and Rugby, and even the other renowned London public day schools, St. Paul's and Westminster, maintained a strict cap on the number of Jewish boys it would admit, the City of London did not. We made up 25 percent of the school. Yet it was a school whose fundament was Christian. Some of the boys were on scholarships provided by the ancient Temple Church for its choristers, and many of us, me included, were to sing in the choir at St. Paul's Cathedral. The school has since moved, but its landmarked Great Hall still sits near Blackfriars Bridge on the Thames Embankment, a gothic construction modeled after the baroque city hall of Belgian's canal city of Bruges. Every morning, our assemblies were held in this august soaring chamber with its stained glass windows picturing Shakespeare, Aristotle, and Aeschylus, and its giant organ. After the berobed headmaster, ranked by the school's prefects, read out the day's notices, he would give a barely perceptible nod to Michael Schwab, who held the school's official and astonishing title of "Head Jewish Boy" (the same title my brother had held). The two hundred pupils "of the Mosaic persuasion" would then stand, our hinged seats would bang upward, and we would file out of the hall. The remaining six hundred students recited the Lord's Prayer and sang hymns according to a tradition that combined the needs of both Church of England and Catholic boys. We strode to a variety of classrooms, assigned by age, where we donned our school caps or yarmulkes, muttered a succession of Hebrew prayers by rote, and sang the hymns I knew from synagogue. Then, and only then, did the school day begin.

On the days when school ended early or I could trump up a reason to wiggle out of going by train to the south London suburb of Grove Park to play rugby or cricket at the school's sports grounds, I would break my journey home at the Underground station at Piccadilly Circus. Dressed in long gray pants, a white shirt and striped tie, black blazer and school cap with embroidered school badge in winter, maroon-and-black striped blazer and straw boater with black-and-maroon ribbon in summer, I would emerge from the tube station and make my way up Shaftesbury Avenue in search of my passions. One of them was to be found in an alley behind the Palace Theatre in Cambridge Circus. A narrow doorway opened to reveal a long passageway in which there stood a nondescript man who would mumble "aft'noon" and say nothing further. On the right wall was a giant trellis of deep shelves with penciled names scrawled on their sides: "Drury Lane," "Haymarket," "Prince of Wales," "Criterion," and more. And on each shelf was a pile of posters of the show currently playing at the relevant theater. I was free to help myself to any, and as many as I wanted. The entire "transaction" was conducted in silence. I took what I needed, drew a rubber band from the container on the shelf near the door, rolled my treasures, said "thank you," and departed.

I retraced my footsteps through Old Compton and Brewer Streets with their peep shows, strip joints, and Chinese restaurants that are now the central arteries of London's gay ghetto. I would pass the Windmill Theatre, the theater that still had "never closed," whose all-day-long revues and restrained female nudity would be immortalized in the 2005 movie *Mrs. Henderson Presents* that starred Judi Dench. But none of this interested me. I was on my way to Regent Street and to Piccadilly, where most of the world's airlines and most of the world's tourist bureaus had their offices. I wouldn't visit them all—there were far too many. But I would call at a select few. At airline offices, I would help myself to timetables and to brochures of the new planes. At the tourist offices, I would ask for posters. And then I would return to the Underground station with my treasures and ride home.

Just as my toy theater had inspired me to design my own scenery, the timetables inspired me to design my own airlines. This was not an elementary project. Using the information I gleaned from the studying of my ever-burgeoning timetable collection, I would devise a new airline—based in London, Paris, Tel Aviv, Rangoon, wherever. I would decide which routes it would fly, how often, and with what aircraft. I would map it all out by hand, and then, with my Bar Mitzvah typewriter, produce the written pages of the timetables, and then complete the project with colored pens, rulers, markers, and staples. The timetable had to include a map. It even had to include a listing of the airline's offices at the rear of the booklet, complete with fictitious yet wholly believable addresses. (To this day, I recognize the leading thoroughfares of tens of cities worldwide because it was in these fashionable streets the airlines maintained their storefront offices in the 1960s.) It was painstaking work that kept me occupied for weeks and months and years.

One does not need a degree in psychology to ascertain that my ventures into both theater design and air routes that spanned the earth were efforts at escape from the claustrophobia of guilt and my mother's barely masked anguish. Only once did these passions lead me to something even I recognized at the time was peculiar. I suppose I was about fourteen when our math teacher asked us to let him know our career goals. While my classmates said athlete, lawyer, doctor, dentist, I announced that my goal was a career in airline catering, with the specific responsibility to decide which meals and which foods were to be served on which flights. The math teacher was polite but perplexed. I knew it was odd too.

(1960)

My mother surrounded herself with eccentric friends, relations, and admirations. Beyond her best and closest friend, my godmother Hilda, whom she had known since their boarding school days, her idols were many, as were her idiosyncratic hates. She adored King Charles II, Oscar Wilde, the Duke of Windsor, Noël Coward, Winston Churchill, Ivor Novello, Cecil Beaton, Benjamin Disraeli, Greta Garbo, Rudolph Nureyev, Anthony Eden (for whom my brother was named), Liberace, and the drag performer Danny La Rue. She despised the Queen Mother, whom she blamed singly for what she perceived as the country's odious treatment of Wallis Simpson. She loathed Archbishop Makarios of Cyprus ("a terrorist"), Betty Grable ("common"), and Barbra Streisand ("a bitch").

There was a clear and definite theme to the qualification of many on the list of those she adored. In 1960 she came home from seeing the Peter Finch movie *The Trials of Oscar Wilde* furious and fulminating at the treatment meted out to Wilde. She admired men who were gentle, who exuded grace, men whom we would now characterize on a scale ranging from "unafraid to show their feminine side" to "ragingly gay." The theme carried over into her social circle.

Harry Isaacs was her second cousin and a noted concert pianist. About twenty years her senior, Harry lived in an oddly cavernous construction in the garden of a once stately mansion in West Hampstead. Downstairs was a vast studio where recitals were given on two concert grand pianos surrounded by a parade of hand-me-down couches and mismatched sagging armchairs. Upstairs were a bedroom, kitchen, bathroom, and a small but gracious living room, with beautifully delicate lighting and dozens of silver-framed pictures of Harry and his family, his students, and his loves arranged atop yet another concert grand. Harry was attractive and ugly at the same time. He had a face rather like that of a trout, with bulging eyes and an unruly shock of thick white curly hair that fulminated atop his forehead and finally veered up and to the left. Other than his talent, what endeared him to me, and I assume to everyone, was an exquisite sense of humor that was perfectly timed and outrageously idiosyncratic. He had the facility of enrobing the relating of a humdrum visit to the fishmonger to buy a pound of haddock in a wrapping of such mirth, delight, and absurdity that would leave all around him with tears of laughter coursing down their cheeks. He couldn't help it. He had the aptitude to scour the everyday in order to discover a germ of the ridiculous that he would then transform into a story weighted with exaggerations, flailing hands, and a rich baritone.

Whenever Harry was coming to our house for dinner, Ma would fret about selecting appropriate dinner companions. After all, Harry moved in circles that included the likes of Dame Myra Hess and Sir Malcolm Sargent and apart from dinner having to be cooked and served to perfection, she was frantic in ensuring that the other dinner guests be of a suitable caliber. Alec Nathan was Harry's "dear friend" and had been his "dear friend" for decades. Alec lived on the other side of London and worked at Bourne and Hollingsworth, now defunct, a vaguely aristrocratic department store on New Oxford Street. Alec and Harry would spend every Christmas and Easter together, as well as frequent weekends, winter breaks, and summer vacations, usually at a boardinghouse in a dreary town on the English Channel called Walmer. Like dozens of obscure resorts portrayed in those posters produced after "the war" by British Railways, Walmer had a seafront promenade; a bandstand; and a procession of Georgian, Victorian, and Edwardian houses owned by genteel ladies and gentlemen who let rooms to equally genteel ladies and gentlemen.

Not until the 1980s, when Harry and Alec were dead and the world sufficiently enlightened, could my parents bring themselves to the acknowledgment that Harry and Alec were gay. Previously, they had been "confirmed bachelors," they were "sensitive," they were "artistic," although I'm sure they had never entertained the slightest doubts they were homosexual. But it was an era when they remained either unable or unwilling to bring themselves to conjure up visions of dear Harry and dear Alec actually engaging in the unimaginable panoply of practices in which "poofs" were rumored to indulge.

Another of Ma's coterie of eccentrics was Sybil Albury. Sybil had been another boarding school friend who, in the 1950s, resided—quite by coincidence—a block from Harry in an oddly shaped apartment attached to the back of a once faintly grand mansion. The flat was full of Tudor hutches, willow pattern china, and the scent of lavender. Sybil, the only daughter of a very wealthy family, had devoted her life to the care and maintenance of her mother in a nursing home in the mountains above Lake Geneva. Now that her mother was dead, Sybil was both too moneyed to require a husband and too old, quirky, and neurotic to consider marriage, even had it occurred to her, which I suspect it probably didn't, and even had she not suffered from catastrophic halitosis. Sybil was not merely thin; she was emaciated. She talked endlessly and mind-numbingly. She wore severe costumes with cinched waists and was never to be seen without a hat from which hung a matching veil. She would telephone my mother and, without a greeting, continue a conversation she had paused three days earlier. She was boring, maddening, amusing, and generous, and my mother loved her.

My father did not. When the Blitz began in 1940, Sybil telephoned in hysteria and declared herself too unnerved to remain in her flat during the air raids. My mother suggested she sleep on my parents' couch for a day or two. Within an hour a taxi drew up and Sybil descended on their tiny two-room apartment followed by the taxi driver staggering beneath the weight of five suitcases and ten hat boxes. Sybil remained on the couch for a year. Sybil died in the 1980s, her will bequeathing an antique writing desk to Anthony, which was duly shipped in a container to Jerusalem, where a Russian émigré restored its Edwardian sheen.

(1940)

In 1940, eight months after the declaration of World War II, the Phoney War ended. The Germans invaded Denmark, Holland, Belgium, and France, culminating with France's surrender, the establishment of the pro-Nazi French government in Vichy, and the miraculous evacuation from the beaches of Dunkirk to England of two hundred thousand members of the British Expeditionary Forces and one hundred thousand French soldiers. The Battle of Britain was on, Spitfires and Hurricanes were downing Stukas and Messerschmidts over Kent, and the lower echelons of the British government—despite the appointment of Winston Churchill as prime minister—were panicked by the presence of so many German nationals in Britain. They had neither the time nor the wherewithal or interest that a vast majority of these Germans were young Jews stripped of their German nationality by the Nuremberg Laws. The fear of espionage was too great and checking for foreskins too irksome and inexact. Thus, almost all were sent to detention camps on the Isle of Man, and, like Pa's friend Herbert Sutton, and an eventual cousin by marriage, Edgar Fromm (whose father had invented the rubber condom), eventually to Australia.

My grandfather was fifty-nine in 1940. Although he had come to England in 1899, he had kept the German "Weill" throughout World War I—the same war that had the royal family discarding the German "Saxe-Coburg" family name in favor of Windsor, while the Battenbergs became "Mountbatten." The war ended and his British life went on, with intermittent visits to Germany to visit his family and for Pa's epic Bar Mitzvah in 1922. What he had never done in his forty-one years living in Britain was to become naturalized. In May 1940, the police came to his apartment to inform him that, despite his age, he was on the list to be interned. Edith, sister of his second wife, Beatrice, worked at the Home Office. The next day an elegant arrangement was wrought: my fifty-nine-year-old grandfather would not be interned on the condition that his thirty-one-year-old son—my dad—volunteer immediately for the armed services. And so it was done, and Pa became a private in His Majesty's Pioneer Corps.

Some thirty months later, Pa had been promoted to staff sergeant. His brigade was lined up at Portsmouth docks ready to embark aboard a ship set to sail to Burma to fight the Japanese. As they stood "at ease" in formation, an officer approached and asked loudly if any of these troops spoke German. Pa paused—considering the army adage: "Never volunteer." Eventually, nervously, he raised his hand, and was ordered out of line. He went on to spend two years billeted at the Grand Hotel in the refined seaside resort of Eastbourne, teaching German to would-be spies. By April 15, 1945, Pa's new brigade was in Germany, and entering the concentration camp at Bergen-Belsen. Pa remained in Germany in military government until late 1946—at first shepherding nearby residents through the camp to witness the horror and subsequently identifying and arresting senior Nazis. Most of his brigade that had shipped to Burma never returned.

1956

When I was working at the Thomas Cook offices on Fifth Avenue, I would often spend my lunch hour at Brentano's bookstore a few blocks to the north. Browsing its graphics department one day in 1974, I came across a travel poster for San Remo, the classic resort on the Italian Riviera. I thought it magnificent and, at under fifty dollars, I could even afford it. It was to be the first travel poster I ever purchased, the start of my official "collection."

The poster dates from 1931, although its style is far older, even Edwardian. It has no streamlines, no exaggerated elements. It is a simple watercolor of

San Remo, circa 1925. Vincenzo Alicandri, artist (1871–1955). ENIT Agenzia Nazionale del Turismo. Printed by Barbarino & Graeve, Genova. (Author collection)

a flower-bedecked terrace that overlooks two tranquil Riviera bays and the Mediterranean. It exudes calm and a sense of well-being. The terrace is bordered by a low balustrade supported by chubby columns. The flowers on the terrace brim from terracotta pots—bougainvillea, carnations, and masses of yellow blossoms that defy classification. In the foreground is a bush of creamy yellow roses. The poster is framed to the left by a palm tree, its trunk woven with ivy. The only hint of the period is the title, "San Remo"—the only type on the poster—whose hand-painted typeface emits the vaguest suggestion of art deco. The poster is signed by the artist and dated and it bears the logo of ENIT—the Italian Tourist Board. This is a poster that tells no fibs, makes no ambitious claims: it simply depicts an idyllic Italian scene. It underscores why the Italian government—in comparison with other European countries—has traditionally spent so little on promoting tourism: because it simply doesn't have to. The notion of Italy seems naturally to exude romance, culture, art, sexiness, beauty, deliciousness, smiles, and bonhomie. Actively promoting the concept of tourism to Italy has always seemed akin to a bank actively promoting the need for money. Even the horrifying death toll suffered by Italy in the early days of the coronavirus pandemic failed to quash the worldwide desire to return to Italy as soon as possible.

I framed the poster in an elaborate gilt frame. For more than forty years, wherever it has hung, its scene of a flower-filled terrace and the serene Mediterranean far below has provided a sense of serenity. It is an icon of peacefulness, beauty, and the restorative quality of the ideal vacation. When I was six—during our Franceitalygermanyswitzerlandliechtenstein road trip—my parents, brother, and I experienced just such a vacation in a tiny town called Menaggio on the shores of northern Italy's Lake Como. At the Bella Vista Hotel, our Italian flower-filled terrace was an elaborate affair that projected on stilts over the lake, atop which we took all our meals. We befriended a Danish family with a son my age, and I gaze now at the tiny black-and-white photos of blindingly blond Lars? Sven? Jan? and me, with our mothers—mine, a cross between Edith Sitwell and Gertrude Lawrence; his, the image of Nina of the once European-famed singing pair Nina and Frederick.

Sixty-four years later, the Bella Vista's website shows that terrace with a swimming pool, but in 1956 there was none. We just clambered down from the terrace to swim in the freezing lake, and we would take ferry rides to places called Bellagio and Dongo and Tremezzo. But the most haunting memory of Lake Como was visiting a modest farmhouse in the hills where, it was explained to me, a gentleman of whom I had never before heard—one Benito Mussolini—had spent his last night, just eleven years previously. We were ushered inside by an aged lady garbed in widow's black and sagging hose and led upstairs to "His" bedroom. The crone knelt and creaked open the lid of a giant linen chest. Reverently, as if unfurling the Shroud of Turin, her gnarled hands retrieved a linen hand towel that she unfolded and held aloft for our scrutiny. And there they were: the yellowing handprints of Il Duce's final handwash. We were then ushered down to the spot just outside the gate where, the now moist-eyed custodian pointed, Mussolini and his mistress were shot by the *partisani*, their corpses subsequently driven to Milan to be draped from the lampposts outside the Duomo.

Our journey to Menaggio had been replete with memorable moments that began with my initiation into luggage labels by the concierge in Reims. Our journey took us through the Jura mountains and into Switzerland, where we paused for afternoon coffee (and milk for me) at a sidewalk café in Lausanne. In the days when parking was effortless, our Anglo-American Vauxhall was parked in front of the café, and I suddenly pointed dramatically at the car to indicate we had a flat tire. My hasty pointing knocked the glass of milk over, my father slapped my face with frustration, and I burst into tears. As half of Lausanne gathered to watch, Pa and Anthony removed our four thousand pieces of luggage and my blue plastic chamber pot from the trunk to locate and extract the spare tire. They jacked the car up, changed the wheel, and—my eyes now dried—on we slogged to the Alpine Simplon Pass.

The Alps were glorious. We climbed and climbed—yes, me on the front bench seat atop my red stool with the prancing bunnies—through meadows of grass and wildflowers and stopped intermittently for my mother to caress the necks of Swiss cows, their bells jangling, so she could smell their breath: an unconventional activity that always seemed to please her immeasureably. As we reached what seemed to be the highest peak of the drive, there came an ominous clunk from beneath the car, and we juddered to a halt. Pa got on all fours to inspect. And while no mechanic, he determined the rear axle spring—whatever that was—had broken. Ashen with despair, isolated atop an Alp, he realized that as we had actually reached the summit of the Simplon, we could, with luck, coast the twenty-five or so miles down into the valley below. Which is what we did, Ma wincing

Anthony, Pa, Ma, and me in front of our Vauxhall Velox, France, 1956. Note the formal attire for a family 1950s road trip. (Author collection)

with alarm at every hairpin bend and yawning precipice; Anthony studied the map while I jauntily sang selections from *Salad Days*, the 1954 musical that Cameron MacIntosh, three years my senior, ascribes as the birth of his passion for theater. Our coasting slid us into the town of Domodossola, where Pa managed to start the engine and, at five miles per hour, slink the car into the nearest garage.

A collection of mechanics in dark greasy overalls surrounded the car, utterly unfamiliar with, yet intrigued by, a Vauxhall Velox. They pushed it over an inspection pit. Down they climbed to examine and scrutinize with flashlights and tap with tools. There was much pointing and rapid Italian discussion. Eventually, the chief mechanic emerged, wiped his greasy forehead, and engaged Pa in lengthy murmuring and dramatic hand gestures. As he spoke, the concern visibly left Pa's face. The repair could be effected, but they would have to work through the night. With 163 kilometers before us to reach Menaggio, we would have to sleep in Domodossola. Ma, Anthony, and I were bundled into a minute Fiat Cinquecento and whooshed off to a tall peeling building with a sign that announced "Albergo." We climbed staircases to tiny rooms that were open to an interior well strung with lines of laundry and infused with cooking smells, where elderly grandmothers in black and Anna Magnani lookalikes leaned out windows to screech to neighbors and their children playing below. It was quite fabulous.

By dusk, Pa joined us, and as it was still very warm, off we went to dinner, me shirtless in shorts and sandals. We ate at a restaurant on a narrow sidewalk, and for me it was a night of two firsts: my first ever spaghetti and my first ever fresh peach. (The reader has to marvel at the austerity and

Me in Italy, my brother in Switzerland, 1956. (Author collection)

insularity of mid-1950s England that at six I had tasted neither.) The peach was massive, and as I ate it the juice ran down my bare chest into my navel.

We slept under sheets in the heat of our rooms and, in the morning, trooped back to the garage. The mechanics told Pa the repair was complete. It was a temporary fix but it would, he was confident, get us back to England. Great stacks of lire were handed over, cheek air kisses were exchanged, and we were back on the road to Mennagio.

The postscript of this vignette is that from Menaggio we drove home through Germany and France and prepared to cross the English Channel from Calais (pronounced "Callous" by Great-Aunt Flo) to Dover. In Calais, we scoured open-air markets, buying wheels of Brie and Camembert and crates of melons and fat peaches that were available only for unfathomable sums in England. The ferry was delayed and the car sat in the July sun until we lumbered aboard. We stood on board the ferry, straining for the first glimpse of the iconic White Cliffs of Dover. As we churned through the waves, Ma hummed the classic World War II song "The White Cliffs of Dover" that glorified those White Cliffs, and explained to me their critical importance in keeping my family and all England safe from the Germans. It was made famous in 1940 by the twenty-three-year-old Vera Lynn, who was subsequently elevated to "Dame." Born in 1917, she died in the summer of 2020, aged 103, happy in the full knowledge that her wartime rendering of "We'll Meet Again" had become a British anthem of unity and hope during the coronavirus lockdown.

Ashore in Dover, we were treated to the habitual customs check of the car—and as Pa opened the door for the inspector, the aroma of overripe cheese and fruit knocked him backward and we were instantly waved on. It was dusk now, and the long journey to London was before us. About fifteen miles from Dover, the ominous clunk we had last heard atop an Alp was repeated and we ground to a halt. Somehow a large Humber taxi was summoned and our vast amount of luggage, bags, Ma's picture hat, wheels of smelly cheese, and crates of aromatic fruit were laboriously transferred. And yet we were happy. The mechanics of Domodossola had kept their promise. Their repairs had gotten us back to England.

1981

I have found myself on dozens of flower-filled terraces similar to that I discovered at six years old on Lake Como. Most seem to overlook the

Mediterranean. They exude a unique air of tranquil comfort. In 1981 Terry, my first cousin and my first wife, and I discovered a perfect flower-filled terrace in Positano. Nowadays, the town's Sirenuse Hotel is considered one of the world's finest. But when we first discovered it in 1981, it was much less known. We had flown from Israel, driven south to the Amalfi coast, and checked into the Sirenuse a few hours before Terry became violently sick to her stomach. Some hours later, with her resting and groaning in bed, I came to the hotel's moonlit flower-bedecked terrace to dine alone—and almost cried at the beauty of the panorama of twinkling lights that accompanied the ambience of crisp linen, courtly waiters, and al dente pasta.

In 1957 Cary Grant invited Deborah Kerr to leave the ocean liner on which they had met and romanced in order to visit "someone" who lived above the tiny French Riviera port of Villefranche-sur-Mer, just thirty-three miles from San Remo, the inspiration for my poster of the flower-filled Mediterranean terrace. Grant didn't really invite Kerr—it was part of a movie called *An Affair to Remember* that would be regurgitated forty years later as *Sleepless in Seattle*. *An Affair to Remember* is possibly the sappiest tearjerker of all time. The "someone" Grant takes Kerr to meet turns out to be his grandmother, played by Cathleen Nesbitt—the same lady who had played Henry Higgins's mother at Drury Lane in *My Fair Lady*. Grant leads Kerr up into the hills overlooking the harbor of Villefranche and through a door onto one of the most exquisite terraces captured on film, where flowers and blossoming trees invite shade and serenity. They spend some time with Nesbitt, who, draped in a lace shawl and affecting vast age, a beatific calm, and a curiously Central European accent, gives the lovers her blessing. The movie wastes no time on explanations as to why the Anglo-American Grant has his grandmother immured on a terrace on the French Riviera, but the ship's siren eventually calls, they bid a tearful farewell, and—we learn later in the movie—Nesbitt subsequently dies happy in the knowledge that her playboy grandson has found the right woman.

Terry and I discovered Villefranche for ourselves after we were persuaded to cancel our planned 1990 Israel vacation in the wake of Saddam Hussein's invasion of Kuwait and threats to bombard Israel with rockets. Villefranche was to become my summer home for almost ten summers, and Terry continues to vacation there annually in the same room of the same hotel. A deep-sea port lying between Nice and Cap Ferrat, Villefranche was passed over by the development of Côte d'Azur tourism precisely because it was a busy port—and, until 1960, a U.S. naval base. Along with five-year-old Benjamin, we checked into the oddly yet aptly named Hôtel Welcome, where our room overlooked the harbor and the main square with its palm trees, cafés, and Sunday antique-cum-flea market. Despite the modernity of its name, the Hôtel Welcome was almost 150 years old and had been a haunt of Ernest Hemingway and Jean Cocteau, the latter having painted the interior of the chapel that abuts the hotel. One afternoon in 1927 the fabled American dancer Isadora Duncan was in Villefranche, and it was on the promenade just steps from the Hôtel Welcome that she and her lover climbed into an open-air car, she flung her long scarf around her neck, the wind caught the scarf—snagging it in the wire-spoke wheel of the automobile—and, as the car moved off, it snapped her neck.

The harbor of Villefranche is overlooked by hundreds of flower-filled terraces identical to that of the San Remo poster. The town dates from the fifteenth century. Its narrow Franco-Italianate alleys utilize steps to convey walkers to and from the upper town. One of my favorite spots in Villefranche, however, is the passenger ship terminal, built in the 1930s, all terra-cotta moderne curves with art deco lettering. Here is where Cary Grant and Deborah Kerr alighted from the tender that had brought them ashore from the SS *Independence*. Villefranche is a town peopled in summer by the middle class, bringing their children, and their children's children, to frolic in the calm bay. A few times a week, a cruise liner anchors in the harbor and thousands of passengers in Lacoste polo shirts and Nike sneakers surge ashore in tenders not, mercifully, to stay, but to be whisked off on bus tours to Monte Carlo, Cannes, and the perfume factories of Grasse. There is not a Missoni or Vuitton or Chanel boutique to be found in Villefranche. Only at night, when the dozen or so wharfside restaurants are open, does the timbre change as Bentleys and Maseratis with chauffeurs and Monaco license plates glide along the very same promenade where Isadora Duncan died to deposit their charges at open-air restaurant tables.

One of the most magical posters produced in the late 1920s by the Paris-Lyon-Méditerranée railroad is for Villefranche-sur-Mer. The poster calls it a "port de tourisme," and it features the profile of the town as it creeps up the Maritime Alps, a scene virtually unchanged ninety years later. In the harbor are fishing boats, yachts, two small steamers, and an ocean liner. The colors are vivid, the scene breathlessly romantic. Were the same poster commissioned today, it would seem entirely accurate. The poster is available widely as a reproduction for a mere $9.95, but I'm still searching high and low for an original. Perhaps Elton John has one in that gorgeous villa of his that overlooks Villefranche's harbor.

(1949)

In another of my forays into Brentano's, I chanced upon an Air France travel poster from 1949. If the 1920s and 1930s were the decades of the classic shipping poster, the fifteen years from 1945 to 1960 were the classic period of the airline poster. Inarguably, Air France was the leader of the genre, with Pan American and BOAC running distant second and third. Air France commissioned artwork from dozens of France's leading artists—including, for an entire country-by-country series, Salvador Dali. Every Air France destination had its own poster—each a work of art, many complemented by art deco type and the image of a tiny Air France Constellation or, after 1958, a tiny 707. Each poster bespoke seduction, portraying the destinations not exactly dishonestly but often with the customary otherworldly, flying-down-to-Rio romance of smiling natives and bucolic scenes. The Air France poster I bought at Brentano's was generic and not for a specific destination. It portrays a globe against a cloud-filled sky. The continents and oceans are defined, and strands of airline routes, as if strung from a parabola and interspersed with silhouettes of propeller aircraft, encircle the planet. At its center, Air France's elegant flying seahorse logo appears as a giant golden-orange trompe l'oeil emblem. "Air France World Air Services" is the poster's only type.

When the poster was printed, Air France was—just five years after the liberation of Paris—the operator of the world's largest airline network, and its posters were designed to be a constant reminder that France was a Great Power. In those heady days when Gene Kelly was tap-dancing through the streets of Montmartre as an American in Paris, France was at the height of its short-lived postwar self-esteem. The boche had been vanquished and carved up into controllable zones. Indochina was yet to be lost. Suez was a canal and not a humiliation. Air France ruled, and hundreds of posters proclaimed it.

In the postwar forties, the nationalized Air France was the world's largest airline network simply because other countries had more than one airline. The United States, where flying was born and where it took instant root in the public's imagination, was, after World War II, home to a dozen or more major airlines—none of whom, alone, was bigger than Air France.

Air France World Air Services, 1949. Air France. Printed by Perceval, Paris. (Author collection)

In the 1930s, three European airlines had competed to link their home capitals—London, Paris, and Amsterdam—with their colonial outposts in the Far East. Britain's Imperial Airways and Air France were the largest, but KLM—whose initials stand for the Dutch equivalent of "Royal Dutch Airlines" (Pa taught me how to say Koninklijke Luchtvaart Maatschappij in perfect Dutch)—had the most modern fleet. KLM was flying the latest American-made DC-2s and DC-3s, while national pride obliged the British and French to fly less advanced, less efficient, and far more eccentric home-grown craft.

The other large prewar European airline was Deutsche Lufthansa ("German Air Fleet"), then known as DLH. The colonies it would have yearned to link had been confiscated by the Treaty of Versailles, but after January 30, 1933, it flew the swastika throughout Europe, to the Middle East (except to "Jewish" Palestine), to China, and to South America. It also had its eye—more so than any of its European competitors—on the North Atlantic. In 1936 Germany's *Hindenburg* "zeppelin" airship made regular crossings from Frankfurt to New York, ferrying ninety people from Germany to the United States in less than three days. But the era of the airship came to its abrupt end in Lakehurst, New Jersey, when the *Hindenburg* exploded at the end of the flight that inaugurated the 1937 season. The moment lives on in spectacular newsreel footage, the newsreel commentator witnessing the gala arrival and lapsing into tears and exclamations as the fireball crashes to earth. The following August, sixty days before Kristallnacht, a twenty-six-seater four-engine DLH Focke-Wulf 200 Condor operated the first ever nonstop commercial proving flight from Berlin to New York, slashing the flying time to exactly twenty-four hours. Had World War II not intervened, there is little doubt that Lufthansa would have won the Atlantic air race—for no American or other European manufacturer was close to producing a plane that could fly the Atlantic nonstop.

While their aircraft competed in the air, each of the European airlines competed for space on the walls of travel bureaus. They produced hundreds of posters whose goal was to make flying appear glamorous, sexy, and—most importantly—safe. A glorious art deco poster produced by Imperial Airways in 1935 depicts a man seated in a moderne club chair to which giant wings are attached, propelling him through the clouds. In my collection, I have a splendid Air France poster from the same period, promoting its service from Marseille to Algeria. Palm trees and a flying boat are painted in tones of yellow and ocher set atop a relief map of the western

Air France: Marseille Iles Baleares Alger en 5 Heures, 1935. Albert Solon, artist (1887–1949). Printed by France-Affiches, Paris. (Author collection)

Mediterranean—the kind of map movies from *Casablanca* to *Indiana Jones* use in dramatic gestures, backed by swelling orchestras, to further the development of the plot.

After World War II, the socialist British government split British Airways (the name of Imperial Airways had been switched to "British" in 1939) into two: BOAC (British Overseas Airways Corporation) and BEA (British European Airways). KLM resumed flying in 1945, but the rebirth of Lufthansa would wait another decade. As a boy in the Britain of the 1950s and early 1960s, I was possessed of the simple notion that each country had a national airline, and it seemed to me that Pan American was the national airline of the United States. It seemed that way also to Pan Am's creator, Juan Terry Trippe. In a saga of exploration and daring, Trippe had transformed a small company linking Miami and Havana into an airline of American imperial might—linking the mainland of the United States with Latin America and forging its way across the Pacific to Manila in 1935. To reach the Philippines, Pan Am built flying boat bases and overnight hotels at Midway, Guam, and Wake Islands—a project of vast ambition. Pan Am's "Clipper" flying boats were crossing the Atlantic in 1939 too—reaching Lisbon and Marseille with intermediate stops in Bermuda and the Azores. The war won, Pan Am was invariably first with everything: the first round-the-world service, some of the first jets, the first jumbo jets, the first sleeper seats in first class, the innovator of "business class," the creator of the "frequent flyer" program. What kept Pan Am back from ruling the world were the U.S. regulations of the time prohibiting it from offering domestic flights within the U.S. So that if a traveler in St. Louis needed to reach Paris, it was only natural to fly TWA all the way from St. Louis, to Idlewild/JFK, then on to Paris. In 1980 Pan Am attempted to right that wrong by buying the ailing domestic carrier National Airlines. For a while it worked, but the borrowing of so much money to buy National and the attempt to integrate the National Airlines fleet of aircraft so different from Pan Am's began a money drain. Then came the coup de grace. Close friends of mine were booked to fly Pan Am from London to New York on December 21, 1988. Upon check-in they had a bizarre falling out with the Pan Am staff and dramatically picked up their bags and stomped over to the TWA check-in desk and switched their plans and their planes. Only on arrival in New York did they learn that the Pan American Boeing 747 they had been meant to fly—and on which their family assumed they were flying—had taken an unusually northerly route to avoid bad weather over the Irish Sea. It had exploded over the town of Lockerbie in Scotland, killing all on board. It was an accident from which Pan Am would never recover.

Just as World War II confirmed America's status as the West's leading power, so it was with aircraft and airlines. Lockheed's Constellation and Douglas's DC-4 would be the airplanes that not only would bring Pan Am and TWA winging across the postwar Atlantic; these same planes would also bring the European airlines back to work when the war was won. As I sat on the floor of my brother's aka my room after Anthony left for Israel, it was the advertisements for Pan American and TWA in the *National Geographic* magazines that—like those for air conditioners, dishwashers, Buicks, and Parker 51s—underscored the lushness, the material superiority, and the seductiveness of postwar America.

1974

Because of my success at that sales counter at Cook's on Fifth Avenue, I was promoted in the fall of 1974 to the position of manager of the Cook's office in Baltimore. Unexpectedly, I liked Baltimore. It was a city that, at its heart, retained a Victorian elegance and an obsession with the eating of hard crabs. An element of Baltimore that shocked me rigid, however, was that it retained the mindset of the segregated south. The Cook's office had a white staff, two of whom—Nancy and Carlotta—insisted I must never take a bus in Baltimore because "colored people smell." The one nonwhite staff member was James, an elderly African American man whose entire calling seemed to encompass fetching milk, unlocking the door in the morning, locking up at night, vacuuming, and shrinking from sight.

The high-rise apartment I rented overlooking Johns Hopkins University was convenient to a supermarket that was part of a small mall with a mélange of unexpectedly high-end shops. Wheeling my cart out of the supermarket one weekend soon after arriving in Maryland, instead of turning directly left to the parking lot, I turned right to window-shop. And in the window of an art store that normally displayed nondescript prints, there was an exhibition of original travel posters. I stopped short. Despite my purchase at Brentano's, it had not fully occurred to me that the genre of travel advertising that spoke to me so fluently and alluringly was actually a valuable art form one could collect. I wheeled my brimming supermarket cart into the elegant store, much to the consternation of its staff, a consternation that rapidly dissolved with my purchase of all three posters in the window—posters that are, almost fifty years later, the most valuable of my collection. Looking back, it remains a mystery why three arguably "Jewish" posters would be on display in the window of an art store in a Baltimore neighborhood called Roland Park that well into the 1950s was restricted. But there they were, beaming at me from the window. I whipped out my American Express card first and asked the price second.

Two of the posters I purchased that day date from the 1930s and one from 1949. The 1949 poster was one of those many produced by Air France after World War II. It contains only three words: "Air France" at the top, and, at the bottom, "Israel." It is the first travel poster produced to promote travel to Israel after the Jewish State was founded in 1948. It was off the presses in Paris before El Al was even founded, and years before Israel would start promoting tourism on its own. It's magnificently romantic. It rehearses the bravery and idealism that had founded the state, when Israel's image in the West was all about heroism, when Israel was considered the "good guy, "the little country that could." The poster was commissioned by Air France before the War of Independence was won, and there it hung, a quarter century later, in a store window in Baltimore. The image is of the impossibly high walls of the Old City of Jerusalem. In the blue sky is an Air France Constellation. The walls sit atop a jagged outcrop of rock at whose base stands a young woman. She's dressed in a white shirt with short sleeves, and very short shorts that lead down to impossibly long, tanned legs. In her arms, she is holding a giant Israeli flag, its blue and white stripes and Star of David flapping in the breeze. The poster's simple naivete is magical.

The second poster dates from 1936. It is a painting of Jerusalem framed by an old tree. By rights, it should be an olive tree, but this seems too large, its trunk too thick. It comes across much more like an oak. This was one of the first posters painted by Franz Krausz after his immigration to Palestine. The panorama of the city has, at its center, the Dome of the Rock, and the poster contains a two-word entreaty: "Visit Palestine." The poster was issued by the Tourist Development Association of Palestine—a department of the Jewish Agency, the organization set up in the wake of Britain's Balfour Declaration of 1917 that promised the Jews a national home in Palestine: "it being clearly understood that nothing shall be done which may prejudice the civil and religious rights of existing non-Jewish communities in Palestine." The organization was, until Israel's foundation in 1948, the quasi-government of Jewish Palestinians. Sixty years after the poster was first published, its reproduction was adopted by the fledgling

Air France—Israel, 1949. Renluc, artist. Printed by Hubert Baille et Cie., Paris. (Author collection)

Palestinian Authority; facsimiles can now be purchased in the alleys of the Old City of Jerusalem, along with my-parents-went-to-Israel-and-all-they-got-me-was-this lousy-T-shirt souvenirs, olive wood camels, and bubble pipes. The poster I bought in 1974 in Baltimore is one of the few originals to have survived.

The final poster of my "Baltimore trio" is for "the Jewish Ships." It is a classic, art deco ship poster, and possibly the most eclectic in my entire collection. Like "Visit Palestine" and the Air France "Israel," it speaks to that fleeting moment in time when Zionism and a Jewish Palestine were part of a courageous attempt to right a wrong committed by the Romans nearly two millennia earlier. Hitler was in power, but the Holocaust was still unimagined and still unimaginable except, perhaps, by the founder of political Zionism, Theodor Herzl. Born in Budapest in 1860, Herzl was a Germanophile who believed that German civilization, culture, literature, science, and royalty were superior to all. Educated at German-language universities yet barred from antisemitic fraternities, he came to believe that the "Jewish problem" could only be "solved" by the Jews leaving Germany (and elsewhere) to return to their ancient homeland. As he traveled through Eastern Europe and was confronted by the poverty and misery of Jewish life in the shtetls, he came to believe that a vast tragedy was inevitably soon to befall the Jews of Europe. And while he never could have imagined the enormity of the horrors that forty years later would devastate European Jewry and his own children, Herzl was convinced that the tragedy he prophesied would have its roots not in the shtetls of Poland or the Pale of Russia or the mountains of the Balkans but in the hypercivilized Germany he so admired. When I hear of those who question the Holocaust and connect it to Israel's right to exist, I look at this poster and remind myself that Israel was well on its way to being founded when the gas chambers and the Warsaw Ghetto were mere twinkles in the eyes of Reinhard Heydrich and Adolf Eichmann.

The "Jewish Ships" poster features in the foreground five oranges, along with the logo and signature, in English and in Hebrew, of Palestine Maritime Lloyd Ltd. At the left, vertically, are the words "Haifa-Constanza-Haifa" and, to their right, is a painting of one of two identical ships, steaming through a blue sea. Palestine Maritime Lloyd placed these two "Jewish" ships in service in 1938, to carry Jaffa oranges from Palestine to the Romanian Black Sea port of Constanza and Jews fleeing the Nazis from Europe to Palestine.

Visit Palestine, 1935. Franz Krausz, artist (1905–98). Issued by the Tourist Development Association of Palestine. Aron Advertising. Printed by Lith. Monson, Jerusalem. (Author collection)

I brought the three posters home. I gazed at them. I took them to Ian, my British-born specialist in New York who repairs aged posters' tears, creases, and folds and backs them onto linen. Currently, one hangs in my office, one in our bedroom, and one in our music room. I can gaze at them for hours. And I deflect the sporadic calls from dealers yearning to buy them.

1962

My brother was a championship swimmer. My parents played tennis. As a kid, my father played soccer and as an adult his idea of the perfect Saturday afternoon was to watch wrestling on television. He would stamp his feet and whoop with joy when one bruising ape caught his opponent in a hammerlock. Every July, our home became akin to an annex to Wimbledon. Each match was watched by my parents, my father reciting the score after each point, my mother's eyes tearing whenever an Australian won. For twelve years at school, I was bullied and cajoled into playing cricket in summer, and soccer, then rugby in winter. To say that I loathed every moment would be to put it mildly. I considered a ball not a plaything but a weapon. I disliked the need to win, because it meant someone needed to lose—usually me. Moreover, sports were never taught, they were played. Nobody ever sat us down and explained rules or tactics. Little boys were just expected to know them by some Y chromosome osmosis and, bizarrely, most of my schoolmates seemed to do just that.

It was in the final weeks of December 1961 that my schoolmaster (British for homeroom teacher), a six-foot-six giant by the name of "Biff" Vokins, asked me in study hall while he was completing our school reports whether my parents had a sense of humor. I couldn't imagine the point of the question but responded "yes." The reason became clear a couple of weeks later when the buff envelope containing my school report dropped through our letter box. I had come first in the class overall, first in French, first in English, first in geography (big shock), second in history, third in science and in Scripture. In twelve years of schooling, it was the best school report I was ever to receive. Yet the point of "Biff" Vokins's question had to do with the area of the report devoted to rugby. "Geoffrey," he wrote, "makes every match a pleasant social occasion." My parents did consider it humorous. So did I. The framed report hangs to this day in my home.

"Biff" Vokins's real first name was Cyril. Apart from the penning of wry school reports, one of his prime fortés was the annual sex education lecture to his eleven- to twelve-year-old students. In 1962 this was an utterly unusual circumstance in England. I had heard about Biff's lecture from older boys and faced it with a mixture of excitement, apprehension, and embarrassment. When the big day came, we sat at our desks and he prepared us. He told us he would be explaining things about which we might already know some or all aspects but, he said, "it is important for you to have all the facts right." He explained that he would be writing words on the blackboard, but he would quickly erase them because as the door to the classroom contained a window, he did not want passersby to see what was written. It seemed clandestine and slightly sinister. I know that other classes of the same age group did not have his lesson—but I have to presume, with the retrospect of decades, that he had the school's approval for this special instruction.

He explained everything rather well. Of course, it was all couched in terms of love, husbands, and wives. We sat at our desks, each one of us, I assume, attempting to smother a trouser-bursting erection as we heard, for the first time in our lives from the mouth of an adult, details of concepts we had heard about only in snickered whispers in the schoolyard. I was proud that very little of his dissertation was new to me—with the exception of menstruation, about which I previously had not the remotest idea. He would write words such as "penis" and "vagina" and "testicles" and "intercourse" and "fuck" on the blackboard, and then immediately erase them. He did not invite questions, nor do I think any of us would have had the wherewithal to ask any. It was all far too stimulating and far too awkward.

This all happened in the winter semester of 1962, the semester that had started on the day of my grandmother's funeral. The school was not informed of what had occurred upon our return from Israel—even in the most cursory way. I was expected just to move on with my life and my studies in that oh-so-English tradition of "Keep Calm and Carry On." It never occurred to my parents that Marmi's death—for whatever cause—might affect my schoolwork, let alone my grip on sanity. Despite the fact that a quarter of the school was Jewish, I was the only Jewish child in Cyril Vokins's class, and the winter semester contained yet another curiosity performed at the City of London School. The teaching of scripture was (and, I believe, remains) a general course in most private and state-run British schools. At the City of London, it was customary that the fall and summer semesters' study was devoted to the Old Testament and the winter term to the New, from which Jewish boys were automatically excused and expected to study in the library instead. My parents disagreed. They saw nothing wrong and everything good in my education being as broad as possible. Knowing what was in the New Testament was, they argued, important and useful. Yet my parents' decision had an unexpected outcome. It made me even more peculiar than I already was. The Christian kids thought I was weird, and the Jewish kids considered me weirder still.

An even more hideous aspect of my being the only Jewish child in the class emerged in that year's teaching of English. We were to study Shakespeare's *The Merchant of Venice,* and there was an unavoidable sadism attached to my English teacher's decision to cast me as Shylock in both the readings in class and the end-of-term performance of the juicier scenes. I wanted to portray Shylock with misunderstood dignity. The English teacher, Mr. Lewis, directed me to play him with every hackneyed gesture of anti-semitism he could muster. I was to wring my hands. I was to hunch my back. I was to exude oiliness and speak with a Yiddish accent. For the end-of-term performance I wore a false beard and skullcap. My gabardine was my late grandmother's floor-length black velvet, burgundy-lined, mink-collared opera cape that dated from the 1920s. I climbed onto the stage and stood tall. I dropped both my hands and the Yiddish accent and played Shylock the way I wanted. Lewis didn't know whether to be furious or impressed. Fuck him: I came first in English anyway.

Antisemitism was prevalent at the school, yet my Jewish peers in other classes just didn't seem to care like I did. But then they didn't have mothers who were half-Christian and who had brought them up to believe that they were Englishmen first, gentlemen second, and Jewish thirty-eighth. The City of London School taught me that being Jewish had less to do with what one considered oneself and everything to do with how one was classified by others. It made me furious.

"Fucking Jew," classmate Keith Clarke spat at me one day in math class in response to my doing something infuriating. He was seated at the desk in front of mine. I calmly removed my geometry compass from my pencil case and rammed it into his right buttock. He shrieked in pain. Biff Vokins asked what happened. Clarke told him of my assault . . . and I told him why. We were sent together to the principal, Dr. Barton, who had been the principal when Anthony attended the school. Barton remembered my brother, whom he had elected "Head Jewish Boy," and who, he recalled, had "moved to Palestine." He was tall, dour, and humorless. Lethargically, he berated Clarke for what he had said, and he berated me for taking the law into my own hands. He made us shake hands. We returned to the classroom and, because I was close to six feet tall, that kind of verbal and physical assault was to reoccur only occasionally. My retaliation, of which I was proud (and for which my parents saluted me), gave me a "don't mess with Jewish Geoffrey" reputation. An interesting sidebar to the anti-semitism issue was that because we swam naked and were curious adolescents, it was apparent who in the class was and was not circumcised. Even though probably 50 percent of the Christian boys were circumcised, the antisemitism I was to encounter in my eight years at the City of London School invariably spouted from the mouths of boys whose foreskins were intact. Intriguing, no?

I had an excellent singing voice and was a member of the school choir, an odd circumstance in that I was absent during most of the choir's performances: the daily singing of hymns after the Jewish boys had filed out of assembly. Yet I was a member of the choir that sang at the school's annual "Founders' Commemoration Service" held annually in the grandeur of St. Paul's Cathedral. The year after the compass-in-the-ass incident, my mother—as did many other parents—attended the service too. The guest speaker was the headmaster of Charterhouse, a venerated public school founded in 1611, whose dreary sermon suddenly took a turn that accused the Jews not only of killing the Savior but also "in our own time" of seeking to undermine His followers. As I looked at my friend Jonathan Silverman and we shrugged and rolled our eyes, there came the deafening scraping of a chair on the marble floor behind us followed by the determined march of high-heeled shoes. I turned and saw Ma storming down the nave of the cathedral to the giant doors. I was very proud. The next day, I brought a letter addressed to Dr. Barton from my mother in which she informed him that I would no longer be singing at the school's commemoration services. Barton conveyed not the slightest comment, explanation, regret, or concern. I received the message that this was a Christian school in a Christian country in which my presence was certainly tolerated but equally certainly not required. (But then, decades later, in 2015, I learned that the tall, dour, humorless Dr. Barton had in 1939 been intricately involved in the Kindertransport project that brought Jewish children from Germany and Czechoslovakia to England to survive the Holocaust that would destroy their parents. Go figure.)

So it was that during this, my twelfth year of life, I gave birth to the notion that when I was old enough, I would leave England. It was a decision I would never come to question, even now, decades later when England is a very different place. When I was twelve, it was not a matter of if, merely of when and where. The when would be as soon as possible. And there were only two possible wheres: Israel or America—the two places where being Jewish would, I believed, not be a drawback.

1967

In June 1967 we and the world had been watching the buildup of President Gamal Abdel Nasser's Egyptian troops on the Israeli border. We watched UN Secretary General U Thant withdraw, at Nasser's behest, the UN forces from Sinai that had kept the status quo since 1957. We watched King Hussein of Jordan fly to Cairo to hug Nasser and proclaim their military brothership against Israel. And even though much was, we now know, going on behind the closed doors of the White House, the Quai d'Orsay, and 10 Downing Street, to the casual or not so casual observer, it truly seemed that the tiny and fledgling Jewish State—along with my brother, Ariela, and their son, Ilan—were in mortal danger of being wiped off the map in an orgy of cruelty worthy of the Saracens. Anthony had never been in the Israeli army, but he was a member of some kind of neighborhood defense force, so our states of mind were not relieved by a telegram arriving in the final days of May asking Pa to express mail him a dozen copies of a Red Cross handbook on how to deal with extreme injuries. On Sunday, June 4, an emergency meeting was called at our synagogue at which Rabbi Cyril Shine, never a ball of jocularity and humor on the best of days, portrayed the possibility of Israel's impending demise with terrifying gravity, urging significant contributions to the United Jewish Appeal. Pa and I drove home in silence.

Over breakfast in the kitchen on the following morning, Monday, June 5, 1967, the BBC radio told us war had broken out between Israel and Egypt. I am not sure what our emotions were other than numb fear, but I got dressed as usual in my maroon-and-black striped school blazer, walked to the tube, and went to school. At lunchtime, I broke a school rule and ran out to buy the *Evening Standard* (published two blocks away in Fleet Street), whose headlines proclaimed Israel had destroyed something like 250 Egyptian aircraft. My classmates snickered that such a thing was impossible, and I didn't know enough to argue. By the afternoon we knew Jordan had joined the war and was attacking Jewish Jerusalem; knowing that the Jordanian border was not more than five hundred yards from Anthony's flat allowed the fear to deepen. We watched and listened to every news bulletin. Somehow, we slept, and on Tuesday Ma received a phone call from Anthony that they were all right. Never one for understating the drama, he quickly explained that they were sleeping in the building's shelter but he had run upstairs to call. He said Jordanian troops had advanced as close as the nearby football field but had been repulsed. By the end of Wednesday, we knew Egypt was vanquished, Israel's counterattack had united Jerusalem, and Israeli troops had occupied the entire west bank of the River Jordan. The relief was immense; the joy intense. It took another three days for Israel to finish off the Syrian threat, and what was quickly to be dubbed the Six-Day War turned out to be one of the greatest military victories in history. Most of the civilized world heaved sighs of relief and marveled at how this tiny little country, twenty-two years after the Holocaust, had managed to rout its far larger neighbors. Nobody for a moment thought that victory would not produce a permanent and just peace settlement.

Six weeks after the war, I was aboard an El Al Boeing 707 on my way to Tel Aviv. I stayed five weeks with Anthony, Ariela, and the now three-year-old Ilan. It was five weeks of exhilaration as the pall of the Jewish State's disappeared fragility was celebrated. The coming together overnight of both halves of Jerusalem had been a daring decision by Mayor Teddy Kollek, whom Anthony knew closely. Instead of a cautious, gradual coming together of the two sides whose inhabitants were enemies, the barbed wire and tank traps were cleared and the barriers bulldozed overnight. To make way for the tens or hundreds of thousands of Israelis expected on the holy day of Shavuot (Pentecost) to stream to Judaism's holiest site, the Wailing Wall—from which they and Jews of any nationality had been barred for nineteen years—much of the Mughrabi neighborhood of the Old City adjacent to the wall was bulldozed, its inhabitants given a pitiful two-hours' notice to be gone. Israelis ventured across the "line," eager to discover what was beyond the vanished border. The Arab merchants of the Old City had a field day as Israelis bought out their stores, where prices were a fraction of those in Israel. Jordanians crossed to "Israeli" Jerusalem too. They stood shell-shocked, applauding at their first encounter with traffic lights. The wealthy among them ventured to the neighborhoods of Katamon, the German Colony, and Talbieh to see what had become of the luxurious homes they had been forced to abandon, and to which many still had keys. The word "occupation" had yet to be born. In Israel, there was just a sense of elation, a sense of relief, and a sense of pride.

Beyond the now united Jerusalem was the West Bank, off-limits to Israelis unless they held a precious laissez-passer. As Ariela was employed at a government ministry, she was able to obtain a permit, so that each weekend we would cross the "border" to see Hebron, Solomon's Pools, Bethlehem, Jericho, Ramallah. We rushed, because we knew these places might shortly no longer be freely accessible once the West Bank was returned to Jordan in the wake of the inevitable peace treaty. In Hebron, we bought its eponymous glass. In Bethlehem, we visited the Basilica of the Nativity and bought olive wood souvenirs. In Jericho, we bought giant pomelos. And in Ramallah, we discovered a dairy serving what I still think are the best milk shakes ever shaken. We got lost on a back track trying to reach Nebi Samwil (the burial place of Samuel the prophet), nervous that we would not make it back to the "frontier" by the 7 p.m. curfew. We also drove north, waving our precious permit, to visit the Golan Heights, wrested from Syria, and in Jerusalem, we admired the Western Wall (the "wailing" was dashed from the vocabulary now that its loss no longer required mourning), the Temple Mount's exquisite Dome of the Rock, the Al Aqsa Mosque, the bazaars, the Church of the Holy Sepulcher, and the panorama from the Mount of Olives atop which Pan American had built the Jerusalem Intercontinental Hotel—shamelessly indifferent to its garden reaching into Judaism's holiest cemetery, its gravestones used for the hotel's foundations. It was a heady moment with, I am ashamed to admit in retrospect, more than a modicum of colonial disdain. Yes, we were the "saved," but we were also the victors, the winners, and we sadly too often behaved like conquerors even in our interactions with shopkeepers. We reacted with scorn that Jerusalem's Old City had no central sewage system or electricity. There was a giant exhibition at the fairgrounds in Tel Aviv, displaying the armored might that had enlarged Israel's area by 400 percent in six days. And despite the unimagined sense of overall pride in which we were all floating, I found myself bothered by the exhibit's gloating, boasting, militaristic bombast. Tragically, within weeks, the assumption that peace would ensue was dashed by Egypt's president and the Arab League proclaiming in Khartoum at the end of August that there would be no recognition of, no negotiations with, no peace with Israel. And so the victory that many of the people I knew expected to evolve into peace evolved instead into occupation, settlements that would ultimately grow into cities, and the insoluble mess that more than a half century later continues to seem impossible to resolve.

But Israel's victory in the war changed me and changed my self-esteem. Within months, the always charming yet comparatively introverted and shy Geoffrey had become—outwardly at least, almost extravagantly—extroverted and gregarious.

1977

Back in New York after my eighteen months in Baltimore, I discovered a poster dealer whose "gallery" was a second-floor garret atop an antique store on what was still marginally unfashionable Columbus Avenue. Indeed, when Terry and I were married in 1976, we moved to a very snazzy apartment near Lincoln Center just off Central Park West. Yet, half a block west, Columbus Avenue was still so seedy one didn't venture there after dark. Phillip Williams was the name of the poster dealer, and he and I would sit on the floor in front of foot-high piles of old posters. I would examine the top one, he would move it to the right to make a new pile, and I would examine the next. We did it often, for hours. One day, he unveiled a poster that featured the Olympic rings and a plane. I stopped him. The poster was pale, beautifully water-colored, and it possessed a lovely symmetry. At the top of the poster, flying over the clouds, was a German-made Junkers airplane, the blue cross of the Finnish flag emblazoned on its tail. The central element of the image were the Olympic rings, below which was a vision of Baltic islands. The poster bore the signature of the Finnish Air Traffic Company. It intrigued me. The Olympic Games had taken place in Helsinki, two years after I was born, in 1952. Yet why would the poster for these games have sported an airliner from the 1930s? It didn't make sense; and then suddenly it did. This was not a poster for the 1952 games. This was designed to promote the Olympic Games of 1940, the games that were never held. It's been in my collection ever since and, despite my antipathy to sports, I confess to loving the pomp and circumstance of the grand openings and finales of the Olympic Games. The games of 1916, 1940, and 1944 were the only games to be cancelled . . . until 2020, of course, with the Tokyo games postponed as the awfulness of Covid-19 encircled the globe.

On another occasion, sitting on the floor in Phillip Williams's attic gallery, he uncovered a poster of a wide beach framed, at left, by tall trees. "Happy Vacations" was its chief title, under which, in script, was added "at Germany's Sunny Seashores." I found the poster graphically beautiful, at the same time as I found its invitation wracked by harrowing irony. Published by the tourism department of German Railways (the ominous-sounding Reichsbahnzentrale für den Deutschen Reiseverkehr, Berlin), the use of the word "vacation" (instead of "holiday") confirmed it was designed for the American market. The poster is undated, but judging from its graphic style, I imagined it dated from about 1928, before the Nazis rose to power; only much later have I come to suspect it was published in the mid-1930s. Even though in the 1920s my father had vacationed at the German North Sea beach resort of Norderney, the love-hate relationship with Germany with which I had been raised made the poster's title seem incongruous. But this was a poster, like that for the "Olympic Games That Weren't," that demanded to be bought. And so it was.

(1938)

In 1936, three years after Hitler's rise to power, the German government tourism board produced a poster whose purpose was to promote travel to Germany from the United States. Designed by the German artist Jupp Wiertz, the poster seeks to appeal to the potential traveler's sense of both history and admiration for Germany's technical prowess. The poster's background contains a faint rendition of the skyscrapers of lower Manhattan. At its center, the art deco bow of the transatlantic steamer *Bremen* looms toward the viewer. Above it, a Lufthansa Junkers biplane soars to the left. In bas relief at the base of the poster are the outlines of Cologne Cathedral, the twin spires of Munich's Frauenkirche, and—at center— the Brandenburg Gate. The message at the very bottom of the poster is "A Pleasant Trip to Germany." One more element completes the poster: a giant image of the *Hindenburg* airship floating above the New York skyline, its tailplane sporting a black swastika in a white circle against a red background. The poster was clearly intended to convey a friendly invitation to whatever American audience would, in 1936, buy the notion of "a pleasant trip to Germany." Yet just as it is impossible for any of us since 1912 to view the word "titanic" with any meaning other than the sinking of an ocean liner, it seems implausible from the vantage point of the first decades of the twenty-first century that this image of the Manhattan skyline over which looms a vast swastika-daubed *Hindenburg* could possibly have been considered anything but ominous to an American audience.

Yet such judgments in retrospect tend to warp and ignore the appreciation of the climate at the time the poster appeared. My godfather, Ferdy, owned *Touring Abroad*, a guidebook to the continent of Europe published in 1938 for British motorists. As an adolescent, I became so obsessed with this book that I arranged for it to become mine. It is divided into sections devoted to individual countries, as well as an introductory section with staggeringly archaic and condescending advice to the British traveler of 1938 on how and what to pack and how to comport oneself in the view of "continentals." The book oozes a sense of the patronizing. "Don't imagine that when you have crossed the Channel you will be removed from civilization in the form of shops," it announces, assuring women that foreign "hairdressers are usually excellent." It advises that "the British visitor abroad should do her best to uphold the prestige of her nation" and relieves the burden of overpacking with the comment that "even if she does not wish to change every night into evening dress, at any rate a neat afternoon frock with small hat should be worn if she intends going out in town after dinner." Women are advised to wear a shantung coat over their suit when motoring, and gentlemen travelers are assured that a tuxedo will suffice for evening wear ("tails may be left at home"). Moreover, it continued, "if one is staying at a hotel where English guests do not predominate, a dark lounge suit will be perfectly correct." Another section of the book deals with picnics; in the days before Tupperware, visitors are advised to buy "peasant pottery, often of local origin . . . of characteristic designs and gay colours to enhance the atmosphere of your Continental picnic." It also recommends they be taken home as souvenirs for the servants.

The month of the book's appearance is unmentioned yet easy to pinpoint: it contains sections on both Germany and "German-Austria" as well as on Czechoslovakia: thus it was clearly published in that short hideous interlude between the Anschluss of March 1938 and Chamberlain's September meeting in Munich with "Herr Hitler" to address the Sudetenland crisis. His flights to and from Munich were the aged prime minister's first— immortalized by the photograph of the Edwardian-era politician at the foot of his Lockheed airplane steps pathetically brandishing the piece of paper that augured "peace in our time."

The section on "the new Germany" is confounding when viewed with postwar eyes. It lauds the efficiency of the new Germany and touts the wonders of the autobahns. It assures the traveler of 1938 that it is "the very genuine and cordial spirit of hospitality which is everywhere evident, which makes a motoring holiday in Germany an unforgettable experience." The book makes no mention of the signs on park benches indicating they're forbidden to Jews. The section on the "New German-Austria" takes the odious surge of appeasement a step further, assuring travelers that "under the new regime the roads are going to be even better."

The distastrous transition from Weimar to Nazis is evident in yet more posters. In 1930 the Hamburg-America Line produced a poster that may just possibly have provided Cassandre with inspiration for his legendary *Normandie* poster. A ship's hull in profile looms in front of the side of another liner with similar colors. "Germany's largest motor ships," it proclaims. The poster is for the line's sister vessels, *St. Louis* and *Milwaukee*. Another Hamburg-America Line poster, resplendent with vivid hues and arching palm trees, advertises the *St. Louis*'s South America cruise of winter 1937. Historic irony is again at the forefront for it was in May 1939 that the *St. Louis* would sail from Hamburg with a manifest of 937 passengers bound for Havana. All aboard were German Jews escaping their homeland to Cuba. All 937 were in possession of entry visas issued by the Cuban embassy in Berlin. The transatlantic voyage was a combination of elegant and mannered service and taunts by a small cabal of Nazi crew members instructed to ensure the passengers' discomfort. On arrival in Havana, a brief delay turned into hours then into days as the Cuban government reversed its agreement to admit the refugees. The *St. Louis* sailed on to Florida. For forty-eight hours, it steamed back and forth from Miami to Palm Beach while telegrams and entreaties to permit the passengers to disembark in America flooded the White House. The pleas were ignored and the *St. Louis* returned to Europe, providing Hitler with the unexpected propaganda boost that neither Cuba nor the United States wanted these people any more than did Germany. Just before docking in the Belgian port of Antwerp, the governments of France, Belgium, Holland, and Great Britain agreed to admit the 937 passengers. Only those fortunate enough to be accepted by Britain escaped the Holocaust. One of them was my third cousin, Kippenheim-born Freya Wertheimer, who lived well into the twenty-first century in the Bronx.

The seductiveness, palm trees, and art deco allure of the *St. Louis* Caribbean poster spew mockery in the face of those 937 passengers. Their tortuous journey round trip across the Atlantic was rehearsed in Gordon Thomas's 1974 book, *The Voyage of the Damned*, which was transformed in 1976 into an aptly tortuous movie starring Faye Dunaway, Oskar Werner, Luther Adler, Wendy Hiller, and Julie Harris.

(1940)

In retrospect, it is not the 1930s posters for ships or planes or destinations that contain the ugliest of ironies. It is the hundreds of posters touting the elegance, chic, and style of the trains of Europe. For while in 1913 the parenthetically antisemitic Henry Ford had perfected the assembly line of industry, it was thirty years later that the Germans perfected the assembly line of death. And central to that assembly line were trains. The Holocaust could not have been achieved without them.

When the Germans invaded Russia in the summer of 1941, the Wehrmacht was followed by Einsatzgruppen, squads of SS, and middle-aged policemen who scoured every captured town and village; dragged the Jews from their homes, synagogues, and workplaces; drove them into the countryside or the town square; and machine-gunned them. The Einsatzgruppen were relentless; men, women, children, babies, young, old, healthy, infirm: all were killed without mercy. It is estimated that a million Jews were murdered by the Einsatzgruppen—but it was slow, cumbersome, and—so one is led to understand—unpleasantly emotionally wearing on the shooters. At the January 1942 Wannsee Conference in the suburbs of Berlin, when the killing of every Jew in Europe became the Third Reich's established goal, it was Adolf Eichmann, Hannah Arendt's embodiment of the "banality of evil," who created the fantastic plan to transport the Jews of Europe on trains from near and far—from Warsaw, Budapest, Salonica, Rome, Copenhagen, Paris, Bucharest, Berlin, and, if things went well, from London and Manchester and Glasgow—to camps in Poland where they would be systematically worked or put to death.

Trains were the currency of the Holocaust. Cynically, the Nazis understood that trains convey optimism. Considered for almost a century as a means of reaching a new destination, perhaps the trauma of deportation was softened microscopically by the semblance of the victims' subconscious hope that at their destination, wherever it might be, life would be hard, even ugly, but it would continue. The deportation of millions of people by train was a giant ruse involving the victims being persuaded, or allowing themselves to be persuaded, that they were being taken to new lives. Without the deception, it couldn't have worked.

In October 1940, Adolf Eichmann had ordered the undertaking of an experiment in deportation designed to test whether German Jews would willingly agree to leave their homes and report for exile. Jews throughout southwestern Germany were given a few hours to pack two small suitcases and report to deportation centers. Without exception, in cities, in towns, in villages, in hamlets, they obeyed. On October 20, 1940, twelve thousand Jews from Stuttgart to Freiburg to Baden-Baden to Heidelberg and to my grandfather's hometown of Kippenheim obediently cleaned their homes, packed their luggage, arranged for the cat or dog to be boarded, and massed at schools and bus stops to clamber aboard trucks that would deposit them at the local train station. They boarded passenger trains whose doors were then locked for a two-day journey that ended in the French Pyrenees. The majority were interned in a camp created five years earlier for refugees from the civil war in Spain, in a place called Gurs. The camp was not run by the Nazis, nor even by the Germans. It was under the command of Vichy France. These benighted German Jews were to remain there for almost two years, in two camps separated by sexes. It was freezing in winter and a sea of mud and swarming with flies in the summer. The only time the genders mixed was at funerals—when a husband would learn that his wife had succumbed, when a mother would learn that her father was dead.

From 1942 until early 1945, the trains of Europe—those gorgeous trains whose images leap from a hundred posters—transported millions of Jews to hard labor, slavery, torment, and death. The majority rode crammed into cattle cars. But there were exceptions: the majority of transports of Jews that traveled through Germany proper traveled in locked passenger trains: the assumption being that the cruelty of transporting people in cattle cars might offend the sensibilities of the German populace.

The Jews of southwestern Germany remained at the Camp de Gurs until June 1942, when further trains transported them north to Drancy, in the suburbs of Paris, where a vast Bauhaus apartment complex had been transformed into a misery-wracked concentration camp. Pa's Uncle Hugo was one of them. Born in 1885, Hugo was a bachelor with a wonderful sense of humor and, according to Pa, "queer." Hugo was a shoe salesman.

He lived in Konstanz, a few hundred yards from the Swiss border. All Pa knew was that he had died in the war, but in the 1970s, after some months of research, I was able to track Hugo's final months. He had been moved from his home into a "Jew-House" and, like all the Jews of Konstanz, had been deported to Gurs on October 20, 1940. After almost two years in the Pyrenees, it was on to Drancy. On September 4, 1942, Hugo was instructed to board convoy #D901/23 for the East. The convoy was a train made up of fourteen coaches carrying 981 Jewish deportees. Its single on-board Wehrmacht escort was Staff Sergeant Brand. The train departed Drancy-Le Bourget on time, at 8:55 a.m. Two days later, on September 6, convoy D901/23 pulled into the station at a place in Poland called Auschwitz-Birkenau. After disembarkation and a cursory life-or-death glance by a German doctor, sixteen of its male passengers were given tattoo numbers 63065 through 63080, and thirty-eight women were branded with numbers 19170 through 19207. For the remainder, including Hugo, the deception continued. They were told to deposit their suitcases. They were led to vast undressing rooms and to remember on which peg their clothes were hung. Then, naked, they were guided into a giant room for a shower. My gay Great-Uncle Hugo was one of the first of millions to die inhaling the fumes of Zyklon B.

1956

I have visited Germany dozens of times, and for many years was filled with the simultaneous senses of like, love, admiration, and abject fury. I could not ride the train from Frankfurt to Cologne and look at the passing cars and not think of the days when they were crammed with Jews on their way to the slaughter. I have been impressed by the majesty of a dozen German cities; I have been moved to tears by the beauty of the Rhine Valley; and I have been moved to tears visiting Dachau, Sachsenhausen, Warsaw's Umschlagplatz, Treblinka, Babi Yar, Theresienstadt, and Auschwitz. I have been moved to tears at the new memorial in Berlin for Europe's murdered Jews; I have been moved to both tears and anger when a particularly officious Germany security guard rubs me the wrong way.

In the summer of 1981, I lectured—in German—at the ceremonies in the hamlet of Weil-der-Stadt commemorating the six hundredth anniversary of the birth in 1381 of my great (x16) grandfather, Rabbi Jakob ben Yehuda Weil. A dozen noted German rabbis were my ancestors and my father's second cousin Kurt, the son of a cantor, was talented enough not only to marry singer Lotte Lenya but also to write the *Threepenny Opera* and, safe from the Nazis in America, to collaborate with Ira Gershwin to write *Lady in the Dark* for Broadway. People often remark we look alike.

In 1988 I attended the memorial service marking the fiftieth anniversary of Kristallnacht at the synagogue in Grandpa's hometown that I had helped pressure to be restored. In the 1960s and 1970s and 1980s, I had gazed into the eyes of old German men hobbling along streets and wondered what they were doing a few decades earlier. I look at young Germans and I think what a terrible legacy has been left to them by their grandparents and great-grandparents. In the 1980s, I even wrote a travel brochure for the German Tourist Board titled "Germany for the Jewish Traveler," in which I pulled no punches. And there it remains in the twenty-first century, on the Visit Germany website.

Berlin is a city that I adore, and I have seen it at its postwar worst and best. I once flew to East Berlin from Moscow, the only passenger in first class, aboard a massive, two-story Aeroflot Illuyshin IL-86 jumbo jet, and then traveled by transfer bus through a series of barbed wire battlements to the West. I flew the Pan Am shuttle from Frankfurt to Berlin and, at home in New York on November 9, 1989, the fifty-first anniversary of Kristallnacht, I watched with tears in my eyes as NBC's Tom Brokaw anchored the Nightly News from atop the Berlin Wall while around him, Berliners from both sides celebrated the demise of the Iron Curtain; I even had the presence of mind to slide a blank tape into the VCR. I was in Berlin in 1990 on the day the East and West German currencies were united. I have been moved by the magnificence of the restored Reichstag and the Potsdamer Platz and I have experienced goose bumps as I admired the vista of the beautifully cleansed Brandenburg Gate from my suite at the reborn Hotel Adlon.

And, of course, Germany was also part of that Franceitalygermanyswitzerlandliechtenstein trip that, at age six, had brought my family and me to Lake Como and to the hotel lobby in Reims where the concierge's luggage label on my toy box gave me the imprimatur of "traveler." After the palm trees and pasta of northern Italy, we passed through St. Moritz in Switzerland on our way to Germany. It seemed immensely forbidding. I'm not really sure why for, apart from the obvious, lurking anathema English people—even English people aged six—harbored toward the former enemy only eleven years after the war, I certainly had been protected from more than the most cursory knowledge of what would one day be known as the Holocaust. It was raining heavily and deeply gray-skied as we drove through the Black Forest—dense and dark-green walls of pine trees obscured by sheets of water—and my mother kept muttering, "I can see SS men behind every tree" and "I can see the swastikas now." And while I certainly didn't understand what precisely she meant, I also knew enough to know it couldn't be good.

Our goal that day was that small market town of Kippenheim from which my grandfather had immigrated to England just before the dawn of the twentieth century. The rest of his family remained if not in Kippenheim, but in Germany, and most did manage to emigrate before World War II. But not gay Uncle Hugo, of course, nor Claire Bloch Weill, widow of Grandpa's brother Fritz, who on Kristallnacht sat before her dressing table mirror and slit her throat. The prime purpose of our detour into Germany was to visit Pa's mother's grave in neighboring Schmieheim, a sad visit made even sadder by the torrential rain and sodden undergrowth that impeded our search for her tomb. Then we continued into Kippenheim itself to visit the family home Pa remembered well and where we were quizzically greeted by the owner of the neighboring pub, an aging, obese, furry-slippered "Frau Kopf," who, remembering my father from his childhood visits, hugged him—and my brother and me—with an almost savage fervor. But the grimmest part of the grim day was our pause at the synagogue, a building we couldn't enter, but which, we could see through the still-broken windows, remained the same wreck into which the Kippenheimers' fervor had transformed it on Kristallnacht, a mere eighteen years earlier.

The change in the weather was fittingly emblematic of the change in our locale. The oppressive rain and gray skies spoke fittingly of our passage through "the Fatherland," as Ma venomously chose to term it. We spent hours driving through the rain in search of a hotel for the night, driving to Lake Titisee and its environs, where hotelkeepers shook their heads and pointed at full guestbooks and choked parking lots. Nevertheless, by nightfall we finally found rooms in tiny Emmendingen, where I was put early to bed beneath an immense duvet of goose down—yet another first. I awoke screaming from a nightmare in what I assumed was the middle of the night and, crying and clad only in a pajama jacket, was escorted by the hotel's proprietress down to the *gaststube*, where my parents and Anthony were eating dinner. I've often wondered whether my absent foreskin peeping from beneath the pajama jacket explained why, the following morning as we departed, the proprietress graciously presented Ma with a beautiful honey container and me with a toy car.

1976

Terry and I were married on January 1, 1976. Yes, I married my first cousin, something not considered abnormal on either side of my family. At our wedding, my father gave a witty speech in which he congratulated us and joked that "it would have been unfortunate for us to have ruined two *other* families," and then we returned to Baltimore. Terry—a BFA in Fine Arts from Carnegie Mellon and now a premed student at NYU—remained in New York and we commuted on weekends. In April I was summoned back to Cook's head office on Fifth Avenue, eighteen months after being shunted to Baltimore: I was considered such a star that I was brought into the company's American management. But I was sorry to leave Baltimore, where I had acquired not only monumental posters but also a substantial coterie of friends. Within two weeks of my return, I was on a plane to Cleveland to dress down the manager of the local Cook's office for some infringement of policy and to review the office's profits. I returned to New York tasked with the analysis of how other Cook's offices were faring financially and given reams of documents and fiscal statements through which to pore. This was so very much not what I wanted to be doing. I could have been working for a bookstore chain or a bank, barking at hapless managers, and squinting at ledgers. Where was the travel? Where was the romance? Where were the air routes? The glamorous hotels?

Six weeks later, outside the patrician Scribners' bookstore, a block from Cook's, I ran into an acquaintance, Yoram Golan, the director of the Israel Government Tourist Office. We chatted. He told me their public relations director had resigned and asked whether I knew anybody who might be suited for the job. I told him I would see if I could think of somebody. I walked on and long before I had reached Saks, two blocks to the north, I had identified the obvious candidate. I knew tourism inside out; I knew Israel inside out. I had no idea what public relations was—but I figured I could learn. I called Yoram and an interview was arranged with a garrulous man with very large teeth, Israel Zuriel, who rejoiced in the quasi-military title of "Israel Commissioner for Tourism, North America." The Israel tourist office was located at the back of the Newsweek Building on Madison Avenue, protected by an alarmingly handsome security guard. It was a windowless and claustrophobic warren of cubicles and offices—but a plus was that it also possessed a giant shelved storeroom full of travel posters.

Zuriel and I hit it off. He asked me all the right questions and I seemed to give all the right answers. Then came the test. He wanted me to go next door to a typewriter and write a press release. A press release? He suggested the topic: a rise in tourism for the previous month. I sat, I wrote, I rewrote. I brought it to him, he read it, he paused, he read it again, he paused . . . he offered me the job. I tried to affect nonchalance but I was beyond thrilled. We barely discussed salary. I accepted. I was to start on September 1, after a vetting process that involved having my fingerprints taken, obtaining proof from the police headquarters in Lower Manhattan that I had never committed a crime, and a rather daunting interview by a security officer, an interview that I apparently passed.

Getting journalists interested in traveling to Israel was, I figured, not really a job; it was a continuation of my dearest hobby. I came to love the work; I liked my coworkers; and I had my very own secretary, Janet, who swooned daily over my English accent. It was Janet who taught me the intricacies of PR with which I was unfamiliar and which were not a great deal more than the ability to write, to be charming, and to know how to whirl a Rolodex.

The following spring, TWA offered us tickets to take a group of six travel writers and me to Israel. I whirled that Rolodex, I made calls, I wrote letters, and, wading through the directory of the Society of American Travel Writers, I happened on the name of one of the society's founders, who—coincidence of all coincidences—was the "Legends Editor" of the *National Geographic* magazine in Washington, DC. I assumed her role was to research into the stories of Merlin or Pocahontas, but when I called Mrs. Carolyn Bennett Patterson, she explained to me in a charmingly aristocratic southern drawl that "legends" was the *National Geographic*'s term for picture captions. "Yah see, dahlin'," she explained, "nobody really *reads* the articles in the magazine: they just look at the photographs and read the legends." I wanted to add that there were also benighted children who just sat on the floor in their bedrooms to read and salivate over the advertisements.

Mrs. Carolyn Bennett Patterson happily accepted my invitation to visit Israel because, she explained, she had never been to the Holy Land and was particularly interested in visiting the Museum of the Jewish Diaspora, recently opened in Tel Aviv. A few weeks later, with husband, Pat, in tow, Carolyn arrived in Israel. We adored each other on sight. She was totally

WASP, totally white, totally southern, but utterly liberal. She had been born and raised in Kosciusko, Mississippi, hence the accent, and I learned that as a high schooler in 1939 she had organized a demonstration demanding that President Franklin D. Roosevelt enable the ill-fated Jewish passengers aboard the SS *St. Louis* to enter the United States. She joined the *National Geographic* magazine in 1950, an era when women were no more than secretaries. She was the first woman at the magazine to be given any kind of editorial task. Her big break came in January 1965 when she was sent to London to cover the epic funeral of Winston Churchill for which, of course, I had remained home from school to watch on television, sobbing, alongside my mother.

In Israel, we toured. She admired. She wept at holy sites. She met my brother. She liked my brother. We became fast friends. And after a week of mirth and fascination and immense quantities of wine, we all flew home.

About three months later, Janet buzzed to tell me that Mrs. Carolyn Bennett Patterson of the *National Geographic* magazine was on line 1. "Dahlin'," she bellowed, "we're going to do you in the magazine." "What?" I countered. And she explained. My invitation for her to come to Israel had been the entirely coincidental culmination of her years of attempts to have the magazine write an epic story on the history of the Jewish Diaspora. Yes, she was the "Legends Editor," but she had pitched the idea to the editorial board of her writing such an article, not as dry history but as Jewish history seen through the eyes and family trees of two brothers—both born in London, brothers who had long and complex lineages that were both Ashkenazi and Sephardic. The icing on Carolyn's pitch was the ultimate finale that brother 1 had chosen to "return" to the Promised Land, and brother 2 had immigrated to that other Jewish Promised Land, America. We would take journeys into our past, accompanied by Carolyn and a photographer, and discover our roots and relatives in the places our families had lived, flourished, been persecuted, and flourished again. Anthony and I would "narrate" our experiences, and Carolyn would edit us and provide the overview that would glue our stories together. And we wouldn't go alone. Our wives were to come too. And our parents.

The fraught little boy who had found solace in the pages of *National Geographic* magazines was speechless. I called Anthony. He originally assumed I was joking. Then he was over the moon. A week passed and a contract arrived at my home. We were to be paid $8,000 (equivalent to

$30,000 dollars today). We would fly all over the world in first class and stay at the finest hotels.

Over the following months, I went several times to Washington, and Carolyn came to New York. We sat at our apartment and pored over family trees. Carolyn's assistant Victoria Ducheneaux was assigned the task of research. I hauled out boxes of ancient documents and albums of family photographs. Carolyn glommed onto a photo of a family picnic in the Black Forest a week after Pa's Bar Mitzvah in 1922. There and then she decided we would re-create that scene to celebrate my dad's seventieth birthday in the summer of 1979. She also decided that she; a photographer; Anthony and his partner, Judy (he and Ariela had separated in 1976); and Terry and I would all meet up in London to start the story and continue to Germany. In February 1980, my mother, Terry, and I would discover our family history in Morocco and Spain. A few months later, Anthony and Judy would travel to Czechoslovakia and Poland. Carolyn would spend Passover with us in New York. Then she would tour Israel with Anthony and his children and they would visit Mount Sinai. It would all be photographed by the charming and handsome and curiously witty Nathan Benn. It all sounded unbelievable.

Carolyn, Nathan, vast trunks of camera equipment, Anthony, Judy, Terry, and I flew to London in June 1979. All the luxurious travel arrangements had been made by the *National Geographic*'s travel office, and in our hand luggage in those days before Excel sheets, we carried our little *National Geographic* expense booklets, into which we were to notate every to-be-reimbursed expense next to a list of categories (my favorite was "Tips to Natives"). My parents hosted dinner in the apartment where I grew up. It quickly evolved into a massive eight-way love affair as a delicious and very alcoholic meal was served in the dining room adjacent to that bedroom where I had discovered both solace and America in those yellow-bound *National Geographic* magazines.

The following morning, we visited the City of London School that Anthony had loved and I had loathed. It happened to be ROTC day, with ranks of sixteen- to eighteen-year-old soldiers being reviewed by a flush-faced Colonel Blimp officer. Nathan was thrilled and took ten trillion photographs. I excused myself to go to the boys' bathroom and there it was up on the wall in front of me as I peed: proof that the antisemitism I had experienced not much more than a decade earlier was still alive and well. "Jews burn easily" was scrawled in big penciled lettering above the urinals.

I sent Nathan to the bathroom to memorialize my discovery in a further trillion shots.

The next day, the eight of us occupied the entire first-class cabin of a Lufthansa Boeing 737 bound for Stuttgart. We retrieved our two Hertz Mercedes for Nathan and me to drive and we headed southwest for the then-122-year-old Hotel Sonne in the hamlet of Offenburg, which was to be the base for our adventure. During the next week, we journeyed far and wide but returned each evening to the gemütlichkeit of the Sonne, where we consumed dozens of pounds of white asparagus, kilos of boiled potatoes, gallons of Hollandaise sauce, liters of Moselle wine, and buckets of fresh fruit salad that exotically contained kiwis and avocados.

First stop was, naturally, Kippenheim. We were photographed outside the former Weill home, where my grandfather, Great-Uncle Hugo, and their siblings were born, and where Claire Weill had ended it all on Kristallnacht. We were photographed peering into the barred windows of the smashed synagogue, which, since our 1956 visit, had been turned into an agricultural storehouse. We visited the Town Hall and were directed to the home of the town "historian," where Carolyn interviewed an aged, bald, pale-blue-eyed Herr Schaubrenner, who mumbled how distressing were the events of Kristallnacht forty-one years earlier. It wasn't until two months later, back in New York, that I was to learn that the sad little bald, pale-blue-eyed Herr Schaubrenner had, in 1938, been the Nazi gauleiter of Kippenheim. It was he who had overseen the tormenting of the town's remaining Jewish population, the vandalizing of the synagogue whose Torah scrolls were unfurled and wrapped around trees, and the deportation of the adult males to Dachau. Nice.

Nathan captured us clambering through the unkempt grass of the cemetery at nearby Schmieheim to recite Kaddish, the prayer for the dead, at our grandmother's and Claire's graves. We journeyed to the sleepy village of Donaueschingen, where the Weills had lived in the seventeenth century. Here we followed ancient maps to find the ancient synagogue, while perplexed ancient crones stared at us quizzically from second-story windows, causing Nathan to quip, "They haven't had this much fun since Kristallnacht." We drove to half-timbered Weil der Stadt, where my great (x16) grandfather was born in 1381 and where astronomer and astrologer Johannes Kepler was born 190 years later. Carolyn orchestrated our borrowing a table from an inn and carrying it to the town's grassy moat so we could pose for the first Sabbath blessing in the town for hundreds of

National Geographic's Carolyn Bennett Patterson with Anthony and me at the
City of London School, 1979. (Courtesy of Nathan Benn)

years. The week's climax was Pa's seventieth-birthday picnic in a sunny glade in the Black Forest, re-creating the 1922 photograph that had captivated Carolyn in our living room in New York.

Our German journey was to end with our various flights from Zurich Airport, but as we had completed our "work," Carolyn suggested we spend our final evening in Zurich and wondered where we should stay. "At the Eden au Lac, of course," I responded instantly. And thus five of the best rooms at arguably one of the best hotels in the world were magically commandeered by the *National Geographic*'s travel office back in Washington. Terry and I then spent a week in Portofino before meeting Carolyn and Nathan at the Ritz in Paris (the Ritz "because Proust had stayed there," Carolyn explained) and where we dined with Joyce and Raymond, Carolyn's first introduction to Ma's side of the family. The following morning, Terry and I boarded the Concorde, and four hours later were home in New York.

1979

Andrew Lloyd Webber, in his memoir, *Unmasked*, wrote that for those of us born sadly too late to have been able to cross the Atlantic in the splendor of the *Normandie* or of the *Queen Mary* in their heyday, nothing, but absolutely nothing, can beat the sheer glamour that was flying on the Concorde. It wasn't just the speed, although that was indeed remarkable: enabling the traveler to arrive in New York at 9 a.m. after having left London at 11 a.m. But, no, it was the cosseting. It was—particularly on the British Airways version—the shamelessly grand way one was treated: as if legions of planners had sat around boardroom tables spending hours and days discussing how to make it seem worthwhile to spend an absurd $8,000 (in 1979 dollars) to cross the Atlantic one way . . . which is, of course, exactly what must have occurred. The Concorde was a joint venture of the British and French governments that poured millions and millions of pounds and francs into what was really a vanity project. The British wanted to call it Concord but that would have been pronounced "Concor" in French—thus it became Concorde.

One drew up at Heathrow's Terminal 3—then still called "the Oceanic Terminal" to differentiate it from Terminal 2, named "Europa," or Terminal 1, which even then was so horrible that I believe it remained unnamed, although perhaps it did rejoice in the title "Britannia"—and entered through a doorway emblazoned with the distinctive navy and silver Concorde logo.

At the grave of my grandmother Gladys Weill (1889–1928), in the Jewish cemetery at Schmieheim, Germany, 1979. (Courtesy of Nathan Benn)

Picnic in the Black Forest to celebrate Pa's seventieth birthday, 1979 (*l to r*): Ma, Pa, Terry, me, Anthony, Judy. (Courtesy of Nathan Benn)

Check-in was effected with such speed, bowing, obsequiousness, and deference that it was barely noticed. Luggage was whisked away after baggage tags of the finest navy polished hide were tied to the cases' handles. One was then ushered across carpets into a private, attended elevator and whisked somehow vertically then horizontally past the throngs and hoi polloi flying—dare one say it: "subsonic"—and steered into a lounge directly adjacent to the tarmac, its windows in full view of the needle-nosed plane.

If it was winter, coats were taken with a crisp British merchant marine "G'morning, Sir" and hung on racks to be later wheeled into the aircraft. Teams of British Airways' most senior and reverent minions were on call to bid one welcome, to offer newspapers, to see to any possible request, and to fawn shamelessly. The point was that every single person in that lounge was either hugely rich, hugely celebrated, hugely well employed, or hugely lucky. Travelers sunk into couches, affecting nonchalance and a weary veneer of ennui amid mounds of Vuitton, Gucci, and Asprey. Flutes of champagne ("White or rosé, Sir?") were proffered from silver trays. One chose several or a dozen of the most elegantly coiffed canapés ever constructed by humans, placed them on porcelain, nonchalantly munched, and wiped lips with linen so starched it scraped.

The clubby atmosphere was not tarnished by loudspeakers announcing the departure. Instead, several of the minions walked gently to each of the one hundred (if it was full) passengers and invited them to board. It was all done with utter calm, utter grace, utter leisure. No standing in line, no foot-tapping as the passenger in front of you tried to cram a roller bag into an overhead bin—just an effortless stroll from the comforts of the lounge to the sleekness of the plane seat.

Unlike the Boeing 747, which preceded the Concorde, it wasn't spacious. But it didn't need to be: just two navy leather seats on each side of the aisle, plenty wide with very generous legroom. There were none of today's flat beds and mounds of duvets and pillows, because the Concorde's fuel tanks were unable to hold more than four hours' worth of fuel. The windows were tiny, perhaps eight inches by five, and set just a little too high to be continuously peered through.

Once strapped in, announcements were made as the Concorde taxied to the runway and given preferential treatment by the gods of the control tower. There was none of the customary waiting in a line of seventeen aircraft for takeoff: the Concorde just wheeled directly onto the runway, quickly gained speed, and pointed skyward. All seemed normal at first. The flight attendants did their usual bustling and butlering and it was only then, if it was your first time, you noticed the digital display at the front of the cabin giving notice of the aircraft's speed. "Mach 0.85," it would read (Mach 1.00 is the speed of sound) for the first thirty or so minutes. Because it made a fearful noise as it broke the sound barrier and showered the landscape with poisonous carbons, the Concorde was not permitted to fly supersonic until it had crossed the coast and was above the ocean, and damn the fish if it was too loud or too toxic.

Aboard Air France flying from Paris, the captain—a latter-day Charles Boyer—made the climactic announcement as we crossed the beaches of Brittany: "Ladies and Gentlemen, we are now going to light the after-burners," with the most erotic French intonation for "burrrrnerrrrz" that could have said, "We are now all going to slowly undress and make passionate love."

Suddenly, but without the least ferocity, there came a sharp increase in engine noise and we were compressed into the back of our seats as the speed dial quickly climbed to Mach 1.00, 1.25, 1.50, 1.75, and ultimately 2.00—the equivalent of 1,400 miles an hour. It was all very *Star Trek*. Gradually, quickly, the crushing into the seat was relaxed as the body adjusted to the speed and it was soon that, peering out the tiny windows, one noticed not ocean below but the curvature of the Earth: we had reached 70,000 feet, twice the average height flown by a subsonic plane. We were aviation royalty tempting to brush the edge of the Earth's atmosphere, no longer blue but violet.

An extremely elegant meal was served with mounds of caviar, reams of smoked salmon, buckets of foie gras followed by delicate main courses and manicured desserts, all washed down with gallons of Pol Roger and Perrier.

The 11 a.m. Concorde from Paris arrived at JFK at 9:30 a.m. We had beaten the sun and an identical pattern of cosseting and reverence greeted our arrival except, of course, for the snarling gentlemen of the U.S. immigration service who, still indoctrinated with the bonhomie and charms of turn-of-the-twentieth-century Ellis Island, cared little if you were entering on the Concorde, the *Lusitania*, or a banana boat. Yet the scowls had an upside: the process of inspection being sufficiently sluggardly to ensure that as soon as one was admitted to the Land of the Free, one's luggage was already circulating on the carousel and Air France's American minions had rolled the coat racks ashore and were considerately enshrouding their owners back into cashmere and mink.

Of course, there were and remain flying experiences that rival the Concorde, but none can ever match it until the day comes when supersonic flight is somehow made environmentally acceptable. For instance, in the early years of the Boeing 747, often termed the "Queen of the Skies," first-class passengers could sashay up that broad circular staircase to the upstairs lounge to slurp caviar and munch filets mignons at tables for four, or laze on the couches lining the windows. It was pretty pointless, but it was also wonderful and entirely the next best thing to getting to one's destination in half the time. Even in the twenty-first century, the opulences and luxuries and showers installed by the heavily subsidized Persian Gulf airlines— not to mention Singapore Airlines, Qantas, or Lufthansa or even plucky old British Airways—do certainly impress, and do certainly make the journey blissful. But what the *Normandie*, the *Bremen*, the *Queen Mary* and *Queen Elizabeth*, the SS *United States*, and—yes—even the doomed *Hindenburg* were able to vaunt was that they were the fastest way to cross the pond. That mattered beyond all else. So it was with the Concorde.

In the twenty-first century, Cunard ships still ply the New York to Southampton route—and other cruise lines seasonally offer transatlantic "positioning" voyages at the dawn of the Baltic/Mediterranean season or Caribbean seasons, but all have given up any pretense of speed: after all, if you wanted to get there fast, why would you choose a boat? Nowadays, the *Queen Mary II* crosses from New York to Southampton in a leisurely seven days.

Ultimately, the Concorde plied only two routes—connecting New York with London and Paris—the most glamorous routes of all time. There were brief experiments with Singapore Airlines from London to Singapore— and with the now defunct Braniff to Houston—but they proved to be unworkable as so much of those journeys had to be flown subsonic over land masses.

All in all, I have been lucky enough to cross the Atlantic by ship six times: once at thirteen aboard the original *Queen Elizabeth*, once on the *Canberra*—my immigration voyage—once in a storm-filled January in the Gallic majesty of the SS *France*, and three times on the *Queen Elizabeth 2*. Aboard the *France*, two of my fellow passengers were Mr. and Mrs. Salvador Dalí. On one memorable evening, they descended the breathlessly elegant staircase into the dining room (the staircase down which elegant women would waft was a feature of all French Line transatlantic liners), Monsieur Dali dressed in a tuxedo and brandishing a sword, Madame in a long red flower power gown and gum boots. On one *QE2* voyage, I was traveling with a convention of members of the Society of American Travel Writers. It was November; the seas were rough; and, for reasons poorly explained, the stabilizers were not employed to limit the ship's rolling. After unloading us all in Southampton, the *QE2* was to continue to Hamburg, where its coal-powered engines would be replaced with oil-fed machinery (some months after the voyage each of us was sent a piece of iron from the old engines encased in Lucite, as a souvenir of the *QE2*'s final steam-powered crossing of the Atlantic). On that voyage, half the passengers succumbed to sea sickness. One always knows when rough seas are ahead as the staff quietly remove unnecessary paraphernalia from coffee tables and add additional rope handrails in corridors. And at a gala cocktail reception on the roughest night of the voyage, a vast and complex ice sculpture—into which kilo cans of caviar were imbedded—crashed to the floor, and Barbara Gillam, the glamorous editor of *Glamour* magazine, and I (she in a ball gown, me in a tux) instantly sat on the floor with large spoons and gulped down great gobfuls of the finest Beluga. On a later voyage on the *QE2*, I was a guest lecturer as we sailed from Southampton to New York. I lectured on New York's attractions and on recommendations of Broadway shows. I always prefer the westbound voyage, because the clocks are set back an hour every night, so that every day is a blissful twenty-five hours. I haven't crossed the Atlantic by ship since the internet was born. I'm not sure I much want to. The whole magic of a sea crossing was that—unless there was an urgent family emergency—there was no connection with the world. We were alone in the middle of the ocean.

So one is left with flying. After literally hundreds of overnight flights to Europe, I have every step down to a fine art. If I am in economy—as I often am—I have a light supper at the airport. I buy a bottle of water and I board. My carry-on bag contains a small square brocade-covered pillow, eye shades, earplugs, a bag containing shea butter cream, toothbrush, toothpaste, electric shaver, a fresh wash cloth, and a bag of pills and unguents suitable for the traveling hypochondriac. (Flying to Zurich in February 2020, as the coronavirus was making its way from China to Europe, I added Purell and masks to my stack of supplies.)

On boarding I change the time on my watch and my cell phone to that of my destination (nothing helps reduce jet lag better than persuading oneself that the new time is the "real" time; nothing exacerbates jet lag more than for days saying to oneself, "Yes, but the *real* time is . . ."). After takeoff I take a cocktail of gin, a sleeping pill, and a tranquilizer; smear shea butter on my forehead and around the eyes; don the eyeshade; insert the earplugs; put the seat back; and within minutes I am asleep on my brocade pillow. The only exception to this rule is if I am sitting up front, I have dinner on board and take just one sleeping pill as the seat is so much more comfortable. The bottle of water is a must—waking up in the night in the dry air, one's throat is usually parched. Almost always, I wake up bright and breezy thirty to forty-five minutes before landing, repair to the bathroom, wash my face and head with the fresh washcloth, brush my teeth (bottled water, never the water in an airplane bathroom), and I am ready for the day.

1980

In February 1980, Ma flew first class from London, Carolyn and Nathan flew first class from Washington, and Terry and I flew first class from New York—to Casablanca. We were now to search into the Moroccan roots of my mother's family. We met at the large and soulless Hotel Casablanca, whose inevitable "Rick's Bar" was staffed by swarthy waiters wearing trilbys and trench coats in an utterly unsuccessful effort to look like Humphrey Bogart. We were joined by Marvin Goldman, a university professor from New York engaged by Carolyn to accompany us, as his field of research was the history of the Jews of Morocco. Marvin had a Moroccan Jewish wife, an admirable trove of knowledge, a total absence of humor, and extreme paranoia. He barely hid his disdain for our quest, which he considered trivial, or for us, whom he considered vacuous. He repeatedly warned that we must not "advertise" the Jewishness of our endeavor. Most importantly, he stressed, we must never, ever, under any circumstances utter the word "Israel" in private or in public. Should we ever have to refer to that nation, we must use the code word "Disneyland." Marvin was quite a challenge.

We were invited to afternoon tea at the home of Doris and Vivienne Afriat, Ma's second cousins whom she had never met. Doris was in her seventies, the oldest of five sisters, rotund, and garrulous. Vivienne was a shade younger, much slenderer, more frail, and almost eerily reminiscent of Great-Aunt Vi. Doris and Vivienne had grown up in one of the Afriat mansions in Mogador-Essaouira and spoke perfect stentorian English—as well as French and Arabic. The apartment and its residents reeked of faded glory, antiques, and charm. As we chatted, Doris suddenly rose from her fauteuil to sweep aside a drape in order to reveal a hole in the salon's exterior wall. Caused by a U.S. navy shell during Eisenhower's conquest of North Africa in 1942, it remained purposefully unrepaired. Doris and Vivienne considered the damaged wall a beloved symbol of their deliverance from the Vichy French, who had planned to arrest and deport Morocco's quarter of a million Jews.

We continued to Marrakech and checked into La Mamounia, then and still one of the most magnificent hotels in the world. With Carolyn, lunch always came before exploration. There was a curious sensuality about the dining room at La Mamounia, where gorgeous men, gorgeous women, and gorgeous waiters made electrifying eye contact and exchanged flirtatious smiles. The sensuality was confirmed by our subsequent discovery of several guest suite doors left purposefully ajar, the occasional hand or pair of eyes extending an invitation.

On that first afternoon at La Mamounia, Terry and I lounged after lunch by its massive palm-shaded pool. Between naps and swims, we were engaged in conversation by a group of middle-aged Americans who just happened to be touring Morocco under the auspices of the American Jewish Congress. They wore giant Star of David and Chai necklaces. They were loudly visiting synagogues, loudly meeting with representatives of the Jewish community—including the minister of tourism, who was Jewish—and loudly conducting Shabbat dinners in their hotels' dining rooms. So much for Marvin's paranoia.

The next day in the souk, we chanced upon a jewelry store whose name was "Afriat." Carolyn marched in. In her fluent Mississippi total lack of French, she announced who we were. The proprietor, Joseph Afriat, embraced my mother—his third cousin—kissed her on both cheeks, and announced that his daughter was to be married a week from now and we must come to the wedding. Carolyn beamed. Nathan beamed with the promise of finally having something interesting to photograph. Marvin looked acid. And Carolyn returned to La Mamounia to telex the minions of the *National Geographic* travel office with the instruction to rearrange our schedule to have us back at La Mamounia a week hence.

National Geographic rented a minivan large enough for the six of us and all our luggage, and I drove us south into the Anti-Atlas region of Morocco, where we would stay overnight in the outpost of Goulimine before venturing on to Oufran, my great-grandfather's birthplace. Goulimine's Hotel

Salaam was not La Mamounia. We walked up endless staircases to rooms where mattresses were on the floor and dank toilets were down murky corridors. We slept in our clothes; Carolyn and Ma shared a room, sharing secrets and adorably gossiping into the early hours. The following day we drove through breathtaking desert to Oufran, an oasis of red-mud houses and palm trees that was once known as the "new Jerusalem." My seventy-one-year-old mother's arthritic knees and ankles clambered down a wadi into the village where her grandfather had been born 130 years earlier. Local boys showed us what they said was once the synagogue, where we lit candles, and then we scaled a cliff to the ancient Jewish cemetery, where barely readable Hebrew names were hewn into gravestones. It was hot; it was moving; it was unbelievable. The local boys were gracious and affable and when they finally escorted us back to our minivan, we gave them a gratuity. Finally, I had something to write in my *National Geographic* expense book's "Tips to Natives" column.

We continued north to our chief goal, Mogador. It was here that Anthony's and my great-grandfather had grown up and from which he had embarked for England. We checked into the only hotel in town, the art deco Hôtel des Iles, where Terry immediately befriended a large ginger cat who guarded our room and whom we named for my great-grandmother Rahma. It was now dusk on a Friday evening and the six of us gathered in the hotel dining room, where Carolyn ordered flagons of white wine and giant platters of freshly caught lobster, crab, and shrimp. Suddenly an elderly couple entered. Short, bald, and peering through Coke-bottle-thick glasses, Levi Ben Sousan, a distant cousin, introduced himself. Thus we learned that Marvin's entreaty of anonymity was not only preposterous but all for naught. The National Geographic Society had alerted the Moroccan ambassador to the United States, who had alerted the foreign minister of the Kingdom of Morocco, who had alerted the governor of Essaouira, who had alerted the small Jewish community of Mogador of our arrival.

Levi and his wife insisted we come with them to their apartment. We waved sad good-byes to the seafood and walked through the sunset into the walled city and the Ben Sousans' home. It was Shabbat in Mogador. Candles were lit, challahs and wine were blessed, and a giant Shabbat dinner was served, involving course after course of soup, salads, pastilla pies, lamb, couscous, and pastries laced with rose water. Conversation, in French, was ebullient and gracious. We learned that the city that was once 50 percent Jewish was now home to not more than fifty Jews. Another cousin, Jacob Afriat—single, sixty, and snazzily outfitted in a very British navy blazer and striped tie—joined us and it was he, the following morning, who led us to synagogue for Shabbat services.

We returned to the Ben Sousans' apartment for lunch to find Madame Ben Sousan and her sister red-faced and in floods of tears. An hour earlier they had received a telegram conveying the news that their sister, who had decades earlier immigrated to Israel, had died. (I don't actually recall how Marvin reacted to hearing the forbidden word.) A happy evening had turned into two full days of three-meals-a-day French-speaking mourning, not easy on any of us, and particularly not easy on Carolyn, who had come to adore the diminutive Levi Ben Sousan, but enough already.

Back at La Mamounia, we dressed in our finery for the Afriat wedding. Despite Marvin's urging of low profiles, it turned out to be a giant celebration for some seven hundred guests, complete with post-vow glass-stamping beneath the traditional Jewish wedding canopy, endless food, endless wine, endless music, and my mother belly dancing to wild applause. Two days later Pa joined us in Tangier—birthplace of our great-grandmother Rahma Toledano Afriat. As we left Morocco to fly to Spain, the passport officer in his glass cage thumbed through my passport, stamped it, and literally threw it back to me, spitting out the word "Yahud" (Jew). So perhaps Marvin did know what he was talking about all along.

We visited Córdoba, Granada, and Seville, where prior to 1492 Jews and Muslims had lived and prospered in what was termed an idyllic golden age. The year Christopher Columbus journeyed westward to reach India was also the year both Jews and Muslims were expelled from Spain. We continued to Toledo—from which our Toledano ancestors had been banished in 1492. We told Carolyn of the doubtlessly apocryphal family legend that one of Queen Isabella's ladies-in-waiting had been Jewish and that despite Her Majesty's fundamental Jew-hatred, Isabella was so saddened by her friend's enforced departure for Morocco that she enobled her as the "Marquesa de Toledano." Nathan leapt at this story, and he photographed Ma leaning on a wooden throne in a Toledo palace. My mother gazes from the photograph with aristocratic splendor.

Over the next months, Anthony and Judy traveled with Carolyn and Nathan to Prague, Theresienstadt, Warsaw, Krakow, and Auschwitz, as well as to Mount Sinai and throughout Israel. In the spring of 1981, we hosted an elegant Passover seder at our home, complete with Weill and Afriat cousins, Carolyn, Nathan, and seventeen cameras.

Ma belly dancing with me at a family wedding, Marrakech, 1980. (Courtesy of
Nathan Benn)

My mother, channeling her fifteenth-century aristocratic ancestors in Toledo, 1980. (Courtesy of Nathan Benn)

There then ensued months of silence from Washington. I left messages for Carolyn; had cryptic conversations with Carolyn's assistant, Victoria; and also tried to reach Nathan. Silence. Eventually Carolyn called. It appeared that the editors were unhappy with the endless, suffocating succession of family pictures. The story on which the *National Geographic* magazine had expended two years and a quarter of a million dollars was canceled. In a gracious and elegant gesture, Nathan gave us all the family pictures he had shot in thirteen countries.

We remained in touch with Carolyn, who retired in 1986. In her memoir, *Of Lands, Legends, & Laughter: The Search for Adventure with "National Geographic,"* she devoted elegant and lengthy chapters to the adventure she had dreamed that enabled Anthony and me to travel in search of our roots. On July 7, 2003, aged eighty-two, Carolyn died after a long illness. She had been larger than life, elegant, grand, a latter-day Auntie Mame, with giant vision, giant enthusiasm, and a giant capacity for love. I still miss her.

1984

Even had I wanted to, it would prove ultimately impossible to have expunged Germany from my consciousness. Indeed, it was at the end of May 1984 that Germany was to lurch into the forefront of my psyche with a wallop I can feel to this day. I was in Minneapolis on business when I received word that my mother had been hospitalized for the second time in six weeks with an attack of angina that her doctors suspected could lead to a serious heart attack or stroke. I made arrangements immediately to return to New York to retrieve my passport and fly that evening to London.

Pa met me at Heathrow airport. He was wearing his tan, checkered tweed suit that always made him look both particularly rotund and as if he were a farmer up from the country for a day in the big city. Pa was five foot seven, and for the first fifty years of his life, he had maintained the physique of a slender fashion model. In his later years, however, he developed a spectacular paunch and his twenty or more suits were tailored to accommodate the protuberance. His pants were worn—a mere smidgen from being clown-like—halfway up his chest. They hung in a row in his closet, arranged by color. Each pair of pants, each with its own pair of suspenders, hung upside down from a trouser hanger. After each wearing, the pair of trousers was aired and then placed into one of two enormous wooden trouser

presses, which consisted of two panels of wood that were clamped together by means of enormous metal screws. They always reminded me of
a device designed to produce a confession in the dungeons of the Tower of
London.

Pa's sense of humor was epic, with the ability to emphasize the ridiculous. Whenever he would meet my brother or me at the airport, he would
stand among the mass of chauffeurs, holding aloft a sign with our name.
This time was no different. We drove straight to the hospital, where Ma
was sitting up in bed looking fresh and calm. Her blood tests and EKGs
were encouraging, and she would probably be able to come home within
forty-eight hours. We stayed awhile with her and then Pa drove me home
to the apartment where I had grown up. After I had unpacked, Pa asked if
I would come with him into his "office."

His "office" was that former maid's room beyond the kitchen where my
grandmother dropped dead in 1962. He motioned me to sit at his desk. He
removed the jailer's key ring that was a permanent resident of his right
pocket, and he opened the black strongbox in which I knew he kept wills,
birth certificates, passports, stock certificates, and records of vaccinations.
He removed a large manila envelope from the strongbox and handed it to
me. On the outside of the envelope was written in block capitals, "TO BE
OPENED ONLY AFTER MY DEATH BY ANTHONY AND GEOFFREY." "But I want
you to read it now," he said.

I sat at his desk holding the envelope. I sensed this was one of life's pivotal
junctures and I felt someone should be standing behind me with a movie
camera to capture every detail. I opened the envelope. It contained a bunch
of letters and some photographs. The top letter was typewritten, from Pa
to my brother and me.

Dear Anthony and Geoffrey,

As you know, during and after the war I was in Germany in military
government for fifteen months. During that time, I had an affair with a
German woman named Christa, and we had a child. This was a true love
affair, not a one-night "accident." We were very much in love, and we
named our daughter Marion. When it came time for me to return to
England in 1946, I thought long and hard about staying but, ultimately,
because of Ma, and you—Anthony, and because of my father, I decided to
come back to England. Christa's response was, "If you go, I never want to
hear from you again."

The enclosed correspondence is clear. Perhaps you will want to contact Marion, perhaps not. Just know that I am your father and I love you both with all my heart.

Your,

Dad

He was watching me as I read. I stood up and I hugged him. We were both moist-eyed. Then I sat down again. The camera behind me was recording an image of a thirty-four-year-old learning for the first time that he had an older sister. I couldn't believe the thirty-four-year-old was me.

The next piece of paper I drew from the envelope had been torn in four and Scotch-taped back together. It was from a Marion Schmitt who lived at Kühlwetterstrasse 38b, in Düsseldorf. It was typewritten in English.

Dear Mr. Weill,

Surely you will be surprised to receive this letter by me. And you will ask yourself what this is all about, if you are not the person I am looking for and want to address myself to.

My name is Marion Schmitt, née Bethke, born in Wunstorf/Neustadt on May 4, 1946. Christa Hähnel was my mother. Some time ago I was told your name as being my father's. Now I would like to find out more about him, although I do by no means want to molest you.

I am writing this letter in German and will have a translation into English made by a friend, since my command of the English language is limited and I want to avoid any misunderstanding.

I should greatly appreciate your cooperation in this matter, because it means a lot to me to find out more about my father and maybe meet him one day in the not too distant future.

Yours faithfully,

Marion Schmitt

I looked at Pa. He looked at me. The camera behind me continued whirring. "Read on," he said, "there's more."

The next letter was a carbon copy of the response he had sent her a few weeks before I arrived in London. It was correct, formal, and disingenuous. He acknowledged their relationship; he wondered how she had found him; he explained that his wife was very ill. He explained that his two sons—who lived abroad—were unaware of her existence, but that he would tell them about her when he saw them next. Part of his letter disturbed me:

> I quite understand and appreciate your desire to know more about me and
> I hope that the following details will help to satisfy your curiosity, which is
> quite natural under the circumstances: I am now almost seventy-five and
> very deaf, nor in the best of health. For these and other reasons I am no
> longer active in business and live on the state pension, which is barely
> sufficient for our needs, but we manage to exist. I am no longer able to
> travel about much, but I would be glad to make your acquaintance if and
> whenever you may be in London.

What crap. Yes, he was seventy-five, and deaf as a post. But apart from obesity and alcoholism, he was in good health—or so I thought. My parents weren't ultrawealthy, but they were comfortable and lived well on a great deal more than the "state pension." They traveled once or twice a year to Israel and New York, they ate out regularly, and my father was a heavy investor in Johnnie Walker. As I read the letter, and at the same time as it disturbed me, I understood what he was attempting to convey to Marion. She understood it too. In her next letter she had written back, saying:

> I personally consider it not important telling your family of my existing,
> and I think it is not necessary. My desire was and still is to come to know
> you, as my father, without any demands, above all regarding the financial
> aspect.

In the same letter she wrote:

> You asked, how I could manage to find you. Well, a long time ago, a photo
> of yours as a child was given to me by my grandmother. On the back side
> of this photo your name was mentioned. A girlfriend of mine—who
> translated my letters to you—who frequently stays in London, searched
> your address in the London telephone directory. So, finally I did find you.

Marion's initial letter had arrived the day after my mother had first been rushed to the hospital with a heart condition. I looked at Pa. His eyes were still moist. I am still trying to analyze what he was feeling. Relief, of course, that he could share the secret, but I wonder what more was churning in his brain: regret, perhaps; sadness; confusion. The arrival of the letter on the initial day of my mother's illness must have seemed alarmingly menacing. In an environment where doorbells could fell grandmothers and rainstorms invoke tuberculosis, letters from illicit daughters could certainly finish off wives with weak hearts.

There was one more piece of paper in the envelope, my father's final response to Marion in which he again thanked her for her "sweet letter" that had also told him that she was married and had a fourteen-year-old daughter named May. She had also enclosed a picture. He also wrote:

My wife is now home again after several weeks in hospital, but is still far from well. For this reason and to avoid further complications, I would be grateful if you did not contact me here again. Although I look forward to meeting you and perhaps your daughter one of these days, I am sure that you would understand my position and I would prefer it if you would leave things in abeyance for the time being, until I can get in touch with you again whenever convenient.

This letter was signed with a tad more warmth: "With best wishes and kindest regards." I was still in a daze, the camera was still whirring, but I was also beginning to confront a measure of disappointment. I so very much wanted to have heard that for the last thirty-six years, in good times and bad, he had been sending Marion's mother five or ten pounds a month.

It was a warm May afternoon and we went out for a walk. We sat on a bench next to the Spanish and Portuguese synagogue. He explained it all at length. That it was a major love affair and how he very nearly stayed. I suppose it gave me a new insight into my parents' marriage that I knew was not much worse than many (indeed better than most) but also far from perfect. He wanted me to understand that there being no contact with Christa and Marion had been at Christa's insistence. As we talked and I became accustomed to the concept that I had a new sibling, I realized he had to do two things. One was to tell Anthony. And two was to give me permission to contact Marion. He agreed to both.

1984

I wrote to Marion as soon as I got back to New York. I constructed a letter that would be welcoming and warm. I had been upset by what I considered

Pa's brushing her off and I felt it important to invite her into the family. I told her about my life, about Anthony's, about our wives and his children, and I also explained how Pa was both aging and terrified my mother would learn about her existence. I sent photos, and I told her I would be in Europe in the fall and I would like to meet her. I started my letter to her in German, then switched to English because, like her, I did not want to be misunderstood. I signed my letter quite formally.

In just over a week, Marion wrote back, in German. She too sent photos. I wrote back, this time in German. And a regular correspondence developed, each letter revealing a gently expanding affection. We wrote about politics, about America, about Germany. We wrote about our marriages and our loved ones. I would stare at her photographs and see a striking resemblance to Pa. She had his eyes: large, with heavy bags beneath them. She had his nose. She had his hair, wiry and thick.

Pa wrote to Anthony and told him the whole story. He was no less stunned than I. He called me, and we talked about it. We were both intrigued, surprised, excited, and apprehensive. Anthony was at somewhat of a disadvantage in that he spoke only a smattering of German. And I think that deep down in the inner workings of his mind, his reaction had inevitably to be different from mine—because he was ten when Pa met Marion's mother, while I had yet to be born. I decided that I would visit Marion as soon as I could.

An opportunity presented itself that fall. In October, five months after Pa shared his secret with me, I was to attend a convention in Budapest of the very same Society of American Travel Writers of whom Mrs Carolyn Bennett Patterson had been a founder. I had first visited Hungary earlier that year on a proving trip to plan side trips to the countryside for the travel writers who would be attending the meeting. Six of us had been flown that April first class on a Pan American Boeing 747 from New York to Budapest. We were given suites overlooking the Danube at the best hotel then in town, the Duna Intercontinental. We went on rigorous tours of the city, with our Communist hosts eager for us to see how suitable Hungary was for American visitors. One afternoon I went for a stroll and happened upon a state-run antique store in whose jumbled window I spied a magnificent art nouveau vase. Two women were in command of the shop, deeply engrossed in conversation when I entered, both irritated at my interruption. I asked if one of them spoke English. One of them nodded.

"I'd like to see that vase in the window," I said.

"We don't open the window on Tuesdays," came the response.

"No, no, you don't understand," I explained patiently, "I'd like to *buy* that vase."

"It is *you* who doesn't understand," Madame riposted. "We don't open the window on Tuesdays."

And so the vase remained in the store, and I didn't.

Travel writers can be a whining, spoiled, and demanding bunch—invariably the least accomplished or influential is the most difficult. After our sojourn in Budapest, our little group was split into pairs to take three-day proving trips into the farthest reaches of Hungary to check on the hotels, restaurants, and tours the conventioneers would experience to ensure that, heaven forbid, they would encounter nothing too foreign. My partner in this venture was Eugene Fodor, the Czech who had come to America prior to World War II and had built a guidebook empire. He was a legend. We shared the back seat of a tiny Polish Lada car for three days as we were driven along narrow highways by an erratic young man with shaggy hair and epic body odor. It was not an easy three days. Fodor had not the slightest facility at small talk. He did not know how to chat or banter. If he had a sense of humor, it seemed he had left it at home in Connecticut. He was courtly, he was intensely knowledgeable, he had been everywhere and seen everything, and one knows now that he was somehow attached to the CIA. It was cold, it rained incessantly, and it was no easy matter being trapped in the back of a small car with the windows sealed shut to keep out the rain, sitting for hours in virtual silence as our pungent driver stamped first on the accelerator and then on the brake, and then on the accelerator and then on the brake as he veered and steered us along rutted lanes.

Our first night was spent in Hungary's easternmost city, Debrecen, a grim and gray unkempt place not far from the border with the Soviet Union. The once grand Aranybika Hotel dated from the early twentieth century, and apart from the installation of neon signs that flickered inconsistently and a sea of sagging scarlet vinyl sofas, it appeared unlikely anything had changed since the Austro-Hungarian celebrations of its opening. We consumed a dreary dinner and a drearier breakfast. The next day the rain increased from a perpetual shower to a perpetual monsoon. Our car, with our driver whose aromatics had not been diminished by a night in the fabulousness of Debrecen, splashed its way across the vastness of the Great Hungarian Plain, as I valiantly tried to find topics in which to engage Fodor in conversation. Halfway through the ride, the heater stopped working, the rain became heavier, and I began to consider shooting myself.

The goal of our drive through the sodden countryside was an ancient restaurant in an unpronounceable hamlet where we were destined to have lunch. Eventually, a building appeared out of the murk, a crumpled farmhouse with smoke erupting from its chimney—a vision from Grimm. In the short distance from the car to the house, Eugene and I were drenched. We shook ourselves free of the largest globules of rain and creaked open a fat wooden door revealing a tableau vivant of gemütlichkeit. Warmth engulfed us. There was a giant fireplace with a giant roaring fire. Tables were laid with plump vases of plump flowers, red-and-white napkins, and beakers of beer. Garrulous Hungarians were tucking into vast plates of meat and dumplings and smacking each other's backs as they roared with laughter, opened mouths revealing strands of beef and beer foam. A gypsy trio played fiddles in the corner, their upper torsos swaying frantically to the three-four rhythm. We shed our sodden outerwear, we sat on benches, and a buxom waitress dressed in a Hungarian version of a dirndl instantly brought us great baskets of country bread and steaming bowls of goulash soup. We both laughed at the contrast, and all of a sudden Eugene Fodor became a charmer. He told anecdotes in his fabulously thick accent. He found witty things to say. It was as if the rain and the fireplace and the goulash had flicked a switch. I knew I would be able to tolerate the next day and a half.

1984

After the October convention in Budapest, I traveled by train to Vienna, where I spent two days before continuing to Düsseldorf. I wanted to see Vienna, but I also wanted to delay meeting Marion. I was beginning to get cold feet. What if we didn't click? What if it all were uncomfortable and dismal and awkward? The what-ifs were growing. I telephoned her to reconfirm the details of my arrival. It was the first time I had heard her voice. She sounded formal and middle-aged. Her vowels were plummy and Teutonic. In the background there was the sound of hammering. She apologized for the din, explaining that her husband was engaged in renovation of the house. I stammered my arrival details and hung up. The noise of the hammering delivered me a fantasy that envisioned Marion's husband as some blue-collar thug who guzzled beer and screamed anti-immigrant epithets at soccer matches.

I trudged around Vienna obsessing. I bought a dark-green loden coat that, I realized after I had paid for it, my mother would tell me made me look like a Nazi. I ate cakes at Demel. A guide showed me the sights. She was a woman in her late fifties and of great dignity and erudition. She strolled me through the Hofburg and made the Mayerling episode and the tragedy of Sissy come to poignant life. She showed me Gustav Klimt's *Woman in Gold* at the Belvedere Gallery that now—after an epic and antisemitic legal battle immortalized in a movie starring the exquisite Helen Mirren—resides in New York's Neue Galerie. She took me to Freud's apartment at Berggasse 19, where I imagined myself prone on the kilim-covered couch talking about murdering my grandmother. She took me to the giant square adjacent to the Hofburg and pointed up to a small balcony. "That was where Hitler stood on the night of the Anschluss," she explained. "This square was full to bursting with perhaps a half million Austrians, their voices shouting, "*Sieg Heil*," their arms raised in Heil Hitler salutes," she said, and then she paused for effect. "Yet not one person in Vienna today will confess to having been there." I browsed in a poster dealership and came upon a portentous find: a travel poster for Düsseldorf dating, presumably, from the early 1930s. "Düsseldorf, Art City of the West," it proclaimed, in overlarge, heavyset Gothic type. The umlaut over the "u" looked like an SS insignia. There were images of Düsseldorf's cultural monuments and, unconnected to any particular site, a tall thin crucifix. The poster gave me the chills. It remained in the shop.

That evening I attended a performance of *Tosca* at the State Opera House. I sat in a box next to a fiercely elegant thirtysomething Austrian doctor who, in the ten minutes before the performance began, told me the entire story of her life and, as the lights dimmed, inched her gilt fauteuil closer to mine so our knees could not help but touch. *Tosca* was sung by the Hungarian soprano Sylvia Sass, who, it must be admitted, was not terribly good. She had a problem with the highest notes, some of which she seemed capable of reaching only by climbing a tremulous scale in their quest. Perhaps she had a cold. At the end of the performance, she appeared spotlit through a parting of the curtains and there rose from the audience a torrent of jeers, booing, and whistling that made my blood run cold. I sat in my box, with its second-floor view of the now illuminated, formally attired audience, as hundreds of people in tuxedos and floor-length gowns rose to shake fists and cup their mouths with their hands to amplify taunts. On stage, the benighted diva, lit by the glow of the footlights, affected a deep, slow-motion curtsey that artfully seemed to combine a shouldering of her humiliation with face-saving gratitude signaled to the scattered number of people applauding. It remains perhaps the ugliest scene I have ever witnessed. A theater full of dignified and highly cultured people had suddenly turned into a mob of ferocious ruffians. It didn't take great leaps of the imagination to see their parents and grandparents thronging outside this very opera house on the day after the Anschluss, mocking the Jews of Vienna as they were made to scrub the sidewalks with their toothbrushes.

I bade farewell to my box mate, who had entertained, I suspect, expectations of postopera Sachertorte and romping sex, and returned to my hotel room. I called Anthony—it was 1 a.m. in Jerusalem—and told him I couldn't go through with it. I was going to go back to New York, not to Düsseldorf. I would call Marion and make the excuse of some kind of business emergency. Roused out of slumber, he proceeded to talk me out of it. "You're there; you've got this far; you're going," he insisted.

1984

I could have flown from Vienna to Düsseldorf. But it would have been too quick. I wasn't ready and I needed delay. And spending an hour aboard a Lufthansa Boeing would not have been a fitting mode of transportation for a journey whose goal was the meeting of a thirty-four-year-old Jewish Anglo-American with the thirty-nine-year-old German Christian sister who, five months earlier, he had no idea existed. The journey begged for a touch of theater.

In 1927 Cassandre had produced a series of posters for the French railways that extolled the glamour of train travel—particularly the romance of an overnight journey. Pierre Fix-Masseau produced more posters, with similar type and images, yet with the addition of scenery, such as that he created in 1929 for the Pullman Express along the Côte D'Azur—just the kind of train that would have conveyed Isadora Duncan to Villefranche so she could break her neck. Comparable posters appeared in Britain and in America too. They were masterpieces of art deco type and dramatic perspectives. Steaming locomotives charged through Alps, Midlands, and prairies or on tracks leading to infinity. Elegant couples perched on armchairs in Pullmans or retired in silk pajamas and nightgowns in sleeping

Nord Express, 1927. Adolphe Mouron Cassandre, artist (1905–68). Compagnie Générale des Wagons-Lits.

compartments. Carole Lombard and John Barrymore rode on the Twentieth Century, Celia Johnson and Leslie Howard fell in love in a train station,
and everyone murdered Ratchett in the Calais coach of the Orient Express.

One of Cassandre's most epic train posters was for the Nord Express.
Produced as part of a 1927 series, it features a massive locomotive with
looming, stylized iron wheels and puffs of smoke flung back by speed as
they pour from the locomotive. The image is surrounded by art deco type
that affirms the poster is issued by a conglomerate of the train companies
of Britain, France, Germany, Poland, and Latvia, and by the Compagnie
Internationale des Wagons-Lits, the pan-European sleeping car company,
created in the 1870s by Georges Nagelmackers, a twenty-seven-year-old
Belgian, who, on a visit to the United States in the previous decade, had been
inspired by the luxurious railroad cars produced by the Pullman Brothers
of St. Louis. The poster also reveals the French names of the cities the train
connects: Londres, Paris, Bruxelles, Berlin, Riga, and Varsovie (Warsaw).

In the 1977 movie *Julia*, Jane Fonda portrays Lillian Hellman journey-
ing by train in 1935 from Paris to Moscow. There is some question now
as to whether Hellman actually made the trip she described in the auto-
biographical *Pentimento*, but in the movie, Fonda / Hellman opts to travel
via Berlin so she can be briefly reunited with her childhood friend, Julia
(Vanessa Redgrave). The real reason she is making the detour through
Germany is that she is smuggling dollars for Julia / Redgrave to relay to the
anti-Nazi underground, the whole event having been decided over breakfast at Paris's sumptuous Hotel Meurice with a shy and kindly Maximilian
Schell, who modestly asks the waiter for one fried egg and a glass of warm
milk. He urges Fonda not to do it if she is too fearful, but she summons
the pluck to agree. That evening, the cash, secreted in a dramatically angu-
lar felt chapeau, is delivered to Fonda in a hat box by an underground
contact as she is boarding the train in Paris. She is late for the train and is
rushing frantically through the Gare du Nord, enshrouded in mink. She
is accompanied by Hal Holbrook and Rosemary Murphy, who badger her
with questions as to why she as a Jew would choose to travel to Moscow
via the capital of Nazi Germany. "You know what they do to Jews in Germany, Lily," Holbrook tells Fonda. She cannot answer, for fear of disclosing
her secret mission.

While all eyes are on the three characters as they make their way
through the crowded station, mine are not. Because the movie's re-created
Gare du Nord of 1935 has each of its cast iron columns plastered with one

of Cassandre's Nord Express posters. It is a scene that jolts me with the reminder that these posters were not designed to be carefully mounted, matted, framed, and hung in galleries or in my living room beneath a perfectly angled halogen spotlight. They were created to be unrolled by workmen with blue dungarees and sweaty armpits and wiped with wet brushes onto station walls and the hoardings that surround construction sites. They were produced to be shellacked onto the blank exteriors of nameless buildings, to be displayed as advertising on the columns, like those in *Julia*, that supported the arching glass roofs of hundreds of train stations across Europe. The sea of Nord Express posters through which Fonda navigates brilliantly re-creates for me the moment when these magnificent graphics that today I cherish, value, and drool over were merely, well . . . posters.

My journey to meet Marion required, I determined, a similar sense of brio. I booked myself on the overnight express from Vienna to Cologne; there, I would switch platforms and catch a local train for the thirty-minute ride onward to Düsseldorf. I rode first class and, at not inconsiderable expense, reserved a single Wagon-Lit compartment. I had traveled overnight by train once before. At sixteen, some family friends and I went by rail from London for a week of skiing in Austria's Tyrol. This had not been an elegant journey: we traveled second class and we slept on red vinyl-covered shelves known as couchettes, six to a compartment. Twenty years later, the journey from Vienna to discover the sister I never knew existed called for the thrum of nostalgia.

I dined at my hotel and took a taxi to the station. I had finished my books and I needed something to read beyond *Time* and *Newsweek*. The station bookstore contained a wonky revolving stand with about a dozen English books, mostly thrillers and mysteries, with one exception: Christopher Isherwood's *Mr. Norris Changes Trains* . . . the book of short stories that had evolved into the play *I Am a Camera* and into the musical *Cabaret*. I had read it more than once, but as I stood in the cavernous Vienna Westbahnhof hearing the garbled German announcements through the mesh of loudspeakers, I couldn't imagine a volume more suited to the requisite theatrics merited by this particular overnight journey.

The train compartment was paneled in inlaid wood. The lighting was muted, exuding just like the Brighton Belle when I was a child—an embracing pink glow. The bed was made up with heavily starched, whiter-than-white linen. Two plumped linen pillows awaited my head. On the floor, a pale-blue linen cloth embroidered with the art deco Wagons-Lits logo awaited my bare feet. The train slowly glided out of the station. I undressed and donned pajamas. I summoned the steward and ordered a cognac. I climbed between the linen sheets, lay my head on the firm linen pillows, and switched on the tiny reading light. Little effort was required to persuade myself this was 1929, not 1984. I read Isherwood, I snuggled the sheets up under my chin, I sipped the brandy and was lulled to sleep by the rhythm of the wheels.

I awoke to the clanking of carriages being detached from the train and the slamming of doors. I peeled open the window blind. It was a sunny morning, and we were in the central station of Frankfurt. Further clanks, jolts, and slams preceded our departure. Whistles blew. I burrowed back into my linen cocoon and when I next awoke, we were riding along the shore of the River Rhine. I roused myself and ordered breakfast. I sat at the window munching a croissant and drinking milky coffee as we rolled through scenery that was simply so breathtaking that my eyes teared. It had to do with the perspectives. There was something unreal about the sharp angles at which fields of vines reared up from the river shore. There was a mysterious beauty to the occasional Gothic or medieval castle high up the hillsides surrounded by manicured green. There was a picture-perfection to the dozens of villages through which the train glided. All of a sudden, I had an inkling of how it might just be possible for this massing of unique scenic, spell-binding Wagnerian splendor to induce a people to believe that nature had granted it a sense of preeminence that could be perverted into frenzied patriotism.

1984

Marion had invited me to stay overnight in their home but I had declined. It was too risky a commitment. I needed a place to which I could escape emotionally should it be necessary. I took a cab from the Düsseldorf Station to the Hilton, where Marion and her husband, Helmut, and her daughter, May, were to pick me up at 9 a.m. I unpacked. I looked at my watch. I showered. I looked at my watch. I dressed. I looked at my watch. I took the elevator down to the lobby. My stomach was knotted and I felt light-headed. Had I received a phone call canceling the whole thing or a telegram summoning me urgently back to New York, I would have leapt with joy.

It was a cold, bright fall morning. I stood outside the hotel and a BMW containing three people drew up. The door opened and Marion jumped out. She was laughing and gleeful. We embraced in one of those hugs that begins lightly and is gradually transformed into a tighter and tighter clutching born of need and emotion. We kissed. We looked into each other's faces and I saw my father's prominent eyes and his elegantly curved nose. We were both grinning with a kind of inexplicable euphoria. I shook hands with Helmut; I kissed May on both cheeks. We all got into the car: Marion and I in the back. We drove off.

It would be the most tiresome of clichés for me to say that within ten minutes it was as if Marion and I had known each other all our lives. Yet there is no other way to describe how we glommed onto each other's humor, character, personality, and being. There was not a moment of embarrassed silence, no looking at the backs of one's hand searching for something to say. We fell into a cauldron of chatter and laughter that was to continue until midnight.

They drove me to their apartment. They led me up five flights of stairs to what had once been the attic of a turn-of-the-century apartment building and was now a duplex home that proclaimed wonderful taste. It was not just good taste; it was *my* taste. It was entirely different from my own home, yet the similarities were thunderous. The same walls of books, the same fiercely orchestrated clutter of objets d'art, the same eclectic mixing of antiques and contemporary, the same tidiness, the same bowls of tightly arranged flowers. I could have moved right in and changed nothing. The apartment was large and every foot of it was interesting. I felt instantly comfortable. Marion saw humor in everything. She spoke with large gestures as she wandered with me from room to room and as I drank in the details. Yet all the similarities and sense of comfort could not have prepared me for an item on Marion's desk: a small blue-and-silver tin that once had contained a historic English confection . . . Harrogate Toffee. Marion used it to hold paper clips. I was transfixed for a moment . . . and then I told Marion why. My father—her father—kept an identical tin of Harrogate Toffee on his desk in London. He too used his to store paper clips.

All the fears that Helmut would be a Nazi and Marion unlikable were not so much eliminated as I forgot they had ever existed. We sat on couches, we drank coffee, and we talked. Marion's life had not been easy. Christa's husband had been killed in the war, leaving her with a daughter, Karin. In 1949 Christa remarried. The new husband wanted only Karin to stay with them, and Marion was sent to live with her grandmother in the Russian Zone that, in that same year, became the Communist Democratic

Republic of Germany. Marion told of her and her grandmother's escape to the west in 1953, clutching suitcases as a paid "smuggler" wove them through thick woods and across the frontier. She grew up in a small village near Hanover and, gradually, was accepted back into her mother and step-father's family—and into the home she would now occupy with her half sister, and the two half brothers Christa produced with her new husband. Marion told me she always felt different from them and how, at age sixteen, she had ridden the streetcar into Hanover to buy the Star of David necklace she was wearing. Her half siblings had straight blond hair and blue eyes; her eyes were brown, and her hair, like Pa's, was thick, curly, and prone to frizz. They were lumpen and stolid; she was vivacious and witty. They were clumsy with their fingers; she excelled at embroidery. Sitting in that cream-colored room, the fall sunshine streaming through the skylight, I came face to face with the power of heredity: my father's sister, mother, and niece were incessant needlewomen, perpetually engaged in petit point, gros point, knitting, patchwork, dressmaking. Marion was one of us.

Marion, the sister I never knew existed until I was thirty-four, in 1986. (Author collection)

We pored over photograph albums. We had lunch. They had prepared salmon just in case, incredibly, I kept kosher. We chattered and nattered and my sense of euphoria grew. Marion explained that she was one of many Besatzungskinder (occupation children), progeny born of liaisons between German women and allied soldiers. And I learned that Pa had either not been totally honest with me or had been forgetful. To this day, I am not sure which, although probably the former. For it appeared that he had returned to Germany in the late forties and early fifties. Marion told me of recalling his brief visits, and I remembered that, when I was a boy, Pa would travel each year "on business" to the Hanover Trade Fair. Of course, the purpose must have been to see Marion. And Christa. In the afternoon, we strolled the Königsallee, the elegant boulevard that is the Madison Avenue of Düsseldorf. We munched champagne truffles. We met friends of Marion for supper, people eager to meet me, people I found warm and engaging.

Just as I had protected myself by sleeping at a hotel rather than risking a stay at their home, Marion too had made similar preparations in case it had all gone uneasily. She had arranged for tickets for us to a concert by the Dutch singer Herman van Veen, of whom I had never heard. It turned out to be the perfect choice. It was a charming performance by a man whose style and songs were a mixture of Pete Seeger and Jacques Brel. The audience was enraptured and so was I. Marion and I held hands as we swayed to the tunes. Van Veen sang of love, of peace, of brotherhood. It was an ideal finale to perhaps the most extraordinary day of my life. At midnight Marion, Helmut, and May deposited me back at the Hilton. My sense of elation was undiminished, we kissed, we hugged, we waved, and I crawled into bed exhausted but in a state of utter jubilation. I not only had met my new biological sibling, but she felt, she acted, she behaved like my sister.

The success of my visit to Düsseldorf was enhanced by Pa's insistence that, from the age of fourteen, I learn German. Indeed, it would have been impossible without it. Marion's English was poor to nonexistent. We could not have communicated and developed so instant a bond without my proficiency in German that Pa had encouraged. I wonder now if it was part of his subconscious plan. As I lay in bed at the Düsseldorf Hilton, exhausted beyond exhaustion yet too euphoric to sleep, a variety of thoughts galloped through my head. Perhaps I wasn't his "real son" because Marion was his "real daughter." I thought of my kindergarten friend Marion Sonnenblick, to whom I had been devoted at the age of five. Marion was rotund and giggly and impish. Pa would pick us both up from "Auntie Lotte's" kindergarten, after a tiring afternoon of making loaves of challah bread from plasticene, and walk us home. He would always call her "Sonnenblick," an endearing and amusing name for a bouncy and plump little five-year-old. That night in my bed in Düsseldorf, I realized that he had to call her "Sonnenblick" because he couldn't bring himself to call her "Marion." I recalled too how, for many years, my brother, as a successful Jerusalem publisher, would journey each fall to Frankfurt to attend the eponymous annual book fair. Pa took to spending the week with him in Frankfurt, and I suddenly had this fantasy that he went to Germany so he could spend the days when my brother was working walking the streets of Frankfurt looking into the faces of young women of the appropriate age to determine if he could detect a resemblance.

In the ensuing decades Marion would become a fixed member of our family but, sadly, she never met her father, although they did speak on the telephone several times. One morning during that earth-shaking visit to London, Pa had, with unsurprising concern, shown me his tongue—which was covered in a film of what looked like brown-colored yogurt. It seemed to get better in a day or two, but it had to have been one of those signals the body broadcasts in order to announce that something serious is amiss. Just over a year later, after some months of inexplicable weight loss, he was diagnosed with lung cancer. He refused surgery, home hospice care was arranged, and in April 1986, exactly two years after he had shared his secret with me, Pa died in his narrow bed in my original small bedroom in that apartment in London surrounded by his wife, his two sons and their wives, my three-month-old son Benjamin . . . but not his daughter.

Some years later, Anthony and my mother were dining and drinking a lot of wine at a neighborhood restaurant in London and the conversation somehow rolled around to the subject of infidelity. He asked her if, during the war, when Pa was overseas and she had taken a job at the pub of a friend in the Kentish countryside, she and "the friend" had had an affair.

"No," she said. "We talked about it, but we never did."

Anthony poured himself another glass of wine.

"And what about Pa, did he ever stray?"

"Well, you know about the woman in Germany, don't you?" she snapped.

More secrets tumbled out. During a leave from Germany in 1946, Pa had apparently told Ma about his affair with Christa. He had told her he was thinking about leaving her. It had not been an easy moment for either of them. Nor, indeed, for Christa. Anthony did not probe further; our mother died six years later and we do not know if she ever knew about Marion. Three years after our *National Geographic* story was canceled, I told Carolyn about Marion. We both marveled at what would have been a captivating postcript to the saga.

After Ma's death in 1994, Anthony and I invited Marion to come to London. She stayed with us in the family apartment where we had been raised. She drank in the atmosphere of the home that in some way might somehow have once been hers. We shared some of our parents' possessions with her. They are proudly displayed in a glass cabinet in Marion and Helmut's living room.

1957

A further element of my developing travel obsession had to do with food. Pa was preoccupied with every aspect of food: eating it, buying it, discussing it, and even, on occasion, cooking it. I lived in a home where daily fare could include toad in the hole, shepherd's pie, steak and kidney pudding, cottage pie, baked beans, and soused herrings. My grandmother would cook Irish stew in a vast cauldron of fatty lamb and vegetables, which I loathed: she rarely managed to remove all the tiny jagged bones. We ate boiled cod with parsley sauce. Breakfasts included kidneys and a holdover from the war: "economizers," little cakes of fried dough. Afternoon tea could involve crumpets smeared with Marmite, and snacks were on occasion melted beef drippings wiped onto toast. Sunday lunch was always a British Sunday "roast," accompanied by overboiled vegetables, mouthwatering roast potatoes, and a wide spectrum of requisite British accessories: bread sauce with roast chicken, Yorkshire pudding and horseradish sauce with roast beef, applesauce with roast pork, red currant and mint jellies with roast lamb. Desserts invariably sat beneath puddles of Bird's Custard, the sweet and milky yellow syrup made from a packet that had been invented during World War I when the ingredients for a traditional crème anglaise were unavailable. My grandmother made rice puddings and tapioca. She baked fruitcakes, cheese scones, and glazed apple tarts. We celebrated Christmas with roast turkey and all the trimmings, followed by plum pudding, into which Ma buried treasures of sixpences. We ate hot cross buns at Easter and made pancakes on Shrove Tuesday.

Yet we also had Passover seders and Rosh Hashana banquets for twelve or fifteen. Most often, the main course at these meals was cold fried fish, a specialty uniquely Moroccan-Jewish. My mother learned its production from her Tangier-born grandmother, Rahma. In her Edwardian four-story house just a few blocks from our apartment, Rahma would descend in a white cotton coat to the kitchen. The cook and sundry maids stood back while she plunged fish for thirty into vats of boiling vegetable oil. With neither cook nor maids, Ma undertook the same task. To defend against the odors of both the frying and the fish, she would enshroud herself in a housecoat reserved uniquely for this sole (excuse the pun) purpose and wrap her hair in a turban. She unpeeled yards of masking tape to seal the door that connected the kitchen with the rest of the house, and flung open all the windows. She would create an assembly line of plates: breadcrumbs, eggs, flour, salt, pepper. Then, one by one, she would seize dozens of filets of plaice (flounder), halibut, haddock, and sole, dip them in flour, then egg, then breadcrumbs, then egg again, and fry them golden brown. The oil spattered the stove, it clung to the walls, it dotted the ceiling, it matted the cat and smeared my mother. Once cooked, the fish was cooled on wire racks. It was never eaten hot: only the next day, and at room temperature. It was arranged intertwined with bunches of parsley on a giant willow-pattern platter. At its center, two of the largest filets of fried plaice were nudged into the center into the shape of a tower surrounded by sprigs of curly parsley. The fish was accompanied by an arrangement of salads.

Most of my school friends' families seemed rarely to frequent restaurants—but we did, on a regular basis. I grew up eating chop suey, sweet and sour pork, and crispy noodles wrapped into a circular contrivance we dubbed "modern hat" at Cathay, supposedly London's first Chinese restaurant. The Cathay overlooked Piccadilly Circus: its prized window tables offering a spectacular view. The restaurant was all ebony, Chinese red, and white tablecloths. Its maître d'hôtel was a tall, middle-aged Eurasian gentleman with slicked-back hair dyed so black it seemed almost navy blue. He wore a tailcoat, striped trousers, and an air of unctuousness. He spoke with a French accent and bowed from the waist as he addressed my mother as "Madame." In another time and another place, he could have been the technician in *Miss Saigon*. I am sure he was a spy.

Near my father's office, in the City of London and close to the Old Bailey criminal courts, was a restaurant named Delano's, where I was taught by an Italian waiter how to twirl spaghetti to perfection. It was at another

Italian restaurant, this one closer to home in St. John's Wood, that I was taught how to set fire to the wrappers of amaretto cookies so they would fly into the air. And it was at the Cresta, in Hampstead Heath, that I learned that a meal of goulash and stuffed cabbage could be accompanied by gypsy violins. But Pa's—and eventually my—favorite restaurant was a tiny establishment on Monmouth Street called Mon Plaisir. (Incredibly, sixty years later, it's still there, opposite Kit Kemp's Covent Garden Hotel, identical and still family run.) Pa liked it not merely because the food was delicious but because in every respect it was ragingly Gallic. Its owner had a pencil-thin mustache and a Gauloise permanently lodged in the corner of his mouth; he shrugged, shook hands, and rarely smiled. The walls were decorated with a collage of French advertisements, graphics, and a giant map of the *départements* of France. The menu was classic: escargots, steak-frites, duck à l'orange, crème caramel, salads of wilted lettuce drenched in exquisite vinaigrette, crisp baguettes, and a platter of aromatic cheeses. Eating at Mon Plaisir was, as I experienced it, tantamount to a brief vacation in Paris. And perhaps that was the whole point of so many of our ventures into eating out. It was as if the consumption of the food was only a device used to enable us to be transported from the drabness of postwar London, if only for an hour or two, to Marseille or Rome or Prague or Shanghai.

One Sunday morning—I must have been about eight—I awoke to a delicious smell of frying. My parents and Anthony had gone to the movies on the previous evening. In the movie, they explained to me, an actress called Joan Bennett had stood in a "vast American kitchen with every modern convenience," soaked slices of bread in a mixture of frothed egg and milk, and then fried them in butter. She served them on plates and covered them with syrup. The three of them were so intrigued that they arose early the following morning in order to fry up batches of what we came to consider ambrosial. We even gave it our own Germanic-sounding name: *"egg schlacht."* It would be decades before I learned this whole gluttonous fuss surrounded nothing more prosaic than French toast.

Food was a central aspect of travel too—not merely the restaurants in dozens of cities and the new flavors that my parents insisted I sample. But our travels to Israel (and later to America) invariably involved the carriage of foodstuffs whose importation was illegal. The whole point was to bring foods unavailable at our destination to those we knew loved them. When we visited the United States, we would bring liqueur chocolates, fresh red currants, veal and ham pies, and bangers—English pork sausages. They would be buried deep inside suitcases to elude the customs agents. When we visited Israel in the early days, we would bring fresh cherries and raspberries for my brother, as well as Lyle's Golden Syrup, lime marmalade, and china jars of Patum Peparium—a vile concoction made of anchovies and God knows what else that was available only in the rarified confines of Fortnum and Mason and which Anthony would spread atop buttered fingers of toast, munch, and beam. Later, the traffic would go in the other direction. My brother would bring Israeli cucumbers to London; I would bring grape jelly from New York to Israel; and, on his day of departure from New York for London, Pa would fill an entire suitcase—incredible as it may seem—with packages of Thomas' English Muffins, a foodstuff entirely American, and unknown in England.

1956

I grew up in a world in which travel was undertaken for pleasure, certainly, and for business. But it was also a world in which travel could be of far greater portent: the means to a new life on the far side of the planet, a means of escape and rescue, a means of discovery. Travel could spell untold joy. It could also, with the ringing of a doorbell, augur unimaginable tragedy. I was raised in an environment where moving from one continent to another was run-of-the-mill. My school friends visited their relatives in Manchester, and their mothers carped if their children moved to a different postcode in London. I visited relatives in Paris, Israel, and Amsterdam and, eventually, in Morocco, Spain, Australia, and America, and my mother griped that she had one son in Israel and one in New York. To me it seemed normal.

In 1940 Pa's sister Esmé had emigrated from England to the United States. She had married her second cousin Ernest in 1936 in a ceremony that involved not only the ministrations of a rabbi but also the presence of a representative of the Home Office—the British equivalent of the Department of the Interior. By marrying, Esmé and Ernest were caught in the sexist Alice in Wonderland of international bureaucracy. Ernest was born German and even though the Nuremberg Laws of 1935 had stripped him and all German Jews of their citizenship, he carried a German passport and was, in the eyes of the British government, German. Under British law, upon marriage to a foreigner, a woman automatically acquired her husband's nationality. Once Esmé had said "I do" and Ernest had stamped on a glass in the age-old tradition recalling the destruction of the Temple in

Jerusalem, London-born Esmé became a German national. The representative of the Home Office was on hand to reverse the process and to complete and sign the forms re-naturalizing her as a British subject.

Born in 1905, Ernest had traveled from his home in Frankfurt to New York in 1928. He stayed on Riverside Drive at the home of his British-born Aunt Lizzie, whose husband held a senior position with Cunard. Ernest worked discreetly and illegally as a runner on Wall Street. He fell in love with the brashness, hope, and anything-is-possible zeal of America. But in October of the year after his arrival, Wall Street collapsed and Ernest returned home on Cunard's *Aquitania*. The journey back to Germany brought him through London, where he stayed at the home of his cousin, my grandfather, whose daughter Esmé was irritated at being deputized to entertain yet another boring German cousin. Within an hour of Ernest's arrival, boredom turned into love.

As the 1930s wore on, Ernest, now a salesman in London, dreamed of returning to America. On Kristallnacht, his father was arrested and given the choice of leaving Frankfurt within twenty-four hours or being sent to Dachau. Unsurprisingly, he chose to flee. His sister, brother-in-law, and son followed, and they sailed directly to the United States, where the Hebrew Immigrant Aid Society (HIAS), an organization that tended to the needs of refugee immigrants, determined that as Ernest's father had been in the wine business in Germany, the family should therefore be resettled in Louisville, Kentucky, where bourbon was produced.

In 1938 Ernest applied to the U.S. consulate in London for immigration papers. The quota for German refugees was filled; he would have to wait. In 1940, on yet another visit to the consulate, a clerk reexamined Ernest's documents and realized he had been born in 1905 in Strasbourg in Alsace—a city that, with the redrawing of borders after Germany's defeat in 1918, had returned to France. The clerk argued with his superiors that Ernest qualified, therefore, as a French national, not a German. Bingo. The French quota for immigration was unfilled and on September 26, 1940, at the height of the Blitz, F. Willard Calder, U.S. Vice-Counsul at London, England, signed their visas. A month later, four days after Esmé's Uncle Hugo was deported from his home in Konstanz, she and Ernest sailed for New York from Liverpool on the last transatlantic nonmilitary westbound passenger sailing until 1945.

(A thought-provoking nugget emerged in my reading of David Nasaw's *The Patriarch*, a biography of Joseph Kennedy, father of President Jack.

Joseph Kennedy was habitually known as an appeaser, an antisemite, and an admirer of Nazi Germany, but I read that this was simplistic and disingenuous. As FDR's ambassador to Britain, he recognized that the Jews had to get out of Germany, and Kennedy petitioned the State Department to transfer the thousands of spaces unused on the United States' immigration quota for British applicants . . . and add them to the German quota—thus enabling thousands more Jewish Germans to escape the Nazis and make it to America. Secretary of State Cordell Hull vetoed the idea.)

After a week or so in New York, Esmé and Ernest moved on to Louisville to join Ernest's father and sister. Esmé was profiled in a Louisville newspaper as a heroine who had survived the Blitz. Ernest landed a job with an insurance company, and Esmé was employed at Stewart's department store, where she was ignominiously fired for allowing a black woman to try on a pair of gloves. It was Esmé who had sent Anthony the *National Geographic* magazines that had provided me so much solace as I imagined myself relaxing aboard a train with a Vistadome, chatting on a Princess phone, admiring a refrigerator with two doors, flying aboard a Panagra DC-7 to Rio, or crossing the Atlantic on the *Queen Mary*.

When I was six, I was taken to Waterloo Station to bid farewell to Grandpa; his second wife, Bee; and their daughter, Ann, as they boarded the boat train that would take them to Southampton and their voyage to New York aboard the *Queen Mary* to visit Esmé, Ernest, and my first cousin, Terry. In 1956 crossing the Atlantic by ship was still the preferred mode of transport. There was enormous bustle at the station: the blowing of whistles, the pasting of labels on luggage that designated which cases were "wanted on board" and which could remain in the hold until arrival in the New World. There was the busy aura of transportation that morning at Waterloo Station rather than the relaxed aura of vacation that today surrounds the departure of an ocean liner. Passengers were boarding this ship in order to reach a destination; they were not boarding a floating hotel to career them to sunshine and a succession of ports to purchase straw baskets embroidered with raffia flowers. Passengers aboard the train flung open the windows and stuck out heads to bid final farewells. The blowing of the train whistle and the whoosh of steam from the locomotive was a prelude to waves, air kisses, damp eyes, and the flourishing of handkerchiefs.

During the Depression, the two British companies that ruled much of the North Atlantic passenger trade—Cunard and White Star—were forcibly amalgamated by the British government. Both companies had long-standing traditions regarding the naming of ships: White Star Line's ships all had names ending in "ic"—*Britannic, Homeric, Doric, Majestic*, and the unforgettable *Titanic*; the names of Cunard's ships ended in "ia"—*Aquitania, Mauretania, Sylvania, Caronia*, and the almost equally unforgettable *Lusitania*. There is a dubious story that when, in 1934, the amalgamated Cunard–White Star shipping company was building its superliner to compete with France's spanking new *Normandie*, the intention was to continue the Cunard "ia" tradition and name the ship *Victoria*. At an audience with King George V, the chairman of Cunard is said to have remarked to His Majesty that the company hoped to name its new ship after the greatest queen ever to have reigned over Britain. King George is said to have responded, "How lovely; my wife [Queen Mary] will be delighted."

In that era before it was de rigueur to pick up the telephone to make a transatlantic call—even on an oval Princess phone with a lighted dial—we were to learn of the details of the voyage's aftermath only from the contents of the folded blue aerogramme letters sent to us by Esmé. She and Ernest had left Kentucky in 1946 and lived now—with their daughter, Terry—close to New York in a place with, what seemed to us, the romantic-sounding name of West Orange, New Jersey. About ten days after seeing Grandpa, Bee, and Ann off from Waterloo Station, the first of many blue aerogrammes began to drop daily through the letter box onto our hall carpet. The *Queen Mary* had docked in New York on a stifling July morning with temperatures and humidity levels in the nineties. After they disembarked from the ship, Grandpa, Bee, and Ann had sat for seven hours on their luggage in the roasting heat of the pier waiting for customs clearance. By the time longshoremen wheeled their luggage through to the outside world and the arms of Esmé, Ernest, and Terry, my seventy-five-year-old grandfather seemed to be intermittently disoriented. He went to bed as soon as they arrived in West Orange. The next day, his condition seemed even worse, and he was diagnosed as having had a mild stroke. He recovered sufficiently to enjoy the rest of the visit to America as well as the voyage home on the *Queen Elizabeth*. But the grandfather I greeted six weeks later at Waterloo seemed older and smaller than the grandpa to whom I had waved good-bye the month before. In truth, he never was the same man again. Over the next five years, he became increasingly forgetful, ailing, fractious, unpredictable, incontinent, and demented, until he died in April 1961, four months shy of his eightieth birthday. But with that same medieval flair with which my family demanded explanations for every calamity, Grandpa's decline and demise were directly traceable to those seven stifling hours on the Cunard pier in the July heat of Manhattan. And perhaps they were.

His widow, Bee, left London and moved to a tiny village in Kent, into the sixteenth-century thatched Tudor cottage—a protected landmark—where her sister, Edith, lived with her lover, Barbara-Allen. It was Edith who had worked at the Home Office and, in 1940, had miraculously engineered Grandpa's freedom in exchange for Pa's joining the army. The cottage sat in a gorgeous flower-filled garden, surrounded by towering oaks. It looked like the box top of the perfect jigsaw. I had always been extremely confused by Edith. Perhaps I was five or six when first we met, and I was totally perplexed by her short, parted hair; her horn-rimmed glasses; her manly suit; her white shirt and tie; and her serious lace-up shoes. Bar Allen—as she was known—was quite a contrast: exquisitely pretty, with dimples, an enchanting smile, flowered dresses, and masses of white wavy hair. Bee, Edith, and Bar Allen lived in that thatched Tudor cottage until each of them died and was buried in the village churchyard.

Dramatic unfoldings related to travel were not restricted only to my assorted grandparents. It was also in 1956 that Paris cousin Raymond's grandmother Cynthia, one of the patrician ladies who would play cards with Aunt Vi in the chill of the beach in Hove, sailed from Southampton to visit her daughter Olga, Joyce's sister, at her home in Cape Town. The two-week journeys aboard the ships of the Union Castle line from Britain to the Canary Islands and South Africa were romanticized in a succession of postwar posters as two-week, fun-filled vacations. The ships are invariably shown from the air, with special emphasis on attractive passengers reclining by the pool or playing deck games, the funnel spewing nontoxic puffs of smoke as they steam through South Atlantic waves. The ships bore names such as *Rhodesia Castle*, *Transvaal Castle*, and *Windsor Castle*, and as the 1950s progressed, the posters' typefaces emit increasingly panicked entreaties to journey to South Africa by ship rather than by the ever-increasingly popular Britannias and Comet jets of BOAC.

After a dawn arrival in Cape Town, Cynthia was met by Joyce's sister Olga, who in her twenties had converted to Christianity only to marry German-born Walter, a survivor of the Holocaust. They drove to Olga and Walter's home in the leafy neighborhood of Oranjezicht that nestles at the foot of Table Mountain. They spent a glorious morning of catching up and playing with Cynthia's grandchildren. They lunched, and Cynthia retired to her room for a nap. At some point that afternoon, she had a massive heart attack and died in her sleep.

1960

Four years after Grandpa's visit to America, Esmé, Ernest, and Terry visited us in London. Ostensibly, they were coming to attend my twenty-year-old half aunt Ann's wedding, but an unspoken criterion for the visit was to say good-bye to my by now seriously failing grandfather. Before the visit, letters arrived from West Orange asking my father to arrange a room at a nearby hotel for Esmé and Ernest—while Terry, nine months my senior, would stay at our apartment.

"Does the hotel have air-conditioning?" Ernest asked in one letter. "Yes," Pa responded with postwar British sarcasm. "When it's hot, you open the windows; when it's cold, you close them." We thought him hilarious.

Esmé and Terry arrived a week before Ernest. The excitement of their arrival was monumental. They flew to London on a Pan American Boeing 707—the first humans I had ever encountered who had flown on a jet. It was as if the all-American opulence of the advertisements in the *National Geographic* magazine suddenly checked in to our apartment. Everything exuded glamour, from their beige vinyl soft-sided luggage to their cameras and the grandeur of their possessions. Esmé, who was two years younger than my father, appeared to me as an American version of my Dad in drag. She was elegant, strong-minded, beautifully coiffed, and her mishmash Anglo-American accent was rather like that I had heard from the mouth of the Duchess of Windsor in a television interview. And then there was Terry. Almost the same age, we were both effectively only children of parents who bore us late in life, at forty-plus. Within hours of their arrival, Terry and I were embedded in endless games of canasta and plans to build scenery for my toy theater. We were to find a bond that united us instantly in a paroxysm of identification, sympathy, necessity, and affection that would ultimately survive decades of cousinhood, friendship, romance, marriage, parenthood, anger, too much alcohol, my dalliances, divorce, and once again—cousinhood and friendship.

At the age of ten, I became a tour guide. Terry and I would leave the apartment after breakfast and catch a bus to whichever part of London was on the day's schedule. We watched the changing of the guard at

Buckingham Palace. We clambered up the monument to the 1665 Great Fire of London. We climbed way up into the cross above the dome of St. Paul's Cathedral. I knew London strangely well, better than most adult Londoners. In addition to having been shown the city repeatedly by my parents and Anthony, for years, night after night I would pore through an illustrated volume published just after the war ended called *The Wonderful Story of London*.

Through Terry's American eyes, I also learned to see London, and to react to London, as if I were showing my city to a reader of the *National Geographic* magazine. The facets of London I considered humdrum— policemen with tall helmets and no guns, double-decker buses, children in school uniforms—fascinated her. It wasn't enough to show her the Beef-eaters at the Tower of London; I had to clarify why and who they were. I had to justify to this questioning republican why we had a queen and knights and lords. I had to justify driving on the left and why there were twelve pence in a shilling and twenty shillings in a pound and twenty-one shillings in a guinea. She badgered me with questions, with an endless succession of whys and argument, and I learned to respond like a tour guide with a bus full of inquiring and sporadically exasperating tourists. Despite her Anglo-German parentage, Terry's attitudes reflected the insularity and un-embarrassed sense of superiority of 1950s America. There was the American way or the wrong way . . . or not exactly wrong, but outmoded, passé, tired, outdated, outpaced. It was a simplistic outlook, somehow both annoying and alluring.

After three weeks in London, Terry and her parents flew to Frankfurt to visit the grave of Ernest's mother and, because Esmé refused to stay overnight in Germany, they journeyed that same afternoon by train to Zurich. After a day or two at the inevitable Baur au Lac, their itinerary through Europe would take them to Lugano, to the French Riviera (the Carlton in Cannes, of course), and finally aboard the overnight Blue Train to Paris, the deluxe rail journey glamorized by countless posters. We had been given a copy of the itinerary prepared by their travel agent in Newark, and Pa made fun of it. He scorned its sense of detail. He mocked its typed suggestion to "gaze from the left side of the limousine" as they were transferred from Lugano station to their hotel so they would have the best view. They scoffed at its cosseting, at its refusal to entertain spontaneity. I thought it was brilliant.

My parents and I flew from London to meet them in Paris. The excitement of my first airplane flight was relentless. For fifty-two minutes I sat next to the large oval window of the British European Airways Viscount and drank in every aspect of the takeoff, the climb, the leveling off, the crossing of the British and French coastlines, the change in engine noise as we descended, and the flawless landing at Le Bourget Airport—not more than a few hundred yards from Drancy, where Great-Uncle Hugo had been immured before entraining for Auschwitz. A brochure in the seat pocket explained the vast change in corporate identity in which BEA was currently engaged. Hardly normal fodder for ten-year-olds, I found it absorbing. The serif type "British European Airways" was being replaced by stark sans serif "BEA" lettering dropped out in white from a red square that could be positioned within either a black or a white rectangle. The modernity was staggering. It was my first confrontation with the science of logos—of how an airline could adjust its identity by means of what the twenty-first century exasperatingly terms rebranding.

Once again, I stayed at the home of Raymond, Henry, and Joyce. The fourth member of the Paris ménage, Aunt Flo, was, as was customary in August, summering and bickering in Brighton with Aunt Vi. My parents and I took a taxi to the very grand fin-de-siècle Hotel Continental on the Rue du Rivoli, where we awaited Ernest, Esmé, and Terry's arrival. They were to be transported by limousine from the Gare de Lyon, where the Blue Train would deposit them after the overnight journey from Cannes. It was doubtless the grandest hotel I had ever entered. Concierges and reception clerks stood tall in tails and striped trousers. The lobby was vast and surrounded by a sunlit interior courtyard, where opulent guests sat at opulently dressed tables consuming croissants and cafés au lait. We sat on Louis XV fauteuils and waited. Eventually, their arrival was heralded by a porter wheeling a cart heaped with the sumptuousness of their beige vinyl soft-sided luggage I had so admired in London.

Terry and my London gang of two became a gang of three as Raymond showed us his Paris. We shared much in common: three effectively only children of older parents; three children who were far too sophisticated for either their good or their years, precociously accustomed to adult conversation, expectations, and mores. We sat in cafés; we climbed to the top of the Arc de Triomphe; we rode the Métro; we stayed home perched on gilt armchairs in Flo's Belle Époque drawing room and engaged in three-way canasta marathons. Esmé and Ernest took the three of us on an American Express bus tour of Paris. Raymond was fascinated by seeing his hometown through American eyes. A photograph of the tour group arranged on the steps of the Madeleine Church memorializes the moment. Half the men are wearing hats, and all are wearing jackets and ties. Many of the women are also behatted, some with short bolero cardigans over their shoulders. Terry, Raymond, and I are the only children. We stand at the front, Raymond and I in shorts, open-neck shirts, short socks, and sandals, admitted briefly into the affluence and care of the American tourist machine.

1963

In July 1963, six months after the celebration of my Bar Mitzvah at the Central Synagogue in Great Portland Street, it became my turn to visit America. The Bar Mitzvah had been a major landmark for a variety of reasons that had little to do with my graduation to Mosaic manhood. The planning and preparations had brought with them a welcome measure of respite from the perpetual mourning of my grandmother. The first visit to London of Anthony with Ariela enabled Ma to set aside her grief in order to agonize over what she deemed as her elder son's horrifyingly misguided marriage and to fight mercilessly over the seating plan for the tea dance at the Kensington Palace Hotel, which would be held the day after the Bar Mitzvah. Vast charts took over the dining room table and there were endless arguments and screeching about who would sit at which table, one of which was titled "The Rich Jew Table." The coda of the Bar Mitzvah weekend was the afternoon reception that, once my speech was delivered, I rather enjoyed, from my choreographed Charleston with Ma, to the waltz with godmother Hilda, to the fox-trot with Ann, to the unchoreographed twist with Marion-once-known-merely-as-Sonnenblick. The entire event was orchestrated by a master of ceremonies in scarlet attire, whose deportment and stentorian "My Lords, Ladies, and Gentlemen, please rise for the Bar Mitzvah boy," would have been far more apt at a state dinner at Windsor Castle than for an afternoon tea party in a middle-class ballroom full of Jews—some rich, some not—participating in a three-thousand-year-old rite of passage.

I accompanied Pa to Lower Regent Street to book our trip to America. Yes, my father was obsessed with guidebooks, but not with travel advice. His preference was for publications that rated hotels in lists graded by stars rather than by florid or critical passages of prose. He was interested only in where to stay and where to eat, and was entirely bored by volumes that explained architecture, recommended sights, and guided the reader through museums. As far as travel arrangements were concerned, he knew what he wanted. Or he thought he did.

The offices of Cunard shipping that Pa and I entered contained vast models not only of the *Queen Mary* and *Queen Elizabeth* but also of a BOAC Boeing jetliner. In 1963 Cunard was engaged in a brief and frantic love affair with BOAC. With the end of transatlantic passenger travel by ship not quite in sight but certainly looming on a not-too-distant horizon, it was a marriage of convenience designed to enable Cunard at least to keep passengers traveling in one direction by sea by offering packaged prices to fly one way to New York and to sail home, or vice versa. Pa's intention was to book us to New York on a BOAC Boeing 707 and home on the *Queen Elizabeth*. He told the clerk at the counter he wanted the least expensive cabin for three that had its own bathroom. The gentleman at Cunard unfolded a giant deck plan and began explaining the options of the three classes of travel, but Pa was not in the slightest bit interested. His only fixation was the insistence on a private bathroom: the location of the stateroom was irrelevant. We were out of the door within thirty minutes, tickets, baggage tags, and baggage stickers in hand.

It's hard to re-create the sense of excitement that surrounded anticipation of that first trip to the United States. America was the beacon of endless possibility, modernity, and grandeur. It was the land of big and loud and lavish and powerful, and everyone seemed somehow to want a piece of it. Yes, many Britons entertained an underwash of resentment at America's crassness, butchering of English, and overall gaucheness—but these were sentiments fueled largely by jealousy and the bile of a nation that until only moments before had an empire. The British still recalled the million GIs flooding England prior to D-Day, who, they complained were "overpaid, oversexed, and over here." But they were familial emotions, readily foregone whenever it was deemed convenient. I had spent weeks poring over maps, trying to pre-learn my bearings. I found West Orange on a map of the New York metropolitan area, and I determined that our route from Idlewild Airport in Jamaica would take us through Brooklyn and across New Jersey's Pulaski Skyway.

We dressed in great elegance for the flight. Pa and I both wore suits and ties, Ma a costume of navy Thai silk, hat, and white gloves. There was a sense of alarm at check-in at the hangar-like North Terminal at Heathrow when the seat assignments on our boarding passes read A, C, and D—but questions to several BOAC clerks as we progressed through the airport were met with assurances that we were indeed seated together. We boarded and learned that without explanation we had been upgraded to first class. The luxury and graciousness were unimaginable. Once in the air, there began a never-ending proffering of menus, cocktails, food, wines, desserts, and gifts. There was an unaccustomed spaciousness not only to our seats but also to the front of the first-class cabin, where passengers could lounge on a semicircular sofa and be plied with more drinks and admire the change of scenery. A route map was passed around the cabin, our course to New York plotted by the navigator in ink and signed by the captain. One of our fellow passengers was actor Hugh Griffith.

After landing at Idelwild, we taxied to the terminal, a vast and impressive steel and glass structure that proclaimed in large letters: "New York International Airport." The plane stopped, the engines were shut down, and a long square tube magically pulled away from the building and connected itself to the aircraft door. It was as if we had arrived not in another continent but in the twenty-second century. We were met by Esmé, Ernest, and Terry and emerged into scorching heat—the kind of heat that had knocked my grandfather, seven years earlier, into a permanent decline. We rode in a long limousine—not over the Pulaski Skyway but through Manhattan and the Lincoln Tunnel to West Orange.

We entered the suburban ranch house that to us seemed like something from a magazine—which, to me, of course, is precisely what it was. There was a den (previously I thought this had something to do with lions) with a giant color television. There were three—count them, three—bathrooms. There was a porch, a patio, and a barbecue. I entered the kitchen and it was all there: the giant refrigerator with two doors, the Formica counter that swept in a U-shape from one side of the kitchen to the other, the machine into which dishes could be placed to be miraculously scrubbed and dried, the two barstools with shiny red vinyl upholstery, the Princess phone—even a jar of Sanka. I had literally walked into an advertisement in the *National Geographic* magazine.

There was an opulence to everything, a vastness, a sense of plenty and magnificent wastefulness that seemed impossible to comprehend and impossible to forgo. Esmé opened the refrigerator and extracted cantaloupes and bags of peaches and nectarines, items that cost the earth in London and were reserved for special treats. She sliced a melon into two halves, scooped the seeds of one onto a paper square torn from a roll of paper nattily secreted in the wall, opened another secret door to tear off a foot of wax paper in which to wrap the other half, and threw the paper and the plastic bag that had housed the melon into the trash. (Paper towels were a completely new experience, and in London, plastic bags and aluminum foil were washed, rinsed, and positioned messily atop faucets to dry and be reused.) The freezer opened to reveal great tubs of ice cream. I had never eaten ice cream in a private home—the tiny freezer compartment inside our flat's fridge barely kept our lonely tray of ice solid, let alone ice cream. We drove to immense supermarkets in Ernest's giant Oldsmobile 88. We ate vast hamburgers and steaks bigger than an English roast beef. I watched color television at all hours. Terry and I took the bus to Korvettes to buy records that were far less expensive than in London and, what's more, came with album covers of thick cardboard that opened like a book—not the flimsy paper shrouds of English records. We climbed the Empire State Building; we ate at Lindy's; we saw Rock Hudson woo Doris Day (in *Move Over, Darling*), and watched the Rockettes kick at Radio City. We circled Manhattan by boat. We drove along massive highways and saw coins tossed into toll buckets. And we took the bus to Washington, DC, a city I found as ominous, oppressive, and cold then as I do more than fifty years later. In Washington we were installed in the colorless and grim Washington Hotel, whose rooftop restaurant peered over the U.S. Treasury. Our Washington guide was Ernest's thirty-eight-year-old Frankfurt-born nephew, William. William never married, but every Saturday night from 1950 until their dotage in the late 2010s, he and his girlfriend, Lucy—who worked at the Library of Congress—went out for dinner, the movies, theater, or ballet. William worked for the CIA—although in what capacity was never entirely clear because he would constantly impart whispered "secrets" that should not have been imparted, including his tale of being parachuted into Chechnya in his late seventies. It was all very charming and all very improbable.

The bottom line was that I was in love with New York. I was in love with America. It wasn't a love born from need, or based on some Third World yearning for democracy—because political freedom, at least, I had in London. Indeed, I had it in greater quantities in Britain, a country where there was no anti-Communist paranoia, no fallout shelters, no huddling beneath desks during air raid drills. No, my love of America was based largely on several esoteric bits of ephemera. One was materialistic: I was enamored of the sense of lavishness, by the abundance, by the plenty. Another was that being Jewish was not, it seemed to me, a disadvantage: Rose Marie on the *Dick Van Dyke Show* had, after all, mentioned Rosh Hashana on television. Third was Esmé, a glamorous, feminine version of

Pa, whose mother had died twenty years before I was born, whom nobody could accuse me of killing. And fourth was Terry, whom I worshipped. And I loved how everyone adored my accent. I didn't want to leave.

Esmé was aghast when she learned we were sailing home in tourist class on the *Queen Elizabeth*. "Nobody sails tourist class," she insisted with a dogmatic wave of the hands. "You have to travel cabin class." Pa's request for the least expensive cabin with a private bathroom had condemned us, it appeared, to a voyage home in steerage. I am not sure my parents were particularly perturbed. Indeed, I imagine Ma—who thrived on "making do" and had not the slightest acquaintanceship with the state of her husband's finances—accepted it with a sort of pride in his prudence and the sniff of delicate martyrdom that was her forte. The day on which we were to sail from New York was August 28, 1963. Two hundred miles to the south, hundreds of thousands of Americans were gathering in Washington for the march on the capital led by Martin Luther King Jr. at which he would proclaim that he had a dream. It was boiling hot. We held a champagne party in our cabin, attended by Ernest, Esmé, and Terry as well as two Manhattan cousins, Hedy and Walter. Ernest presented my mother with a giant orchid corsage. It turned out that our cabin was actually a cabin class stateroom, even though we would eat, be entertained, and stroll on deck in the tourist class section of the ship. Esmé was somewhat mollified.

After tearful farewells, we stood on deck as the *Queen Elizabeth*, then the world's largest ocean liner, was pushed out into the Hudson. We threw streamers at Esmé, Ernest, and Terry, and we waved until our arms were sore. The giant liner crept downstream, past the Statue of Liberty, under the cables of what would shortly become the Verrazzano-Narrows Bridge, and out into the Atlantic. It was a five-day crossing notable for mirror-like seas and our clambering up and down endless staircases to reach the dining room, the lounges, the bar, and the tiny patches of deck allotted to tourist class passengers. While the layout of the *Queen Elizabeth's* first and cabin class public spaces were horizontal and gracious, tourist class was a vertical arrangement crammed into the aft of the ship atop the propellers. The cuisine was British boardinghouse and the entertainment limited to nightly rounds of bingo and the conga. Movies were screened every afternoon in the library, the projector standing atop a wobbly table. My mother left the evening gowns, and my father the tuxedo, in the luggage.

Back in London, I aped everything American. At times, I even affected a few mild vowel changes in an effort to appear more exotic, more transatlantic, and less definable. It must have been extremely annoying.

On a Friday night four months after our return, my parents went out for dinner with friends, and I snuggled on my bed with Teetoe the cat to watch one of my favorite TV programs. Suddenly, there was a blank screen, then the BBC newsroom. I was momentarily livid that my favorite show had paused, then a somber-faced news anchor announced a report from Dallas that President Kennedy had been shot. Fifteen minutes later, he announced that the president had died. Some minutes later, the anchor returned with the bulletin that Jackie Kennedy and a new president were flying back to Washington on Air Force One with the dead president's body.

I sat spellbound, horror struck, disbelieving. I watched the pictures of the Washington I had just visited. I watched interviews with New Yorkers sobbing in the streets. Nothing would ever be the same again. This had been the American president with whom the whole world was besotted. It was a few weeks later that the Port Authority of New York and New Jersey announced that the Idlewild Airport at which I had landed 150 days earlier was to be renamed JFK.

1964

Because theater and travel had become my two escape valves, I look back at my teenage years and see a progression of trips interspersed with theatrical landmarks. There was the euphoria of seeing Noël Coward's *Hay Fever* at the National Theatre in a production directed by the playwright "Himself." It starred *Brief Encounter*'s Celia Johnson plus a collection of young unknowns named Maggie Smith, Robert Stephens, Derek Jacobi, and Lynn Redgrave. Describing the production with his customary wit, Coward said, "I am thrilled and flattered and frankly a little flabbergasted that the National Theatre should have had the curious perceptiveness to choose a very early play of mine and to give it a cast that could play the Albanian telephone directory."

Next, there was my friend Stephen and I standing for more than an hour in the teeming rain outside the stage door of the Piccadilly Theatre waiting for a surly Barbra Streisand to deign to autograph our playbills after a performance of *Funny Girl*. And a year earlier, after a long wait at the stage door of Drury Lane following one of the first performances of the London production of *Hello, Dolly!*, whoops of glee heralded the arrival of Mary Martin shrouded in white mink, who graciously signed our playbills and embraced us.

Insignificant are the successes at school, the news, and almost all the political developments save the imposition of currency restrictions in 1964, and the Six-Day War of 1967. Even my first encounters with sex seem to pale into insignificance—from the fumblings in parked cars on Hampstead Heath, to a sweaty and impossibly exciting one-afternoon stand with a Brazilian student in a bedsit in South Kensington (Biff Vokins's lecture had made no mention whatsoever of fellatio), to the formal loss of my virginity during a weekend arranged specifically for that purpose at the stately Grand Hotel in Folkestone. No, what remains at the forefront of my recall is where I went when and when I went where. The summer of 1964 was Israel; Christmas 1964 was New York; 1965 was the Italian Riviera; 1966 was skiing in Austria, then Israel again; 1967 was Israel; 1968 was Israel; 1969 was Amsterdam, Barcelona, Frankfurt, and Paris.

There was a new facet to many of those trips. Even more momentous in recollection than my first sexual intercourse when I was nineteen was my first flight alone in the summer of 1964. I was fourteen. I flew to Israel to stay with Anthony, Ariela, and my new baby nephew, Ilan, born that April. It was an El Al flight. There was something devastatingly grown-up about making the journey alone. I didn't look fourteen—I was already six feet tall. I was issued my first passport, and I gaze from it like an innocent small boy, years away from shaving. Yet I seemed to carry myself with a maturity borne of living in a home with two adults who treated me in too many ways as their equal. I was seated in a center seat in the back row of the aircraft in those days when smoking was not only permitted on planes, but planes were not even separated into smoking and nonsmoking sections. It was a Boeing 720, a rather charming slightly shorter version of the 707, notable for a ceiling that combined giant oval lights with a cut-out network of stars so that at night the interior of the plane took on the spectrum of a starlit sky.

I spent six weeks in Israel, alternating between Anthony and Ariela's apartment in the Jerusalem neighborhood of Bak'a and Ariela's parents' house near Tel Aviv. I learned faulting Hebrew from Ariela's younger brother, Naftali, and sister, Chaya, with both of whom I played not infrequent and explicit games of "doctor." We camped overnight at the Dead Sea, we climbed up to the freshwater pools where David hid from the wrath of Saul, and we didn't visit Masada because it was not yet open to the public: 1964 and 1965 were the years of the great archaeological excavation that was to reveal many of the mountain's secrets. I rode the bus all over Jerusalem to visit Anthony at his office, the bus route skirting the giant barbed-wire-crowned barrier that separated Jerusalem, Israel, from Jerusalem, Jordan.

A friend of Anthony's, Yona, ran a travel agency. I would visit her office regularly, climbing winding stairs to the second floor of a seedy commercial building in the heart of Jerusalem. I would collect timetables and schedules, admire the posters, and breathe in the travel atmosphere. I was an absolute pest. About halfway through my stay in Israel, I determined that to fly back to London on the same airline and the same kind of plane would be a totally boring thing to do. And in that era when a plane ticket was valid for any airline, I plagued Yona into changing my reservation home. But first I researched which airline would enable me to have the most interesting journey, and I eventually plumped for a connection with Swissair that would have me fly from Tel Aviv to Zurich aboard one of its spanking new Convair Coronado 990 jets, and then from Zurich to London on a Caravelle. By making the change, I would add a new name to my list of airlines flown, two new names to my list of aircraft flown, plus a new airport. Wow. Yona indulged me—and that was indeed how I flew back to London.

My parents had been meant to meet me in Israel that August, but instead they decided to spend two weeks at a small resort called Spotorno, on the Italian Riviera. Here, the argument went, Ma, who had undergone foot surgery that spring, could aid her recovery by swimming daily in the warm Mediterranean. My parents often made bizarre choices and here was yet another. They had chosen not to attend Anthony's wedding in the summer of 1961 because, they argued, they would be unable to spend sufficient time with him because of the preparations and the honeymoon: thus, they elected to visit Israel five months later. Similarly, neither of them had flown to Israel when their first grandchild was born, and now, apparently because my brother had been lax in writing to them, they chose to travel to Italy instead. I suppose it was—in twenty-first-century parlance—all about them. I thought I understood their argument; in retrospect, their decisions were narcissistic and close to appalling. And if healing Ma's foot was the issue, Israel also shared the very same warm Mediterranean.

That Christmas, my parents finally decided to fly to Israel to meet their grandson, now eight months old. These were heady times, and this indulged teenager decided he didn't want to go back to Israel after just four months and boldly suggested he go to New York instead. Incredibly my parents agreed. This time, TWA was added to my log as well as my first movie aboard a plane—indeed, I chose TWA because it was the only airline offering this innovation; the movies turned out to be projected on a screen about

176 rows in front of mine and the headphones were agony. In New York, I saw my first Broadway show—*High Spirits*, the musical version of Noël Coward's *Blithe Spirit*. Its star was Beatrice Lillie, an Anglo-Canadian aristocrat who became a comedy star in the 1920s. By 1964 she was still brilliant yet a trifle addled (she would later lapse into dementia), but it didn't matter as the role of Madame Arcati required a large measure of dottiness. Her costars were British actor Edward Woodward (Noël Coward said his name "sounded like a fart in the bath"), and Canadian Tammy Grimes as the returned-from-the-dead Elvira, who stopped the show with a vamp-and-shimmy-filled "Home Sweet Heaven." A Broadway show seemed so much more glamorous and electric than London theater. And playbills were given out for free.

My parents would return to Spotorno the next summer, along with me, and with their friends David and Vanessa and their daughter, Clara, who was my age and to whom I was very close. Vanessa was terrified of flying, and before we boarded the British United Airways BAC 1-11 jet at déclassé Gatwick Airport to fly to Genoa, she needed to be loaded with whiskey. We stayed two weeks at the beachfront Palace and Grand Hotel, a turn-of-the-twentieth-century moderately palatial, moderately grand hotel, where we ate all our meals in the regal dining room. Days were spent on the pebbly beach and in the warm Mediterranean. After dinner, evenings were spent strolling into the village to eat ice cream and watermelon (to a Londoner of 1964, highly exotic), or in the hotel's outdoor garden bar—where a band played Europop. Guests danced; Pa, David, and Vanessa got shitfaced while my virtually teetotal mother looked on with acidity; and Clara flirted with waiters, a project resulting in her losing her virginity to the dining room's middle-aged maître d' in a compartment within the servants' dormitory.

And so it would go on, year after year: a new airline, a new country, a new plane. Just as I would one day come to divine that the clients I encountered at the counter at Thomas Cook on Fifth Avenue were unconsciously more interested in having been places than in actually going to them, I wanted to have been to as many countries and cities, to have flown on as many aircraft and airlines, to have slumbered in as many hotels—as would expand my already burgeoning and compulsively compiled logbooks.

1968

I wrote earlier of my glorious 1935 Air France poster for its flights from Marseille to Algiers (see page 127). It was in July 1968 that the world of travel was transformed forever when another plane touched down at the airport of Algiers. A group of armed men had taken over an El Al Boeing 707 after it had taken off from Rome for Tel Aviv. At gunpoint, they forced the captain to fly to Algiers, where on arrival they demanded Israel release Arab prisoners held in Israeli jails; in exchange, they would release the passengers. Five weeks of negotiations ensued, prisoners were ultimately released, the passengers were ultimately flown back to Rome, and—many weeks later—the plane was released too. Even though the hijacking of planes from Cuba had been taking place for some years, those incidents were invariably masterminded by passionate asylum seekers or crackpots. The El Al Algiers diversion was the first political hijacking planned by armed terrorists. In its wake, El Al determined that it would be its last, and ever since, no El Al plane has been successfully hijacked. It would be another twenty years, after my New York friends elected not to fly over Lockerbie, before the airlines of the world would beg El Al to teach them how to keep their airlines safe.

A few weeks after that first and only El Al hijacking, I enrolled in the Hebrew University of Jerusalem. I had graduated that summer from the City of London School with A-Level passes in French and German—and I went to Jerusalem for a year's study at Israel's leading university before ostensibly returning to university in England.

None of this was really what I had wanted to do. When I was eleven, I started taking ballet lessons on Saturday mornings at the Arts Educational School, an institution that occupied a rather ragged, once aristocratic six-story mansion overlooking Hyde Park Corner. The building would eventually be torn down and replaced by the hideous stressed concrete London Intercontinental Hotel. I was a very good dancer. It helped that I was almost six feet tall, slender, and enormously lithe, and my teacher told Ma that if I kept at it, my career could be extraordinary. Yet I didn't like being the only boy in the class, nor did I particularly enjoy the endless repetition of exercises. I wanted to fling myself around the studio according to my own choreography. I wanted to devise my own modern dance steps. I didn't want to conform to rote, nor did I want to perform endless thigh-aching pliés. Eventually, the ballet lessons, which coincided with puberty, were stopped by my father because, he suspected, it might turn me queer. I weep every time I see *Billy Elliot*.

Instead, it was decided that I would take up judo at night classes held in a church hall in Hampstead. On the first evening, I was thrown to the floor by my sparring partner, who jumped around with enthusiasm, exclaiming how super it all was. I thought it was contemptible and never went back. Next came fencing, a sport I started to undertake at school when I could no longer bear the coarseness of rugby. Fencing involved the donning of fencing garb, endless sadistic exercises, and performing hundreds of lunges until my thighs screamed with agony. But I put up with it for a year or so. I even became marginally good at it.

In addition to the mansion overlooking Hyde Park Corner, the Arts Educational School ran an arts boarding school in Tring, not very far from London, in the county of Hertfordshire. I studied the brochures and, when I was about fourteen or fifteen, decided that I wanted to leave the odious City of London School and enroll there, where I would learn acting, singing, dancing, directing, and scenic design.

Why I chose to discuss this with my father rather than my mother, I will ever never know. Perhaps I believed that if I could persuade him, she would be a pushover. I chose to raise the subject one day in the car when Pa was driving me home from school. Our journey home involved a route that would excite the most jaundiced tourist—along the Thames Embankment, through Trafalgar Square and Admiralty Arch, down the Mall to Buckingham Palace, through Green Park to Hyde Park Corner. I was making my argument to Pa about my school plans when, near Wellington Arch, a policeman raised his hand to stop our car and all those behind us. The Queen and the Duke of Edinburgh were returning from a state visit to Ethiopia and her car was due to cross in front of us as she returned to Buckingham Palace. As Her Majesty's Rolls-Royce approached at a glacial pace, Pa emerged from our car, stood erect, removed his hat, and bowed his head in deference. It was fabulously archaic and fabulously moving.

He got back in the car and brought our conversation about schools to a close. "No," he said, "you don't want to do that." And there my theatrical career came to a juddering halt. My malleability was epic. I was committed, in every sense of the word, to remain on at the City of London School.

Pa was adamant about what he did not want for me—but utterly lacking in inspiration about what he did want, with one exception. Perhaps it had to do with his own mangled education that had been so horribly mismanaged by his parents, a charming and charismatic couple too immersed in their own pursuits to devote more than cursory attention to their only son's schooling. At one point, I assumed they were curiously abnormal, but they weren't; ignoring one's children's needs and happiness was endemic, it seems, a condition brought home to me by reading of Winston Churchill's youth and education a few decades earlier, his needs brazenly ignored by his illustrious and syphilitic father, Sir Randolph Churchill, and his phenomenally attractive and man-obsessed American mother, Jennie Jerome.

Pa attended Ascot House, a preparatory school in Brighton, until he was fifteen, and was then sent to the same City of London School that Anthony and I were later to attend. Except it wasn't the same school. After the first week, his mother found the time between playing cards and visiting music halls to ask him how he was faring, and he responded that it was fine, "except that all we seem to do is learn to type." She had signed him up for the City of London Secretarial College. He appeared to have no idea how the mistake could have been made, and why it was never corrected, nor did he seem particularly aggrieved. Thus, at sixteen, Pa was withdrawn from formal education; his father took over the planning of his career by pressing overseas business colleagues to take Pa on as an apprentice, so that he could then return to London and join him in his business of selling imported paint and bicycles. Pa was sent to Arnhem in Holland for nine months to learn Dutch and to work in a bicycle factory, and then for a further nine months in another bicycle factory in Villingen, Germany, where he perfected his German and would visit his aunts, uncles, and cousins in nearby Kippenheim. Thus, Pa's chief recommendation for my further education was that I too be sent for six- to twelve-month periods to France and Germany to perfect my command of the languages.

Ma's education was more formal and given greater concentration— not by her parents but by her Anglo-Moroccan grandfather, who footed the bill. After her arrival in England in 1918 at the age of nine, she was sent to Mrs. Nijmegen's Preparatory School in Kew, an academy that concentrated more on the teaching of cross-stitch, petit point, and overall poise than on the three Rs. The pupils would spend an hour a day perfecting their deportment by strutting around the school with books balanced on their heads and taking daily walks to admire Kew Gardens. At thirteen, Ma was sent to Brighton, to Mansfield College, a boarding school for the children (or in her case, grandchildren) of Britain's wealthiest Jews; she would tell me often that it was more expensive than Roedean, considered the Eton of British girls' schools. The education was good and she made friends that would be with her all her life, including my godmother Hilda, Alicia

Marks (who would go on to become the ballerina Alica Markova), and Esmé—who, at a weekend at the family beachhouse in Shoreham, would introduce my mother to her brother, Bernard, my Dad.

It was never for a moment expected or encouraged that either of my parents would go on to a university. Yet, despite their unusual—and, in Pa's case, criminally foreshortened—educations, they both managed somehow to turn out cultured and worldly. They read voraciously. They succeeded in exhibiting a veneer of learning and a sense of both knowledge and class that belied their fantastically neglected schooling.

Other than working overseas and perfecting my languages, Pa had few suggestions about what I should do after graduation from high school, but my mother wanted me to go to university. Yet her ambitions on my behalf had little to do with academics and everything to do with her belief that university would be wonderful for my social life. She saw me, I fancy, in a college cap and scarf, performing in Gilbert and Sullivan operettas and punting down the River Cam with my patrician friends. I was rescued by neighbors whose daughter Aviva was graduating the same summer as I and was going to the Hebrew University in Jerusalem for a one-year foreign students' course in Jewish and Israeli studies. I leapt at the idea, as did my girlfriend of the moment, Leslie Kaufmann.

1968

Pa was devastated by my departure for Jerusalem. Even though I wasn't "his *real* son," he adored me, he adored my company, and, in retrospect, I think he was not ready to remain home alone with my mother. As the day of our departure neared, the atmosphere in the apartment took on an increasingly gloomy timbre and the hour at which my father would extract the bottle of scotch from the dining room liquor cabinet moved gradually from noon, to eleven thirty, to eleven, to ten thirty, to ten. Leslie, Aviva, and I left for Israel three days before that El Al flight was hijacked to Algeria, and I will never forget the look of grief on my father's face as he hugged me good-bye. Our journey was a complicated one, the result of Aviva's father's search for the most economical student fare. We took a British European Airways flight to Brussels, and then connected to Sabena, the Belgian airline, to continue via Vienna to Tel Aviv.

Our new home was the Hebrew University's student dorm in the suburb of Kiryat Yovel. Leslie and Aviva shared a room with a third girl—

Sharon, who had come to Israel from Manchester and endeared me with her Lancashire accent. I was housed in an adjacent building, in a room for two. My roommate—who was also enrolled in the same one-year program as we—was Henning Weiss from Copenhagen. His English was as good as mine with the merest hint of an accent. He was extremely good looking and when he wasn't sitting on his bed naked, clipping his toenails or writing letters, he wore ridiculously short shorts that were at least a size too small so that everything they contained appeared to be magnified—an affectation his frequent nudity affirmed was, to put it delicately, extravagantly redundant. He was followed around by a string of the course's most attractive girls, and I would return to my room with regularity to find the door locked. Henning was my age, and yet his handsomeness, liberated Scandinavian sexuality, self-confidence, and presumed prowess in the bedroom accentuated my feelings of being an adolescent disaster.

Our initial two-month course was designed to improve our Hebrew. In addition to several Scandinavians, several dozen assorted "continentals," and about fifteen students from England, almost the entire makeup of our course was all-American. Because the Israeli (and British and European) school systems were considered superior to those of the United States, American students needed to have completed two years of college to be considered our academic equals; hence, they were older and more seasoned than we Europeans.

Every morning—except Saturdays—we took a city bus to the campus, where, divided into groups according to our existing Hebrew prowess, we toiled at mastering the language that a mere seventy-five years before had been reserved exclusively for prayer. I was assigned to an intermediate class, less advanced than Aviva, more advanced than Leslie, Sharon of Manchester, and Henning of Copenhagen. Our teacher, Sarah Eynor, was an elegant woman whose husband had served as Israel's ambassador in Senegal. Her teaching of Hebrew grammar was innovative and thorough. She corrected our Hebrew handwriting, instructing us in the correct direction for forming every letter—because, it seemed, most of us wrote Hebrew letters with the mindset of the left-to-right Latin alphabet. She taught us to think like a Levantine; to write from right to left as if we were born to it.

It was now August 1968. That spring in Prague—"Prague Spring," as history would come to term it—a vast freedom movement came to the surface as Czechoslovakia attempted to detach itself from Soviet domination.

On August 20, Soviet tanks rolled into Prague and the budding attempt to find freedom was extinguished that Prague Summer. We demonstrated against the USSR on campus. Czech flags flew from the flagpoles. We sat on the lawn and sang "Kumbaya" and "We Shall Overcome." It was a summer of protest—particularly for the American students: August 1968 was also the month of the apocalyptic Democratic National Convention in Chicago.

At the end of the month, my entire class was invited by our classmate Salwa to her sister's wedding. Salwa lived in Bethlehem. A year before, Arab Bethlehem had passed from Jordanian to Israel's control in the Six-Day War, viewed as a positive step by the Christian Arabs of the town where Jesus was born in a manger. Hence, Salwa had registered for the Hebrew University.

On the day of the wedding, I barely recognized my classmates. Gone were the shorts, T-shirts, sneakers, and backpacks. Long pants, crisp white shirts, silk dresses, clutch purses, and high heels had been hauled out of suitcases and irons had been pressed into service. Hair had been set in rollers and blown dry. We cleaned up well. We rode the bus to Bethlehem, disembarking just beyond Rachel's Tomb at a large elegant house of pinkish Jerusalem stone. We brought gifts. We were treated as honored guests and plied with endless courses of food. We returned to Jerusalem drunk, sated, and warmed. It was a brief and naive moment in time when peace in the Holy Land seemed actually possible.

1968

Aviva and Sharon leapt into the new adventure with gusto. Leslie hated everything, and her disaffection began to infect me. She and I had been dating for more than a year in London. She had a troubled relationship with her parents, and an equally tortuous relationship with me. In that era—in England, certainly—when "going all the way" was unimaginable, we had spent months going to movies, going to the theater, performing in youth group performances; and we had spent hours parked in one of my parents' cars engaged in fervent sex that involved everything but actual penetration. Mostly, however, we engaged in tormented and convoluted psychotherapy sessions whereby we examined every nuance of our feelings and our relationship. As if in analysis, she would free-associate her doubts and misgivings about everything in a paroxysm of tears, anguish, and neurosis that could rarely be palliated. We called these sessions "traumas," which is exactly how each one of them felt. Once in Israel, away from her family structure, and clobbered by the sweltering Jerusalem heat in our un-airconditioned dorm rooms, Leslie became more and more unhinged. She was joyless, homesick, fretful, and unbalanced. It was torture, because no words, no thoughts, no idea would calm her negativity or her pain. Leslie was, in fact, descending into agonizing mental illness that—a half century later—continues to beset her.

On September 1, she fled home to London. Her departure both upset and relieved me. It was as if a giant weight had been lifted. I was suddenly released from the agonies of a liaison that was coming close to destroying me too. With Leslie gone, I began to strengthen my bonds in the dorm. I made friends. I ate pizza with the Americans. I sat on beds and listened to the LP of *The Graduate* with which the American students were obsessed. I sat in the lounge waiting for Henning to finish fucking. I wrote letters on my portable typewriter. I invited friends to my dorm room to listen to my oddly eclectic collection of records.

Two weeks after Leslie's departure, I participated in a sightseeing tour to Bethlehem organized by the university. We saw nothing I hadn't seen a dozen times before—Shepherds' Fields, the Basilica of the Nativity, Manger Square—but it was the group camaraderie I sought. Twenty-four hours later, on a weekend when, thankfully, Henning had left for Tel Aviv to celebrate Shabbat with relatives, I started to experience sweats and stomach cramps that quickly turned into an all-night bout of simultaneous diarrhea and vomiting—in itself a logistical nightmare. Much of the dorm was empty as many students were away, and I didn't have the strength to climb down to the lobby to the pay phone to call Anthony. Eventually the dorm mother summoned a doctor, who diagnosed amoebic dysentery that I (still possessed of the family requirement of blaming illness on a concrete happenstance) immediately linked to the falafel I had bought from a street stall in Bethlehem.

I lost ten pounds in five days and even though Anthony and Ariela eventually were called and came to visit and express concern, I felt weak, bereft, abandoned, and alone. I began to miss my parents. I began to detest the dorm's public showers and their row of toilets with their dysentery memories. I began to be not merely discomfited by but unremittingly jealous of Henning's beauty and rampant sexuality. I began to dislike the whole shebang and to believe that dorm life—and certainly dorm life in Israel—

was not for me. A few weeks later, my parents came to visit and I decided—with not the slightest hint of discouragement from Pa—to cut and run. Anthony was silently and acidly livid but my mind was made up. I had arrived in Israel on July 20, and on October 20, seventy-two days before my nineteenth birthday, I boarded a BOAC VC-10 with my parents and my seven pieces of luggage and flew back to London.

It was the fall of 1968. Most of the Western world's late teens were wearing their hair to their shoulders, backpacking through Morocco, taking buses to India, smoking cartons' worth of marijuana, dropping acid, singing Hare Krishna, or demonstrating against the war in Vietnam. It neither occurred nor appealed to me to join them, or simply to pause and do nothing for a while. Certainly, the specter of backpacking held little thrall, as did the specter of youth hostels or camping or the kind of expedition that might involve sleeping in an establishment where the sheets were changed less than daily. Pa had (thankfully) bribed me not to smoke, I didn't see the point in drugs, I thought long hair looked grubby, and I was altogether disenchanted with a mode of living that was anything other than what I considered "adult." Perversely, perhaps, I saw my parents' generation—rather than the teenagers whose rebellion or joint smoking were de rigueur—as my peers. I suppose much of the explanation is that to have signed on to the ubiquitous inclination to rebel would have been to risk the wrath of my mother—for I remained steadfastly engaged in surging atonement. And finally, it was with a nauseating measure of naivete that I could not bring myself to accept that the America of the curved Formica kitchen counters and Princess phones might have purposefully enmeshed itself into a cynical war both unwinnable and spurious. (It would take another war, thirty-five years later, to bring me furiously to that realization.)

So it was that within ten days of my return from Jerusalem, I found myself seated in a dour room at Lloyds of London opposite a dour man who peered over his rimless glasses at a curriculum vitae that was neither long nor particularly distinguished. He asked me listless questions with dubious enthusiasm and when his eye fell upon the Hebrew University, there was the merest suggestion of a grimace. The interview continued lethargically. I reacted with neither shock nor disappointment when a thin buff envelope arrived a week later bearing a form letter whose crookedly mimeographed words regretted that my services were not required by Lloyds at the current moment in time.

The entrée to Lloyds had been masterminded by my godmother, Hilda, who worked at an employment agency, and upon hearing of Lloyds' expression of disinterest, she set about looking for additional opportunities. I asked her to wait awhile.

In the spring of 1965, I had accompanied Pa to the head offices of Thomas Cook in Berkeley Street, where the arrangements for our two weeks in Spotorno were made by a supercilious clerk who, with patronizing punctiliousness, demanded that Pa bring our passports for his inspection to ensure they were valid. Yet, despite our irritation with the travel clerk, our travel arrangements were effected flawlessly, and what had remained was the memory of the grandeur of the booking hall in which this clerk labored. It was a vast oak-paneled expanse, two stories or more in height that occupied an area literally the size of an entire New York City block. There was a huge square central counter of polished oak manned by dozens of clerks who bestirred themselves purely for those seeking European travel. Similarly imposing counters were devoted to travel solely within the British Isles, and others for travel "overseas." To the side was a vast banking area for the sale of foreign currencies and travelers' checks. At the opposite side, a series of giant oak desks that sat behind a wooden balustrade was the kingdom of additional clerks who saw to the needs of an elite that didn't stand at counters. Appended to high walls and columns, oak-framed travel posters hung everywhere—each more tasteless than the other. The late 1960s were the last gasp of the travel poster's heyday, as cheesy contemporary typefaces clashed with cheesy color photography in a vain effort to continue alluring travelers by means of what had devolved into a hackneyed form of marketing.

Yet that enormous booking hall continued to hold a thrall in my recollections, and so down I sat at my Bar Mitzvah typewriter and composed a letter to the staff manager, c/o Cook's. I have no memory of what I wrote, but within less than a week, I was seated in another dreary office off a dreary corridor that overlooked the interior well of 45 Berkeley Street, and after a short conversation with an exceptionally dreary gentleman, I was hired as a trainee. I recall being elated. What I didn't realize at the time—not that it would have made a difference—was that after World War II, Cook's had come under the control of the newly nationalized British Railways and was, effectively, akin to a minor branch of the civil service—hence the dreariness, hence the unremarkable lack of refinement or intellect of most of those shortly to become my colleagues.

Yet it mattered not at all to me. On my first day—December 2, 1968—
I learned that I was assigned to Cook's Autotravel Department, whose staff
of about thirty were engaged solely in the confection of travel arrangements for English families taking their own cars across the Channel on
motoring holidays throughout the Continent. Somehow, without an inkling
of my years of weekend bath times planning continental car trips with my
father, some cipher in the personnel department had plunked me down at a
desk in an area of the business in which I had been engaged as an amateur
for approximately 70 percent of my close-to-nineteen-year life. The largest
section of the department made hotel reservations, but the area to which
I was consigned had to do with the reserving of space for travelers' cars
on cross-channel ferry boats. To say this required little brainpower would
be to put it mildly—yet it was an activity that was so thrilling that I didn't
mind in the least. Within two weeks it was realized that I could take
on weightier challenges—and I was switched to the section that planned
routes, where I marked driving directions on blank maps and amassed
appropriate Michelin and Hallwag maps for each passenger's use. It was as
if I was flung into a time machine back to the Sunday mornings with Pa,
planning routes as we bathed, and once dried, inspecting the map drawer.

Autotravel was staffed by a diverse collection of people aged from sixteen to sixty-five, several of whom were enmeshed in torrid affairs with
others, invariably older married men with younger single women. Married
Frank, the "chief clerk," was sleeping with Christine; married Jerry was
sleeping with Nina; and all four of them assumed none of us knew. Pete
would sing impossibly vulgar drinking songs with lyrics that referred to
cunts and bollocks and wanking. Alan and Derek would each make shud-
dering puns; Mike would pity me because I was Jewish and had therefore
suffered the removal of my foreskin. Ron, from Malta, would walk daily to
Soho and return with a baguette and slices of odiferous salami and cheese
that he consumed at his desk. Maria's entire life was devoted to eight hours
a day typing identical itinerary forms on a manual typewriter amid dreams
of wedding plans. Nick would endlessly quote, "If music be the food of
love . . . I'll have a roasted violin," or versions thereof. Eileen—sixty, single,
and refined—detected my similar level of refinement and taught me the
intricacies of map drawing. A second Maria, from Spain, was assigned to
the task of shrieking on the telephone at the reception clerks of Iberian
hotels that had not responded to telexes (I was put to a similar task where
a facility with French or German was required). Yolanda—fifty, with an

impenetrable Italian accent and a cardigan balanced over her shoulders—
tottered on high heels and oversaw Maria #1 and Eileen. Michelle—the
youngest member of the staff, with a cockney accent, shaved eyebrows,
long legs, and miniskirts that barely concealed her pubis—made deliveries
around the building, and, twice a day, marched atop platform shoes the
length of the department bringing a cup of tea and a biscuit to the office
of the manager, John Martini. The tea was obtained from a drone whose
11 a.m. and 3 p.m. task was to trundle a vast metal tea trolley from department to department. And last, but by no means least, was Brian, thirty-five
and single, the keeper of the maps, a rather well-meaning yet unsurprisingly lonely man who sat adjacent to the map safe and morosely func-
tioned within a fog redolent of unwashed socks, underpants and armpits,
and seldom-brushed teeth. He chatted lengthily with himself and devoted
untold hours to the excavation of his nostrils and the extraction, inspection,
and ingestion of his discoveries.

Yet I loved the work. Indeed, booking hotels, looking at maps, planning
routes, chatting to hoteliers on the phone in French and German was not
work; it was playtime. For most of my colleagues, the work was drudg-
ery at worst, but for me it was bath time with Pa. This was the work for
which I had been in training since the age of five. "Where the fuck can
these fucking people stay overnight if they're driving from fucking Basel
to fucking Venice?" Pete-with-the-toilet-mouth would yell with frustration. And because I was a "junior," and Jewish, and didn't want to come
across as overly smart, I would surreptitiously sidle up to him and whisper,
"Try Lugano . . ." "Whoah, fanks Geoff!" he would boom with cockney
wonderment.

And there were toys. In the decade before computers, copying machines,
faxes, calculators, and—in the Autotravel department—even typewriters
that were attached to an electric current, a whole section of a lower floor
was devoted to the compilation of vast manuals that contained Cook's
own critiques and gradings of European hotels, manuals that I would read
and study till my eyes were sore. And deep in the bowels of the building was the massive catalog room, where brochures of every hotel in the
world were stored. Nina—a devotée not only of the married Jerry but also
of hotels—and I would spend hours poring through the manuals in search
of the hotels graded "LX," and we would summon their brochures from the
catalog room to spend further hours "learning" their contents and admiring their four-color opulence.

1969

Now that I was back in London, Leslie and I resumed our tortured courtship. She had begun work at an advertising agency near Grosvenor Square, an occupation she deemed superior to my employment at Cook's, which she regarded with undisguised disdain. By the spring of 1969, we came to realize that our multiple everything-but-penetration Saturday night sessions on the floor and back seat of my mother's Morris 1100 were insufficient for our needs, and we embarked on the epic planning of our formal introduction to "going-all-the-way," as the first actual fuck was still termed in that distant epoch. Before I had left for Israel, Pa had come up with the colorful proposition that he should take me to Paris for a weekend, where he would engage a prostitute who would initiate me, but the plan had thankfully seemed to wither.

Curiously, it was Leslie, not I, who proposed that our mutual deflowering be performed in the vaguely sumptuous Edwardian confines of the Grand Hotel in Folkestone rather than in the back seat of a car or furtively at her or my home when our parents were out. Indeed, I cherish the memory of my affair with Leslie if for no other reason than for so elegant a plan. A half century later, Grand Hotel remains a turn-of-the-twentieth-century pile atop the chalk cliffs at Folkestone, a stone's throw from Dover, built to accommodate both genteel Edwardian vacationers and genteel Edwardian travelers about to board the ferry to France.

Folkestone was a three-hour drive from London. We roared up the circular gravel drive, and Leslie and I, each with our own small suitcase, entered a soaring lobby whose fin-de-siècle proportions, aspidistras, Turkish carpets, and aroma brought back memories of the Metropole in Brighton. And, because it was still that cusp of time when it remained unthinkable for unmarried people—especially those aged nineteen, for heaven's sake—to stay at so august an establishment as a couple, we registered for the two single bedrooms without private bathrooms I had reserved by telephone.

To describe it as somewhat less than an idyllic night would be to resort to the grossest of understatement. After dinner, I snuck into Leslie's room and into her stark twin bed, and our lovemaking devolved into an agonizing half-hour assault on her hymen, a battle exacerbated by our joint ignorance of the need for artificial lubrication—yet another omission, it seems, from the lecture eight years earlier at the City of London School. As the dry condom made its attack on her virginity, Leslie, who had neither ridden a horse nor performed the splits on an Olympic cross beam, was in untold agony, an agony made worse by our fear that at any moment the general manager, or the police—alerted by her screams—would come hammering on the door. When it was done, we turned on the light to discover a sheet and undersheet and mattress literally soaked in blood, and we were to spend the next hour scrubbing, soaping, and nail-brushing the bedclothes and ourselves. As we toiled, I couldn't escape thoughts of Stravinsky's ballet *Les Noces*, which we'd both recently seen at Covent Garden, whose climax—you should pardon the expression—has the mother of the bride displaying during the wedding feast the bloodied sheet that proved her daughter's just-lost virginity. Exhausted physically and emotionally, and Leslie in continued pain, we fell asleep in each other's arms.

Thankfully, we had had the foresight to bring our passports. And in large part to take our minds off the horrors—and the disappointment—of the night, we jumped into the car after breakfast the next morning, drove the mile or so down to Folkestone Harbour, and hurled ourselves onto the first ferry for France. We both needed an escape, we both spoke French, and it seemed the ideal distraction. We stood on the deck as the ship bounced through the Channel, the wind soothing us both, the sea spray washing our faces. We spent a day in Boulogne, walking, shopping, avoiding the intermittent rain, and lunching on roast chicken and the thinnest of French fries—for Leslie, the first time she had ever eaten non-kosher meat, yet another milestone in a weekend of firsts. By the time we boarded the late-afternoon hovercraft back to England, it seemed the excursion had somehow served to salve a measure of our physical and emotional injuries.

We returned to the embrace of the Edwardian stateliness of the Grand Hotel. And over a melancholic dinner amid the hushed solemnity of the vaulted dining room, we arrived at the joint conclusion that we were loath to chance another night either of pain or detection by the management. And, unspoken though it was, it seemed we could also live without night-long cuddling. We kissed chastely and each retired to our own single rooms without bathroom, to our own severe single beds. I recall a sense of liberation both that the deed was done—and, for the moment, did not need to be repeated—and that I was serenely alone in a monastic bedroom not so very different from those I had occupied ten, twelve, and fifteen years earlier at Brighton's Metropole Hotel—a mere hundred miles to the west.

Almost fifty years later, her parents dead, her sister estranged, her income assured, Leslie lives alone—not in an apartment or a house but in an

Edwardian country-house-hotel in England's New Forest, the ancient region of Hampshire where Henry VIII was partial, between executing wives, to hunting. Leslie had become a recluse in her thirties, barely leaving her bedroom in her parents' semidetached suburban home, complaining of burning skin and suffering from demons and the tortured thoughts that cut her off from friendships and the socializing she had once enjoyed with enthusiasm. As her parents aged and agonized about her future and ultimately died, Leslie too found her ultimate solace in a hotel. She breakfasts alone; she lunches alone; she dines alone; she reads; she occasionally chats with itinerant guests who waft in and out of her adopted home. Her wit remains, but her glumness is overreaching. The hotel is her anchor.

1969

One of the perks of working at Cook's was that staff were entitled to a 75 percent discount on air tickets. Imagine, if you will, offering a cocaine addict the availability of the finest white powder at 25 percent of its street value. Welcome to my world. As Cook's was the world's largest travel agency, there was no limit to how many tickets were available, and I leapt at the opportunity. The only limit was the amount of time off granted— but if you smartly worked in vacation days, weekends and bank holidays, there were occasions aplenty. Strangely, few of my colleagues were remotely interested in taking advantage of the offering—their jobs in travel were just that: jobs. They could have been ledgering sales of halibut or arranging refrigerator deliveries as long as their meager monthly salary clanged into their bank accounts on time. But for a nineteen-year-old with an unquenchable travel obsession . . . well . . .

In May 1969, I flew with my parents, my recently bereaved American aunt Esmé and cousin Terry to Barcelona. The purpose was to visit Esmé and Pa's first cousin Richard, who had moved from Weimar Germany to Barcelona in 1922, to New Jersey after the war, and then back to Barcelona in 1960. He and his Turkish-Jewish-Spanish wife, Selma, who spoke in Ladino-laced nasal Spanglish, lived in a penthouse apartment in one of the city's wealthiest neighborhoods. Richard and Selma were in their late seventies— an age that seemed much more aged in 1969 than it is now—and lived in genteel and moneyed retirement attended by uniformed maids. We stayed at a luxurious hotel nearby; we toured in the day and ate 11 p.m. dinners with them after late-afternoon passeggiatas and drinks at sidewalk cafés. In their rooftop triplex, we ate elegant meals and stroked their extremely aged dachshund, Umberto, whose testicles were so curiously low-hung that they swept the parquet as he waddled.

The Barcelona of 1969 was not the hip, trendy, over-the-top glitzy Barcelona of today. It was rigid, correct, and Franco-fascist, and everybody observed a stultifying level of decorum. One stood rigid at traffic lights even when there was no passing traffic. To walk to the corner, one was "dressed." There was no jaywalking, no graffiti, merely stultifying rectitude and very little joy. Despite the grimness, Richard and Selma had somehow arranged for Terry and me to be invited to a rooftop party at some American educational institution where we frugged to Fleetwood Mac.

That fall came Frankfurt, again at 25 percent. I accompanied Pa on his annual pilgrimage in unadmitted search of his daughter, a pilgrimage explained by his desire to spend time with Anthony during his annual visit to the Frankfurt Book Fair. We flew to Frankfurt on a BOAC VC-10, a British-built airplane whose four jet engines seemed perilously attached to the rear of the plane, an aircraft that despite its efficiency, its state-of-the-artness, and its aim to compete with the Boeing 707 was, nevertheless, an economic disaster. We stayed at the Excelsior Hotel—a dingy hotel utterly undeserving of its name—opposite the grandiose central Frankfurt station, and for reasons I can no longer divine, while Pa and Anthony spent all day at the exhibition, I never once visited the book fair or went for a walk except to explore the murkier corners of the giant station. Instead, I spent most of my days in bed masturbating to German soap operas and eating marzipan.

Perhaps the increasing downfall of my affair with Leslie had something to do with my listlessness. Back in London, Leslie and I continued to have sex in the back of my mother's Morris 1100, an act that was performed more out of rote than excitement. Her ongoing denigration of my choice of career and her continued and unintentional insistence on being in a constant state of mental turmoil drew the affair to a close.

1970

The relationship with Leslie ended and for reasons still not entirely clear to me decades later, I took up with the micro-miniskirted, platform-heeled, shaved-eyebrowed Michelle, my coworker at Thomas Cook. What was the attraction? She had a beautiful figure, yes, and a sense of humor so ridiculous and outrageous that we spent much of our time together cramped in half, wiping away tears of laughter. She seemed to adore me, and the sex was more than satisfactory. Yet there was so much wrong, especially her accent, which was unashamedly cockney. Michelle lived in a once gorgeous terraced Georgian house in south-of-the-river Kennington—gentrified in the second decade of the twenty-first century but, in 1970, severely down-market, nudged between working-class Lambeth (as in the "walk") and even further down-market Stockwell. Her nebulously Jewish father, a law clerk at the offices of patrician barristers, oozed refinement and gentility. His favorite party piece was to read aloud at breakfast the Court Circular in the *Daily Telegraph*, detailing Her Majesty's appointments du jour in an accent even more stentorian and aristocratic than usual. Michelle's Calvinist French-Swiss-English mother also spoke with upper-class tones, yet Michelle herself—and her older brother and younger sister—spoke in a way I was taught from birth to disparage. Somehow, unaccountably, I chose to over-look it and, for even more unclear reasons, my mother also chose to ignore it as she inexplicably warmed to Michelle.

Perhaps it was easy. And, for this queerly travel-obsessed twenty-year-old, a great attraction of dating someone who worked with me at Thomas Cook was that we were both able to obtain those delicious discounted airline tickets and could and would zip away whenever possible. Not long after our relationship began, we flew on a giant Pan Am Boeing 747—two of about twelve passengers in a plane built for four hundred—from Lon-don to Frankfurt, where we enplaned for the German domestic Pan Am flight to West Berlin. We stayed near the Kurfürstendamm in a hotel called the Sylter Hof (it's still there and still awful) and toured the truncated city.

On our first full day, we took a bus tour to East Berlin. As the West Berlin bus neared Checkpoint Charlie, our escort warned us that East German soldiers would "process us," and we must take it very seriously and, heaven forbid, not be tempted to giggle. At the border, a trio of unsmiling East German soldiers boarded, sporting starchly pressed uniforms that were identical to those of the Nazis, except hammers and sickles replaced swas-tikas. They walked up the aisle, stopping at every seat to scrutinize each of us and, ominously, to read every page of our passports. Outside the bus, we spied other soldiers checking the underside of the bus with mirrors on long poles—as if anyone in their right mind would want to be smuggled *into* East Berlin. Finally "approved," the bus inched forward and we were joined by an East Berlin guide. As our East German journey began with our drive up Friedrichstrasse—the Oxford Street of prewar Berlin—it was as if we had been magically transported from Times Square to an alien city suffused with gloom, grime, oppression, and depression. Welcome to my first piercing of the Iron Curtain.

We were shown the sights of East Berlin: Alexanderplatz with its hideous TV tower, and the once noble Unter den Linden—now lined by socialist office buildings. We were taken to the Russian war memorial in Treptow and we saw the bullet-riddled Brandenburg gate, just inside the Russian side of the Berlin Wall. But what I recall most vividly was the guide's discourse as we rambled through the decrepit city, whose acme was the enlightening news that "during World War II it was the *West* Germans who had murdered six million Jews." I looked at Michelle, she looked at me, we snickered, as did other passengers, but on we drove until finally it was time to return to the West. Back to Checkpoint Charlie: the same soldiers, the same glaring into the eyes, the same studying of passports, the same mirrors underneath the bus, which at least this time would have made sense.

The next day, Michelle and I decided to venture back to East Berlin, this time on our own. We rode the West Berlin subway to the Friedrichstrasse station, at which we alighted—because, in any event, the train was not going anywhere but back to West Berlin. Within the confines of the steel-and-glass-domed station, we were ushered along the platform through a "foreigners only" concrete corridor topped with barbed wire that led to a staircase whose descent led to a vast claustrophobic chamber crammed with visitors lining up for passport inspection. This was my first encounter with the totalitarian-country passport check procedure, one meticulously designed to intimidate and strike fear. (I would later encounter the identical technique arriving in pre-1989 Warsaw, Budapest, and Moscow as well as Hanoi and Havana.) The passport clerks perched in glass booths atop stools designed to enable them to gaze with hostile, impenetrable stares downward at cowed visitors. Our uniformed becapped clerk, like his friends aboard the previous day's bus, read each page of our passports. He gazed intensely at us and ostentatiously held our passports up to compare them with our faces and then, to be sure we were sufficiently submissive, repeated the activity. It was all so menacing that one completely forgot that by international law we, as British subjects, could not be barred from visiting the Eastern sector of the city as much and as often as we desired. Eventually, after more passport reading, thumbing through binders, and furious stamping of documents, we were allowed to pass. Next, we were directed to a counter for the mandatory exchange of twenty-five West German marks into twenty-five worthless East German marks. Finally, we were free to enter the paradise known as East Berlin. Friedrichstrasse was gray. And, of course, it was drizzling. The brickwork, where it wasn't still pock-marked from the Russians' final assault on Berlin in 1945, was gray and grimy. We peered through unwashed shop windows at displays of shoddy merchandise. We strode on. Fifty yards from the station entrance, we were buttonholed by a group of twentysomething East Germans who, very politely, asked if they could swap our jeans for the polyester trousers they were wearing. Uncertain if this was some kind of trap that would end with us incarcerated in some East German Lubyanka, we shook our heads and walked on. We were accosted again with the same offer. We were too naive, too intimidated, to slink into alleyways and take off our pants—even had we been persuaded our gift of jeans was a charity or, even less likely, had we lusted for pairs of bell-bottom polyester pants or the gentlemen wearing them. On we marched to Unter den Linden, turned right, and strolled along the carless boulevard, past the Stalinesque Russian embassy, toward the Brandenburg Gate. After a few blocks, we came to a mostly empty lot to the left where a small gray building stood—called the Hotel Adlon—not more than a student dump. And it was there that the stroll ended and the concrete, tank traps, and barbed wire of the Berlin Wall began. Depressed and dour, we retraced our steps, gave our unspent twenty-five East German marks to some lounging youths, and made our way back up the stairs of the Friedrichstrasse station, back to the glaring passport Nazis, back to the S-bahn, back to the bright lights of West Berlin.

Two months earlier, I had availed myself of the Thomas Cook discount and made my first trip to America in six years. I planned it meticulously: first New York, then San Francisco, Los Angeles, New Orleans, and on to Pittsburgh—where Terry was in college—and finally back to New York. The ride to New York was aboard a spanking new TWA Boeing 747—the world's most exciting plane of the moment—with a crew so new to the aircraft that they seemed as enthused and delighted to be aboard as I was. The stay in New York was suffused with visits to Broadway shows: *Applause*, the stunning musical version of *All about Eve*, starring Lauren Bacall; *Company*, Stephen Sondheim's still impenetrable examination of sin-gledom in a world of couples; and *Two by Two*, Richard Rodgers's musical version of the story of Noah and the flood, in which Danny Kaye in a wheel-chair (he had broken his leg some weeks earlier) infuriated his fellow cast members by changing the lines, improvising, cracking up, and mugging. It was vaguely hilarious—vaguely.

I crossed the United States from Newark Airport aboard an empty United Airlines Douglas DC-8, the plane that the Boeing 707 had beat to supremacy. Its seats were wide and its oxygen mask containers were weirdly concealed not in the ceiling above one's head but secreted in a compartment adjacent to the headrest. I left from Newark's original art-moderne-meets-the-1970s terminal—the one that opened in 1939, knocking Tel Aviv's Lydda Airport from its position as the world's largest airport terminal—which still bore traces of the elegance of pre–World War II air travel, with its soaring WPA wall murals, all propellers and promise and progress. The decades had not dealt with it kindly—as Coke machines and other contemporary paraphernalia had been trucked in to sully the original clean lines.

San Francisco was an eye opener. A giant one. It was my first real traveling alone, and it was in San Francisco that I first truly discovered—although I wasn't yet able fully to identify it—that my travel obsession was indeed all about the conveyances and the hotels, and that the sightseeing obligatorily performed in the interval between arrival and departure was the price to be paid for travel passion. I dutifully took Thomas Cook bus tours to the Embarcadero, Chinatown, the Golden Gate Bridge. I rode cable cars—which was fun because these were all about actually getting from point A to point B. The hills frightened me—too steep to feel comfortable ascending, too steep to feel safe descending. And yet I never really explored the city so beloved by so many and to which thousands of peoples in search of their inner truth or sexual liberation were streaming. With my Thomas Cook 50 percent discount, I was ensconced at the gigantic and colorless San Francisco Hilton and counted the hours until my next flight.

Back aboard United, I flew to Los Angeles, where I was met at the airport by my cousin Pia, a professor of dance at UCLA, and her daughter, Vivian. Pia had been born in Kippenheim and had immigrated with her parents and younger brother, Hans, to America in 1937. Her youth was spent in New York, where she graduated with heaps of honors from the Juilliard School of Music long before its removal to Lincoln Center. Her marriage brought her to Los Angeles and divorce, and she brought up Vivian in a smallish, very California house in arty Westwood, convenient for UCLA and the LA equivalent in population to the Manhattan's Upper West Side—except with cars and palm trees instead of buses and the homeless.

She and Vivian showed me the houses on the beach in Santa Monica where Mary Pickford and Charlie Chaplin and Douglas Fairbanks had frolicked a half century earlier, and up on the cliffs, we strolled the palm-treed promenade where Pia would tell me she had watched Thomas Mann strolling and debating Arnold Schönberg. Schönberg's atonal and—to me unfathomable—music was the genre she not only comprehended but also enjoyed, and which she taught to her eager students at UCLA. Pia had a charmingly German-American accent—ungutteral and perhaps just generically continental, interlaced with the kind of haute American spoken by the ultra-educated.

Once again, the obligatory sightseeing was scheduled, including the supposed highlight—a visit to Disneyland, my first and, sadly, not last encounter with what I term Tourist Fascism, in which hordes pay vast sums to stand in endless lines in order to be channeled through 120-second experiences, some of which are, admittedly, faintly enjoyable. This was long before the princess mania and the brutal commercialization of the Disney machine; Walt had died only four years earlier, and minions remained committed to ensuring his handiwork remained closer to Tivoli than to Wall Street. Yet the Stepford smiles and regimentation were in full force—so that any attempt to waver from the regulations was met with barely disguised disapproval and an enforced return to structured behavior. Also on the schedule was Universal Studios—less fascist than Disneyland—and a peek behind the scenes of moviemaking, whose apex was a trundling tram ride through the parting of the Red Sea manufactured for the 1956 *Ten Commandments*.

Next came New Orleans—once again aboard a DC-8 (this time Delta Airlines)—with its stay at the decrepit Sheraton St. Charles, the obligatory strolls through Bourbon Street, and a tour through the city's unique above-ground cemeteries. It was also a visit to a curious bookstore where racy magazines were sold and where the young and fey manager asked if I was interested in addresses of bars. As I didn't drink alcohol and was preposterously unaware of other purposes for visiting bars, I declined his offer.

Lastly came the flights from New Orleans to Chicago and on to Pittsburgh to visit Terry, then a sophomore studying acting at Carnegie Mellon University. She met me at the airport in her shiny blue MGB and whizzed me to her pretty apartment in the leafy neighborhood of Shady Side, not far from the university and the district called Squirrel Hill, which because of its large Jewish population was affectionately known as Sqvirrrrrel Hill.

I attended classes with her with a mixture of joy and sadness—the joy because it was "theater," the sadness because this had been my dream too, a dream I allowed my father to extinguish six years earlier on a car ride home from my hated London public school. I met her classmates— Michael Pace, a gay actor and singer, who a few years later would be one of the three founders of a singing group called Gotham and who was to become godfather to my son Benjamin. And Judith Light—now an award-winning actress—who delighted me by remarking on what she termed my "perfect sense of comic timing." I basked in that compliment for days. No, actually, for years. Oh, all right, I still do.

I returned to New York from Pittsburgh, and one day I strolled into the Thomas Cook office on Fifth Avenue, the same vaulted homage to travel where this book began. I met a group of people with whom I had corresponded in my days in Autotravel. And so was sown the beginning of the germ of an idea that this temple of travel in this city of wonders was where I absolutely needed to be.

1970

And so the subsidized trips continued. Some were with Michelle—to Paris, Israel, and a large journey to Athens, Eritrea, Ethiopia, and Kenya. And some alone, including my twenty-first-birthday adventure to Israel, Bangkok, Hong Kong, Japan, Honolulu, Pittsburgh, and New York. Back in London, the affair with Michelle churned on, and she became a permanent part of my twenty-year-old life. At Thomas Cook, it was finally realized that I could do more than book hotels and car ferries, and I was promoted to the heart of the organization called the management secretariat. Here I learned the bones of what made the world's oldest travel organization tick. Decades earlier, Cook's had introduced a scheme whereby the staff were invited to come up with suggestions that, if adopted, earned the suggester the princely sum of five pounds. One of my tasks was to wade through acres of aging files and discard anything too ancient to be considered of any use. It was a Herculean task that took months, as it required my careful reading of each document in order to decide on its retention or trashing.

It was during these searches that I discovered one of the reasons for Cook's profitability. In the 1970s, everyone still used to journey around the world with traveler's checks—a form of "currency" largely in the hands of American Express and Cook's—that were the "safe" way to travel with however much money was needed for a vacation or business trip. And what I learned was that Cook's had a "float" of hundreds of millions of pounds of uncashed traveler's checks. Both Cook's and American Express encouraged travelers to keep their unused traveler's checks for their next trip rather than cashing them in—enabling both companies to live and prosper on the millions of dollars and pounds worth of cash sitting in their naive clients' dresser drawers, not to mention the further millions lost, thrown in the garbage, sunk in shipwrecks, or burned in airplane crashes.

Another discovery was even more trenchant. In the "suggestions" file, I came across a letter from an employee written, I think, in 1947. The suggestion posited that as Cook's was a worldwide concern and as travelers were always paying for hotels, meals, and shopping, they could open an account at Cook's; instead of carrying cash or even traveler's checks on their journeys, they could pay for purchases in Bombay or Buenos Aires or Birmingham by presenting a special card, and then have that sum deducted from their account back home. And, the suggester continued, if the traveler was deemed to be trustworthy, Thomas Cook could, in essence, advance the cost of purchase and he or she would be billed for such outlays. Atop this letter of suggestion was a diagonal red-ink stamp bearing the single word "REJECTED." And so not only did the suggester not receive his five-pound reward; Thomas Cook lost out on what would have been its greatest profit-maker of all time.

1971

Yet again I was promoted at Thomas Cook. I moved down the hallway to become the personal assistant to the sales manager overseeing the more than twenty-five retail Cook's offices in London. The job involved moving staff around, chatting with the branch managers, dictating letters on a Dictaphone, and—the most interesting part of all—doling out to the staff of the various retail stores hundreds of free trips offered by airline and shipping companies to familiarize Cook's staff with their services. I was even permitted to nab some for myself. One was an overnight crossing from Cherbourg to Southampton on the *Queen Elizabeth 2*; another was a day trip on the new Lockheed 1011 TriStar from Luton to Amsterdam and back: this was a fabulous eight-hour adventure—the plane felt so new it seemed to be space-age. And it was so casual and confident that we were all strolling around the cabin sipping champagne not only during the flight but also during takeoff and landing. And a third was a weekend trip to New York aboard a BOAC 747. The trip included staying at the Summit Hotel on Lexington Avenue, a modernish hotel located next to a fire station. Sirens blared all night, and my roommate on this familiarization tour was a man of about thirty with body odor. It was not a happy night. I moved into Terry's apartment for the remaining two nights and made my regular pilgrimage to the Thomas Cook office on Fifth Avenue.

But there was another aspect of the job that was interesting—yet troubling. For it was also here that major complaints had to be handled—hence the Dictaphone—for it was my job to compose responses for the sales manager's signature. And here, once again, there were the inevitable anti-semitic slurs whenever one of the complaints or demands for reimbursement came from a client named Goldberg or Silverman.

1972

In February 1972, Aunt Esmé died of colon cancer—a month shy of her sixty-first birthday. Terry, at twenty-two, was an orphan. There was a part of me that felt a sense of responsibility to attempt to take care of her. New York—and that Thomas Cook office—was calling out to me. In retrospect, I was also looking to escape . . . escape from London, escape from my parents, escape from Michelle, escape from myself. And so I talked to my boss to see if I could be transferred to the New York office. I was told it couldn't be done because while they were all part of the Cook's family, they were somehow separate. I mulled, I thought, I deliberated, and finally without even discussing it with my parents or Terry or Michelle, I decided to take the leap. I would resign, make my own way to New York, and beg for employment at Cook's. I knew it would not be easy. I had no idea or concern about the visa obstacle. But I had the confidence and naivete of youth. I somehow knew it would all work out. I composed and handed my letter of resignation to my boss, giving the customary one-month notice. He was crushed. But I explained that New York was my dream and working—by hook or by crook—at Thomas Cook on Fifth Avenue was my goal.

It was a week later that my boss and I—and a Mr. Derek Burrell, the deputy managing director of Thomas Cook, a man of enormous gravity, tallness, and slimness—traveled by train to a weekend seminar at Oxford University arranged by some now defunct travel research association Cook's had encouraged me to join and from which I had graduated with flying colors. For a reason I cannot begin to remember, I had been inveigled into addressing the seminar on some long-forgotten aspect of the future of the travel industry. And so I did. The speech seemed to be very well received. Apparently, I learned later, Burrell leaned over to my boss and whispered how excellently I had spoken and what a credit I was to Cook's. My boss responded in agreement and said, "But he's just resigned; he wants to work at Cook's in New York." Burrell apparently turned to him and said, "Resignation my eye. We're not losing him. We'll arrange to transfer him within the company."

And so it was done. A well-delivered speech had intervened on my behalf. I was on my way. There were visits to the American Embassy in Grosvenor Square, lungs were x-rayed, I certified that I was not a prostitute, not a communist, my blood tests showed no signs of syphilis, my working visa was issued, and my first-class passage was arranged—at Cook's expense— for January 23, 1973, on the *Canberra* from Southampton to New York.

In a replay of seeing Anthony off on his departure for Israel in 1958, tearful farewells took place at Waterloo Station, departure point for the boat train to Southampton. My parents were grief-stricken because even though I had presented this adventure as something temporary, we all knew it wasn't. Michelle was bereft. And yet, curiously, despite my long history of acquiescence and fawning, I was oblivious or uncaring or both. I was doing what my brain and my heart needed me to do.

After seven days churning through the Atlantic, it was on January 30, 1973, that the *Canberra* crept up the Hudson on a freezing morning. I and my seventeen pieces of luggage had arrived. Which is where this memoir began.

Arrival

I T IS FEBRUARY 2020, and I am driving from Lugano to St. Moritz, replicating the exact route I drove with my parents sixty-four years ago. Instead of sitting perched without seatbelt on my red wooden stool with the white prancing bunnies, placed between my father and my brother, I am behind the wheel of a BMW 7-Series. Instead of struggling with Anthony's stack of maps and then misfolding them, a woman with an upper-class British accent is telling me robotically when to make a left, when to merge right. I am not singing tunes from a 1954 English musical; I am listening to Freddie Mercury's "Bohemian Rhapsody." But the scenery remains the same, albeit whiter in February than in July. Lake Como is still there, to the right, and as I climb higher through the Julier Pass, the peaks are as grand as they always were.

Six weeks earlier, on December 31, 2019, I turned seventy. It had been a week of surprise family arrivals from Israel, Australia, and South Africa, orchestrated entirely without my knowledge by my wife, Noa. People who love me congregated at our house in the village of Haworth, New Jersey, with, at its height, eleven people sleeping and consuming three riotous, delicious meals a day. A ten-foot-tall Christmas tree sparkled and was surrounded by an obscene number of gifts. For eight nights, Chanukah candles were lit and songs sung. The extravaganza climaxed on New Year's Eve, with a birthday party in my honor. The theme was the Roaring Twenties, with forty guests dressed appropriately, including my niece Elinor sporting a headband and an eau-de-nil velvet flapper dress sewn with hundreds of shiny beads, a hand-me-down of my mother's from 1927, stored for decades in wads of tissue paper but still eminently wearable. We danced the Charleston, we sang karaoke, and by 4 a.m. we had consumed an array of elegant foods and cases of art deco Corbet Champagne.

What we didn't know as we reveled that New Year's Eve was that on that very same day, officials of the health commission in the city of Wuhan were reporting a burgeoning number of cases of a devastating influenza-like illness. As January and February progressed, reports of the disease's spread became more and more troubling. While I traveled through Switzerland, people were already using hand sanitizer by the gallon, but I assumed that this disease wouldn't be much more devastasting than the SARS that had caused Noa's and my 2003 honeymoon to be switched from Vietnam to Tenerife. How very wrong I was.

Reveling in nostalgia can be glorious. But it can sometimes be maudlin, and even pretty pointless. Yes, it would be nice to be able to press rewind and be six again, and even nicer to know what one knows at seventy. And yes, of course, it would be nice to be driving with my parents. But I am sure the drive from Lugano to St. Moritz is easier now, with dozens of tunnels easing the endless hairpin bends. And a 2019 BMW (coincidentally my father's initials—Bernard Max Weill) is a lot zippier than a 1954 Vauxhall Velox.

I hear constantly about the Golden Age of Travel, as if it is some long-lost phenomenon. And yes, crossing the Atlantic in first class on the Aubusson- and Lalique-clad *Normandie* was undoubtedly fabulous. But was it more fabulous than flying first class on Emirates to an enchanting $2,000-a-night overwater resort in the Maldives?

Yes, I would have loved to have been alive in 1936 and sufficiently moneyed to fly on a spanking new KLM DC-3 from Amsterdam to Batavia (it's called Jakarta today). The one-way fare was 1,300 Dutch guilders, equivalent to a fantastic $12,700 in 2020. The journey comprised a week of hops from one desert or jungle outpost to the next, sleeping in the crisp linen sheets of the airline-fostered guesthouses along the route, and re-embarking in the morning for another day of bumpy unpressurized flight. But would it have been "goldener" than flying the Concorde from London to New York? It's all a matter of perspective. Rose-colored glasses are just that: rose-colored glasses. As Carlotta Campion declares in the rewritten 1987 London production of Stephen Sondheim's musical *Follies*, "The good old days? They were never that good. They were merely old."

In the twenty-first century, I've thumbed through the guest book at Mnemba Island resort in Zanzibar and read Mick Jagger's comment that his lips were so sunburned that he "couldn't get no satisfaction." I've watched

Donatella Versace swimming topless and then being massaged and hair-brushed by the pool at Marrakech's La Mamounia. I've watched Prince and Princess Michael of Kent scarfing down spaghetti alle vongole at the Regina Isabella in Ischia, the very same hotel to which Elizabeth Taylor and Richard Burton escaped to embark upon their affair during the filming of *Cleopatra*. The retired maître d' who was then the pool boy once told me their fighting was so raucous and violent that Signora Taylor once threw all Signor Burton's clothes from the balcony of their suite into the swimming pool. So can one really say that the golden age of travel is behind us?

Then there are the efforts of the travel nostalgists to re-create that which is no more. In 1930, when Air France, Imperial Airways, and KLM had been blazing wobbly trails around Europe and connecting their capitals to their colonies, one could take a plane from Paris to Istanbul. It was comparatively fast, but the expense was daunting, the discomfort of flying below or through the clouds made air sickness and splashed drinks de rigeur, and all in all it wasn't terribly safe. Far more alluring was the chic and style of the Venice Simplon-Orient-Express, with its—for a train—comparative speed, its staff intent on pampering. Its navy-blue-and-gold Wagons-Lits train carriages were outfitted with sleeping compartments done up in velvet, inlaid marquetry, and the crispest linen on Earth. The dining car was all Lalique panels, white damask, crystal, and delicious cuisine. The passengers ranged from businessmen to dowager duchesses, and Agatha Christie had a field day with her now epic tale of a dozen of them serial-stabbing the killer of the faux Lindbergh baby.

In 1982 the Orient Express was reborn and became an overnight success. Europe was scoured in search of the original discarded and dilapidated railway cars (including the *Brighton Belle* that had so seduced me as a child), and tens of millions of dollars were invested in restoring them to their Roaring Twenties gorgeousness. Thousands of people ride it annually, dressing up for evenings of 1920s glamour, but they're taking the ride to engage in the show, not actually to reach anywhere fast.

And so it is with the North Atlantic. On a good day, London is six hours from New York. On a really good day, it can be as little as five. Nowadays, sailing the Atlantic has became all about pretense, a theatrical anachronism obligating passengers to imagine it is 1930 aboard the *Ile de France* and that the jumbo jet roaring above is a clap of thunder.

Of course, everybody aboard today's *Queen Mary 2* is making the trip for the joy of being at sea for a week, with an array of activities from deck sports to lectures to theater to movies to spa treatments to dressing for captain's dinners. Some of the passengers aboard are veteran cruisers for whom a week without the bother of trundling around intervening points of call is elating. There are those who don those metaphorical rose-colored glasses and make believe it's 1935 or 1955 and this is "the only way to cross." They lie on deck chairs swathed in dark-blue blankets, gazing at the horizon as the giant liner mows through the swells. At dusk they repair to their stateroom, dress to the nines, plant themselves in the bar in the vain fantasy of spotting Cole Porter or the Duchess of Windsor and hearing the band playing Rodgers and Hart. And the loveliness of the illusion almost works—until they return to their balconied stateroom (the great transatlantic liners of yore never had balconies). The room is cozy and well lit, and the bed is invitingly turned down, a nightgown or pajamas waiting eagerly. But . . . but . . . but there, on the wall, a flat-screen TV connects them to CNN. And emails and WhatsApp messages are rolling in to their devices. And suddenly it's not 1925 or 1955. The ship is not steaming through an unreachable void that presumes a sense of calm and disconnection from the reality of dry land. Because the latest news or the inescapable leap to share the day's highlights on Instagram shatters the illusion that it's 1930. One is no longer "at sea." One is "online."

The truth is that the actual characteristics of traveling were always fabulous. Or they were middling, or they were vile. And they still are. I just was lucky or strange enough to be someone who was and remains enthralled by it all. I watch *Downton Abbey* and see the family arrive in Yorkshire on that beautiful maroon train and yes, like all of us, I think how romantic it was, as they tote their leather suitcases and are met by a liveried chauffeur and jump into a Rolls-Royce. But that very same train wasn't "romantic" in third class, any more than it's "romantic" today to fly on Ryanair from London's woebegone Standsted Airport to Krakow or on Spirit Airlines from Newark to Fort Lauderdale. Except, of course, if you're obsessed, *comme moi*, with every facet of traveling, grand or not . . . it's still phenomenal. The backpacker staying in hostels and tramping through the Andes can be in as much ecstasy as the Vuitton-toting jetsetters flying first class on Singapore Airlines to reach the latest Aman resort.

It's all about attitude. It is truly extraordinary and beyond comprehension that my mother's voyages from Australia to England in 1912 and 1918 each took six weeks—with all its leisure and grace and lack of jet lag—when the same journey can be achieved now in twenty-two hours. And if those twenty-two hours are spent in the front of the plane, it will be all champagne and flat beds and wonder. But if they are spent back in economy, it's pretty damned grim; as grim, indeed, as those ocean voyages would have been in third class or, heaven forbid, in steerage. Except, of course, in the Roaring Twenties there were always those first classers who slipped away from the dullness of the card room and crept down staircases to third class to snort cocaine and dance the Charleston with the flappers.

In the opening scene of Mart Crowley's groundbreaking 1968 play *Boys in the Band*, the multi-cashmere-sweatered Michael tells his friend Donald about his travels in search of love or sex, and he says, "Well, I'm here to tell you that the only place in all those miles—the only place I've ever been happy was on the goddamn plane." At the age of nineteen, when I first saw the play in London, that line resonated so much that I was jolted by empathy. And to this day, there are times when I just don't want a flight to end.

In the spring of 2019, I lay under a goose-down duvet in my flat-bed seat in business class on China Eastern Airlines en route from Shanghai to New York. The cubicle was snug, arranged in such a way that I was facing the plane walls as I slept. I woke from a deep gin-and-Klonopin-induced nap to discover that only four of the flight's fifteen hours were left. And I was actually disappointed. As much as I wanted to get home to my family, I wanted to stay here. I wanted to remain stashed away in my cozy little compartment disconnected from the Earth, disconnected from the complications of life, disconnected from reality. I was as sheltered, tucked up in my travel cocoon, as I had been forty-six years earlier in my cozy wood-paneled first-class cabin on the *Canberra*, as it slammed through the January waves to bring me to New York.

One hundred and six countries, 4.5 million air miles, 9,200 flying hours (one year and eighteen days of my life), a dozen oceangoing transatlantic crossings and cruises, scores of trains, a dozen safaris, 1,200 hotels, and hundreds of Michelin-starred meals later, there is ample evidence of my obsession. Since the age of fourteen, I had kept logbooks of every flight I ever flew—airline, aircraft, distance, hours. In 2002 my soon-to-be second wife, Noa, secretly arranged for a website to be constructed whereby all these and future flights would be recorded, enabling me, with a click of the mouse, to tell how many hundred thousand miles I have flown in a Boeing 707, or how many times I have flown Air France. Appropriately its URL is www.geoffreyweilltraveladdict.com—but it is password protected and only

I (and probably the Mossad) can access it. I sit at my computer like some crazed robber of a priceless Goya painting that only I can admire. And then there are complex Excel sheets recording every country I have visited. And another listing every hotel I have ever stayed in—and when and in what room. My older son, Benjamin, had his own logbook too, and now my younger children, Zoë and Liam, have their own travel Excel sheets, which I scrupulously maintain and update—although they possibly will never care.

My first marriage, to my cousin Terry, on to whom I had glommed like a limpet at the age of ten, lasted for twenty-five years, the last ten of which were miserable for us both, and for our son, Benjamin, who was sixteen when we divorced. Those ten years saw a collapse of a marriage that was held together mostly by our cousinhood, by our dependence on each other, a marriage made untenable by our individual needs to seek solace elsewhere. I had not intended to remarry—indeed I expected my life to be very different. But when my deep friendship with Israeli-born Noa turned into a

My family, 2019 (*l to r*): Me; son Liam; daughter-in-law, Courtney; son Benjamin; daughter, Zoë; my wife, Noa. (Author collection)

furtive postprandial kiss on the neck, then dating, then love, then living together, it seemed the inevitable thing to do—and eighteen years on, Benjamin has a half sister, Zoë Ann, born in 2006, and a half brother, Liam Hugo, born three days before Christmas 2008. What is it with me, I wonder, that has seen me have a succession of girlfriends and two wives with pansexual names? Michelle, Leslie, Terry, Noa. It could just be coincidence. Or not.

After Terry's and my utterly fraught-free division of furniture, paintings, assorted kitchenware, tchotchkes, and books (I kept the posters), it was on September 1, 2001, that I moved to a new Manhattan apartment building in gentrifying Hells' Kitchen at 54th Street and Tenth Avenue. The apartment had two bedrooms—assuring one for Benjamin, who spent one week with Terry, one with me—and on an eighth-floor setback, it had a 1,000-square-foot terrace facing south and east, with views of the towers and lights of Times Square, the Empire State Building, and the Twin Towers of the World Trade Center. From the master bedroom and the living room, one could see the *Queen Elizabeth 2* docked in the Hudson when it was in town, and I could stroll down and peer lovingly at its giant prow after its arrival was announced by its deafening horn.

Ten days later, New York, America, and the world changed drastically, and my apartment's view of the Twin Towers was no more. I had planned a housewarming party for Sunday night, September 16, the first night of Rosh Hashana—the Jewish New Year. I decided to keep the party happening as it could only help, I thought, to lift everyone's spirits in the wake of the trauma of five days earlier, from which we all remained benumbed. On Saturday morning, one of my friends, *New York Post*'s celebrity columnist Cindy Adams, called me.

"Damn," she said. "I forgot I was meant to have dinner with Liza tonight!"

"So bring her along," I said. And she did. Liza Minnelli was due to appear on NBC's *Today* show the following morning, to sing "New York, New York" live from the field at Yankee Stadium, a sequence designed to underscore New Yorkers' determination not to be cowed by the tragedy that had befallen the city six days earlier.

Guests started to arrive, including my friends David and Brian, and their Jack Russell terrier, one of those dogs that is totally sweet but highly excitable and prone to jumping up and down with friendship or enthusiasm. Others arrived. Drinks were poured. There was plentiful alcohol and delicious food laid out in the living room and on the terrace that overlooked a floodlit, crippled New York. The doorbell rang, I answered, and there was Cindy, clutching her Yorkshire terrier, Jazzy, and Liza Minnelli, looking lovely yet sans makeup, and somehow shy. They entered, handed over gifts, and Cindy put Jazzy down on the floor. Jazzy took one look at the Jack Russell, yapped, and immediately darted to my living room's new sisal carpet to eject a torrent of diarrhea deep into its weave. After I laughed and Cindy picked Jazzy up, the next thing I spied was Liza, kneeling on the carpet with a spray bottle of Fantastik and brushes and sponges, scrubbing furiously at the sisal. I told her how sweet it was of her to do it, but "please get up" and have fun. Which she did.

Cindy and I had become fast friends in 1999 when she alerted the Israel consulate that she wanted to be in Israel for the turn of the millennium and we met at La Goulue to discuss the arrangements. Over lunch, we became instantly besotted with each other, sharing a kind of eclectic and absurd humor that besets us to this day. After the Jazzy poop incident, Cindy whispered to me that because of Liza's performance early tomorrow morning, she shouldn't have alcohol. So I concocted exotic teetotal cocktails complete with pineapple wedges, straws, and paper umbrellas, which Liza took outside to the terrace and dumped into a plant, and then poured herself tumblers of vodka. We performed all the appropriate Rosh Hashana ceremonies: lighting candles, eating challah with raisins, dipping apple in honey—and soon after discovering that I had not yet unpacked sufficient Liza Minnelli CDs to be played, Jazzy, Cindy, and a sweating and wobbly Liza made their exit.

The next morning, I woke at seven to watch Liza perform "New York, New York" alone in the vastness of Yankee Stadium. The sweats and the wobbles of the night before had vanished. The face and the hair were perfect. I watched a superstar perform the haunting tribute to our damaged but undaunted city with total verve and class and brilliance, and tears rolled down my cheeks.

From my office on the twenty-second floor of an exquisite landmarked art deco skyscraper in lower Manhattan, I can gaze at the Hudson River where the *Canberra* had unloaded me to take up my position at the Thomas Cook office on Fifth Avenue. In 2019, after decades of acquisitions and mergers, Thomas Cook—the world's first travel agency and, for more than a century, its most prestigious—collapsed into bankruptcy. Hundreds of thousands of passengers of its eponymous Thomas Cook airline were stranded across six continents. Hotels worldwide were owed millions of dollars, pounds, and euros. It was an appalling ending to the grand era of the Cook's Tour.

After my eight years with Thomas Cook and a further eight with the Israel Tourist Office, I was offered a whopping salary increase to become International Director of the American Jewish Congress. In the early 1960s, the "AJCongress" had opened a travel department to operate tours to Israel. The effort was led by the charismatic Betty Weir Alderson, who charged around America whipping up tens of thousands of bookings to Israel. Long before the United Jewish Appeal, the Jewish Federations, individual synagogues, and Birthright brought America's Jews to admire the Promised Land, it was Alderson who single-handledly built the concept of American Jewish group travel to Israel. With the success of the Israel tours, Alderson widened the program to include tours to Europe and Asia and Morocco—with each tour a brief glimpse of Jewish life overseas—and it was one of those groups that Terry and I had befriended in 1980 at the pool of Marrakech's La Mamounia. It was the largest Jewish tour program in the world; with some seven thousand travelers in 1985, it funded the organization's political and legal work in defense of Israel and for civil rights and the separation of church and state in America.

By the summer of 1984, Alderson was ready to move on, and I was hired to replace her. A year later, an Italian cruise ship, *Achille Lauro*, was hijacked during a Mediterranean cruise by members of the Palestinian Liberation Front. A wheelchair-bound American cruise passenger by the name of Leon Klinghoffer was shot, killed, and thrown overboard for no other reason than he was Jewish. By 1986, with more terrorist attacks in Israel and in Europe, whizzing around the continent on a tour bus reserved for Jewish Americans began to seem less than appealing. In 1987, during the first intifada, an American woman was injured in the face when a stone was thrown at her American Jewish Congress tour bus. The program continued, with fewer thousands continuing to travel, and so it was that while continuing to run the declining tour program, I came to open my own public relations company specializing in travel, tourism, and hotels.

I was very lucky. After I left the Israel Tourist Office in 1984, it had churned unhappily through two PR managers and three PR firms in eleven years. In 1995 my former boss, Uzi Michaeli, a man of gruff prickly-on-the-outside-and-sweet-on-the-inside Israeliness, called me and told me that they wanted me back. He explained they couldn't afford to hire me, but if I were to open my own company, Israel's Ministry of Tourism, North

America, would be my first client. And so it was. An acquaintance, Janet Kaplan Rodgers, came to work with me. She had lived in Jerusalem in the 1970s and, with the Canadian Judy Stacey Goldman, had written the charming *Underground Jerusalem Guide* and *Underground Tel Aviv Guide* (books parenthetically published by my brother) and which made these cities seem charming decades before anyone really believed they were. In a tiny corner of the American Jewish Congress mansion on East 84th Street, Geoffrey Weill Associates was opened on June 1, 1995. The very grand mansion, with its ballroom and sweeping circular staircase, was the former home of Ogden Reid, a scion of the family that owned and published the *New York Herald Tribune*. In 1959 President Eisenhower appointed Reid U.S. ambassador to Israel. Despite its conversion into offices, many of which were unkempt and hideous, the grandeur somehow remained.

Uzi Michaeli was more than a friend—he was also wise. He told me never to rely on just one client. And so I went about acquiring others. I determined that I wanted to avoid being classified as the "Jewish travel PR firm," and so I approached two potential clients who, were they to hire me, would relieve me of that classification. One was the German National Tourist Office, whose director I knew. And the second was La Mamounia in Marrakech. I figured that working with Germans and Arabs would free me of my yellow star. They both hired me. The deed was done.

Twenty-five years later, the company had grown from Janet and me to a staff of fifteen, and from three clients to close to thirty. I never wanted it to be a massive corporation—I had learned from my experience at Thomas Cook that promotion to management was boring, when what I wanted to do was plan people's vacations. And so it is to this day. I don't want to spend my days overseeing accounts and dealing with personnel problems—I want to gush about hotels. And I want to travel endlessly and repeatedly. And, incidentally, some twenty of those trips have been to six continents with Cindy Adams, trips that are a magical blend of touring, eating gargantually, and, mostly, spent in paroxysms of preposterous mirth so frenetic that once, at Johannesburg Airport, we were laughing so uncontrollably and for so long and over something so utterly ludicrous that our traveling companions—Judge Judy and her husband, Jerry—quietly tiptoed into the distance to avoid embarrassment.

In 2004 I detached the company from the American Jewish Congress and we moved to a cavernous loft in the once grubby Flatiron District. By 2017 the still grubby neighborhood had become chic and the rent was doubled:

At Kronenhalle in Zurich, my favorite restaurant in all the world, 2020. (Author collection)

hence our move to Lower Manhattan, where the office is admittedly glamorous, spacious enough for fifteen of us to persuade the media of the glories of our clients . . . mostly some of the world's finest hotels. It is not your average office space. The walls are Majorelle Blue, a color produced in 1931 by painter Jacques Majorelle for the walls and buildings within his gardens in Marrakech, later bought, expanded, and glorified by the brilliant and tormented Yves Saint Laurent. I had brought a small can of the paint from Morocco, and after many tries at paint emporia in New York, it was a paint store in Englewood, New Jersey, of all places, that succeeded in reproducing gallons of it.

Vintage belabeled suitcases are topped by a circular glass tabletop, around which, on most days, the staff eat lunch. The walls are decorated with perhaps 35 percent of my collection of vintage travel posters. Eighty-year-old cabin trunks—complete with hanging rails and drawers for shoes and lingerie—act as stands for art and storage for stationery. There are travel memorabilia everywhere: An original metal sign pointing the way to the

Golden Arrow train from London's Victoria Station (Aunt Flo would have loved it). Ashtrays and assorted china from hotels around the world. Moderne airplane models. Vast tomes about travel. Yards of ancient Michelin guides. The entry is a giant wall mural of an airport departure board.

Every time I walk into my office, it's as if I am being given a shot of travel cocaine. It is the ideal aerie for someone whose lifelong obsession has always been to be all abroad.